Favorite Recipes®
of Home Economics Teachers

BREADS

© Favorite Recipes Press/Nashville EMS MCMLXXXI
P.O. Box 77, Nashville, Tennessee 37202

Library of Congress Cataloging in Publication Data
Main entry under title:
Breads.
   Includes index.
   1. Bread I. Favorite Recipes Press.
TX769.B777   641.8'15   81-5413
ISBN 0-87197-139-9   AACR2

Dear Homemaker:

You don't have to be a grandmother in a starched white apron to appreciate baking delicious homemade bread. Because here's the first complete cookbook on bread making ever published using the favorite home-tested recipes of Home Economics teachers across the country. Now, you have their expertise at your finger tips. (Can you think of a better place?)

Yeast breads . . . quick breads . . . dietetic breads . . . even foreign and holiday breads are all here to become traditions in your family. Nearly 400 fabulous recipes — plus valuable tips, and cooking terms — everything you need for a bread baking bonanza right in your own kitchen.

The editors of Favorite Recipes Press are extremely proud of our new *Breads Cookbook.* It's our way of making bread baking a joy for you and your family. So tie on your apron; get out the flour scoop. With the new *Breads Cookbook,* it won't be long until you'll be proudly announcing that you bake your own bread!

Happy Baking,

Mary Jane Blount

Mary Jane Blount
FAVORITE RECIPES PRESS

Board of Advisors

Favorite Recipes Press wants to recognize the following who graciously serve on our Home Economics Teachers' Advisory Board:

Frances Rudd
Supervisor, Home Economics
   Education
Arkansas Department of Education

C. Janet Latham
Supervisor, Home Economics
   Education
Idaho State Board of Vocational
   Education

Catherine A. Carter
Head Consultant, Consumer
   Homemaking Education
Illinois Division of Vocational
   and Technical Education

Barbara Gaylor
Supervisor, Home Economics
   Education Unit
Michigan Department of Education

Louann Heinrichs
Home Economics Teacher
Greenville High School
Greenville, Ohio

Roberta Looper
1982 President, National
   Association of Vocational
   Home Economics Teachers
Livingston, Tennessee

Phyllis L. Barton
Past President, National Association of
Vocational Home Economics Teachers
Alexandria, Virginia

CONTENTS

The Bread Board

Serving freshly baked bread is a truly satisfying experience. Bring out a steaming, crusty loaf of whole wheat bread, and you're bound to get more "ooh's" and "aah's" than the fanciest flaming dessert or an elaborate entree.

Fortunately, once you learn the basics of bread making, you'll see how easy it really is. If this is your first time, you'll appreciate the easy quick breads that don't require rising or kneading. Then, move on to yeast, sourdough and unleavened breads for more creative baking. And if you really want to be a hit hostess, try serving homemade hamburger buns at your next cookout!

QUICK BREADS

Using baking powder, baking soda, air, sourdough or steam for leavening, quick breads can be made on the spur of the moment. They rise in the oven during baking and emerge as piping hot delights.

It's important to stir, not beat, quick breads just long enough to mix the ingredients. After baking, cool on a rack, wrap, and store in an airtight container or serve immediately while still warm.

YEAST BREADS

Who would have thought the wonderful aroma coming from the kitchen on bread baking day is really the expansion of gases released by the yeast's action, and gluten stretching in the wheat?

But that's only the beginning step in creating perfect yeast breads. Kneading comes next — to spread the gluten throughout the dough and thoroughly blend ingredients. There's a proper way to knead dough, but don't worry about perfecting your technique at first. Just do the best you can.

When You Need to Knead . . .

1. Place dough on a floured board, flatten out lightly.

2. Pull a corner towards you with fingers close together.

3. Then, press down and forward with the heels of your hands.

4. Give dough a quarter turn and repeat — continuing about ten minutes — until the dough is smooth and elastic.

5. Kneading's complete when small bubbles appear under the surface.

Then, Let the Dough do its Thing . . .

1. Place the dough in a greased bowl; turn to grease the surface so when dough rises, it does not dry out.

2. Cover dough with a towel and place in warm place (80-85 degrees), free from drafts.

3. Let rise until doubled in bulk (1 to 1½ hours).

4. Punch dough down.

Now, Get it into Shape!

LOAVES

1. With knife, divide dough into loaf-sized portions. Shape into ball; then flatten into rectangle, carefully squeezing out gas bubbles.

2. Roll into loaf shape, tucking the ends under.

3. Place into greased loaf pan, seam side down. Let rise until doubled in bulk. Bake according to recipe instructions.

ROLLS

Parker House Rolls

Roll dough out to about ½-inch thickness. Cut with a biscuit cutter. Using the dull edge of a knife, crease the round of dough to one side of the center. Brush with melted butter and fold large side over small side. Seal edges. Place about 1" apart on greased baking sheet. Cover and let rise until doubled in bulk. Brush top with melted butter.

Clover Leaf

Form dough into three small balls about the size of large marbles. Have melted butter on hand to dip balls into. Place three balls in each greased cup of a muffin pan. Allow dough to rise until doubled in bulk.

Butter Flake or Fan Rolls

Roll dough into a thin rectangular sheet. After brushing with melted butter, cut into strips about 1½" wide. Place about 5, 6 or 7 strips on top of each other. Cut 1½" long and place end down in muffin pans. Allow dough to rise until doubled in bulk.

Pan Rolls

Form dough into balls about one-third the size of a desired baked roll. Place balls about ¼" apart in a shallow baking pan. Cover and let rise until doubled in bulk. Brush with melted butter.

Crescent

Dough should be divided into three equal parts and rolled into a circle about 10-12" in diameter. Each circle is then cut into pie-shaped pieces. Roll each pie-shaped piece beginning with the larger end and sealing the small end. Place about 2" apart on a baking sheet. Be sure the point of the dough is underneath. Curve each rolled pie-shaped piece to form a crescent. Cover rolls and let rise until doubled in bulk. Brush with melted butter.

WHAT WENT WRONG . . .	. . . AND WHY
Bread and biscuits are dry	Too dry mixture; too slow baking; or over-handling (To remedy, dip quickly in milk, bake for a few minutes; serve hot.)
Bread is very open and has uneven texture	Too much liquid or over-handling in kneading
Gray crumb; slightly heavy taste	Over-rising or over-fermentation

WHAT WENT WRONG . . .	. . . AND WHY
Strong yeast smell from baked bread	Too high proportion of yeast or over-rising
Tiny white spots on the crusts	Too rapid rising; dough not covered properly
Crust has bad color	Too much flour used in shaping
Small flat loaves	Old yeast; not enough rising or rising much too long; too hot an oven
Heavy compact texture	Too much flour worked into bread when kneading; insufficient rising time; oven temperature too hot
Coarse texture	Too little kneading
Crumbly bread	Too much flour, under-mixing; oven temperature too cool
Yeasty sour flavor	Too little yeast; rising time too long
Fallen center	Rising time too long
Irregular shape	Poor technique in shaping
Surface browns too quickly	Oven temperature too hot
Bread continues to rise too long and is porous in the center and upper portion of the loaf	Oven temperature too cool
Overall poor texture, color, flavor and volume	Inferior flour

SEASONINGS FOR BREADS

Caraway Seed — good for seasonings, as well as toppings, particularly in whole grain breads. Store in the refrigerator.

Celery Seed — adds a mild flavor when sprinkled on, or combined with, dough for herb breads, rolls and bread sticks.

Chervil — a staple of French cooking. Try a pinch of this parsley-like herb in your next corn bread.

Chive — a mild-flavored member of the onion family. Add to dumplings or to cheese or garlic bread doughs.

Cinnamon — popular in rolls, coffee cakes, and even waffles and pancakes. Delicious mixed with sugar as a topping for French toast, biscuits and other quick breads.

Cloves — a heady spice with a strong aroma and flavor. Use carefully in combination with other spices such as nutmeg, mace and cinnamon in sweet rolls, coffee cakes and dessert breads.

Dill — a delightfully flavored herb that's part of the parsley family. Try it on biscuits and other onion or cheese breads.

Ginger — a dried and peeled root used frequently in coffee cakes or sweet rolls. Try it in your next waffle batter too.

Nutmeg — comes from the fruit of a tree similar to the rhododendron. Often used alone as a topping. A touch of nutmeg added to herb breads will highlight other seasonings.

Oregano — also called wild marjoram, it's best in breads served with Italian foods.

Parsley — this herb provides vitamins A and C. Adds both flavor and color to biscuits, dumplings, herb breads and other quick and yeast breads.

Poppy Seed — Tiny dark granules with a nut-like flavor. Sprinkle on rolls, biscuits and loaves; or mix with sweet bread dough or batter.

Rosemary — often used in combination with sage or savory in dumplings or biscuits.

Saffron — from the dried flowers of the crocus plant. Used in many breads for flavoring, and by commercial bakers to lend color.

Sage — a strong-flavored herb often added to herb breads. It's almost always combined with other herbs and should be used in moderation.

Sesame Seed — sprinkle on breads, rolls and biscuits. Most recipes call for the seed to be toasted in your oven at a low temperature.

Thyme — often featured in quick and yeast breads, it's good in combination with sage.

Note: In using herbs, remember that ¼ teaspoon dry herbs is equivalent to 1 teaspoon fresh herbs.

GLOSSARY FOR BREAD BAKING

All-purpose flour — the back-bone ingredient of most baked goods. It's usually a blend of hard and soft wheats. "White" is synonymous with wheat or plain flours.

Baking powder — a leavening agent, more reliable than baking soda, which reacts with liquid to produce bubbles of carbon dioxide that are trapped in the dough or batter causing the mixture to rise.

Baking soda — a leavening agent of pure sodium bicarbonate which produces carbon dioxide when heated. ¼ teaspoon baking soda plus ½ cup sour milk is equivalent to 1 teaspoon baking powder (double acting) and ½ cup liquid.

Batter — a mixture of flour, moisture and other ingredients.

Biscuit — a tender flaky bread leavened with baking powder and shaped into a small cake with light brown crust.

Blintz — a thin pancake folded around a filling. Often served with a topping of sour cream, jam or sauce.

Brioche — a soft, muffin-shaped roll with a small tuft on top — made of butter, eggs, flour and yeast.

Buns — individual breads, often containing candied fruits or raisins, molded or baked in muffin tins. The most famous variety is the Eastertime favorite — Hot Cross Buns.

Buckwheat — a dark flour, obtained from the seeds of the buckwheat plant. It's usually combined with white flour.

Cake flour — for delicate cakes, it's softer and whiter than all-purpose flour.

Citron — a fruit resembling a lemon, but is larger and less acid. The thick skin is candied and used in many baked products.

Coffee Cake — a rich sweet bread shaped in various ways and sometimes iced. Usually leavened with yeast, it may contain spices, nuts and fruits.

Corn bread — a quick bread prepared from cornmeal, flour, sugar, shortening and baking powder.

Cornmeal — coarsely ground corn, available either as yellow or white meal.

Crust — the outside of the bread formed by the intense oven heat and drying of the loaf's surface.

Dough — an unbaked mixture of flour, water, yeast and other ingredients stiff enough to be kneaded with the hands.

Doughnut — a small ring-shaped cake made from leavened and sweetened dough, then fried in hot shortening — may be glazed or filled with jelly or custard.

Fermentation — a chemical change in organic substances caused by microorganisms. In bread making, fermentation causes the dough to rise.

Gluten — the protein of wheat and other cereals which, when kneaded, allows dough to expand evenly.

Griddle — a flat, often rimless, metal pan.

Kolachke — a yeast-raised bun filled with apples, prunes, figs, nuts, poppy seed or jam.

Loaf pan — a 9" x 5" x 3" baking pan of metal or glass which gives bread its characteristic shape.

Muffins — small cup-shaped breads sometimes flavored with nuts or fruits.

Oatmeal — a meal made from ground or rolled oats.

Pancakes — flat, round cakes made from a variety of batters and cooked over direct heat on a griddle.

Pumpernickel — a dark bread made from either unsifted rye flour or the combination of wheat and rye flours.

Quick breads — breads such as biscuits, muffins, corn breads, nut, fruit breads, griddle cakes and doughnuts which are leavened with baking powder, soda, air or steam instead of yeast.

Rye flour — dark, tasty flour which lacks gluten-forming protein. Most frequently combined with other flours to produce loaves of smooth, porous texture.

Self-rising flour — contains leavening and salt. When used in quick breads, omit baking powder, soda and salt. Do not use in yeast breads.

Sourdough — a portion of dough stored in a covered container that is living in continuous fermentation. Used in preparing leavened bread.

Sponge — a dough formed either from flour, water, yeast and other ingredients or from starter dough.

Starter dough — an old-fashioned method of preparing yeast breads which uses a brewing mixture of hot water, flour and sugar to allow fermentation.

Stollen — an oval-shaped German yeast bread. It contains almonds, candied orange, lemon peel and currants.

Waffles — batter cakes crisper than pancakes that are baked in a waffle iron.

Whole wheat, graham or wheat flour — unrefined flour from wheat grain ground to a powdery consistency. Wheat flour is rich in vitamins and roughage content because most of the bran is retained during milling.

Yeast — Available as compressed yeast or active dry yeast. A vegetable substance which, when activated by the proper conditions of temperature, moisture, air and food, results in a fermentation reaction. (Before using active dry yeast, soften in warm water for 5 to 10 minutes. Soften compressed yeast the same amount of time in lukewarm water or other liquid.)

BREAD BAKING TIPS

- Rather than making large loaves of bread, shape small, individual loaves for two and three member families.

- Most sweet breads freeze well. Be sure and let cool thoroughly — preferably overnight — before freezing.

- All baking powder breads improve if allowed to stand at room temperature for 20 minutes before being placed in oven.

- Shortcut, quick breads can be made with prepared biscuit mix.

- Grease finger tips before starting to knead.

- The choice of pan affects the crust. Glass, dark tin and dull aluminum pans produce a thick crust.

- Glass and enamel pans require a lower temperature.

- Milk, cream or butter, used in the recipe or brushed on at the end of the baking period, gives a good, over-all brown color.

- For a glazed crust, brush the top with an egg wash near the end of baking time.

- To keep the crust soft, brush with butter after the bread's baked and removed from pan.

- To test for doneness: Notice if the loaf has shrunk from the sides of the pan or test by tapping the top of the loaf and listening for a hollow sound.

- If you heat chopped fruits and nuts for sweet bread mixtures, then dust with flour before adding to the dough, they won't sink to the bottom of the pan.

- For variety, don't use bread pans when baking. Instead, shape free-form loaves on cookie sheets.

- Save wrappers from butter and margarine and use later to grease pans for cakes and breads, or for greasing potatoes before baking. Store wrappers in the freezer to use when needed.

- When substituting one yeast for another, remember: one packet dry yeast is equivalent to 3/5-ounce package compressed yeast.

- It's better to use too much yeast than too little. The dough will simply rise faster.

- The richer the recipe is with shortening and sugar, the more yeast will be needed for the dough to rise.

- Use ingredients at room temperature; cold ingredients slow yeast action.

- Scald, then cool milk, before adding to dough to destroy any organisms which might interfere with yeast action.

- If you have trouble getting whole grain breads to rise, use a little extra yeast. After you get the feel of kneading breads, reduce the amount of yeast.

- Old bread — especially if it has nuts, fruit or sugar in it — makes excellent bread pudding.

- Cool breads before slicing.

- Slice loaves before freezing.

- When you slice homemade bread, save the crumbs. Store in a covered container in the freezer until needed.

- Turn stale bread into croutons by slicing in ½" slices. Remove crusts; cube. Bake at 325 degrees for 15 to 20 minutes, stirring occasionally, until golden brown. Save crusts for crumbs.

- To fix herb-seasoned bread crumbs, dry leftover bread slices in a 250-degree oven until crisp, but not brown. Break up dry bread and place in blender. Blend at medium speed until fine crumbs are formed. Stir 1 cup crumbs, 1 tablespoon oregano, ½ teaspoon thyme, ½ teaspoon onion salt and 1/8 teaspoon pepper.

- Every bag of flour has a slightly different moisture content, so you may have to increase or decrease the amount of flour kneaded into the dough.

- For high, light biscuits, cut them quickly and place close together on the baking sheet. For crusty biscuits, cut thin and place far apart on the sheet.

- For a different dinner treat, stack pancakes in a casserole with filling between layers. Top with sauce.

- Add small amount of vinegar to deep fat while frying doughnuts to eliminate the greasy taste.

YEAST

ANGEL BISCUITS

1 pkg. yeast
5 tbsp. sugar
5 c. flour
1 tbsp. salt
1 tbsp. baking powder
1 tsp. soda
1 c. shortening
2 c. buttermilk

Combine yeast, 1/4 cup warm water and sugar in small bowl. Stir until yeast and sugar are dissolved. Sift dry ingredients together in large bowl. Cut in shortening until crumbly. Add buttermilk and yeast mixture; mix well. Let rise in warm place until doubled in bulk. Roll onto floured surface. Cut as desired. Place on greased baking sheet. Let rise in warm place until doubled in bulk. Bake at 400 degrees until lightly browned. Dough keeps for several days if covered and refrigerated. Yield: 100 biscuits.

Mrs. Obera B. Pruitt
Belton, South Carolina

BAKED ALMOND DOUGHNUTS

3/4 c. milk, scalded
8 tbsp. oil
1/3 c. sugar
1 1/2 tsp. salt
2 1/4-oz. packages dry yeast
2 eggs, beaten
3/4 tsp. nutmeg
4 1/4 to 4 1/2 c. sifted all-purpose
*   flour*
1 to 1 1/4 c. diced almonds, roasted
1/2 c. butter, melted
1/4 c. corn syrup
1 6-oz. package chocolate chips

Mix milk with 6 tablespoons oil, sugar and salt; cool to lukewarm. Dissolve yeast in 1/4 cup warm water in large bowl. Stir in milk mixture, eggs and nutmeg. Blend in flour and 1/2 cup almonds gradually. Turn onto floured board. Knead until smooth and elastic. Return to bowl. Grease top of dough; cover. Let rise in warm place until doubled in bulk. Turn onto floured board. Roll to 1/2-inch thickness. Cut into 2 1/4-inch rounds with doughnut cutter. Place 2 inches apart on greased baking sheets. Brush with 1/4 cup melted butter. Let rise in warm place for 20 to 30 minutes. Bake at 425 degrees for 8 to 10 minutes. Brush with remaining melted butter. Bring corn syrup, 3 tablespoons water and 2 tablespoons oil to a boil in

saucepan. Remove from heat. Add chocolate chips, stirring until mixture is smooth. Dip warm doughnuts into glaze and remaining almonds. Let stand until glaze is set. Yield: 1 1/2 to 2 dozen.

Photograph for this recipe on page 6.

YEAST BISCUITS

2 pkg. dry yeast
6 c. flour
1 tbsp. baking powder
1 tsp. salt
2 tbsp. sugar
1 1/2 c. shortening
1 c. milk
Melted butter

Dissolve yeast in 1/2 cup lukewarm water. Sift dry ingredients together in large bowl. Mix in shortening until crumbly. Add milk and yeast. Knead until smooth and elastic. Roll onto floured surface; cut with biscuit cutter. Dip in butter. Place on greased baking pan. Let rise for 30 minutes or until doubled in bulk. Bake at 400 degrees until brown.

Mrs. Janice W. Hill
Panama City, Florida

DELICIOUS CRULLERS

2 pkg. dry yeast
1/2 c. milk, scalded
1/3 c. sugar
1 1/2 tsp. salt
1/4 c. shortening
3 1/4 to 3 3/4 c. sifted flour
1 egg, slightly beaten

Dissolve yeast in 1/2 cup warm water. Mix milk, sugar, salt and shortening in bowl until shortening is melted. Cool to lukewarm. Add 1 cup flour; beat well. Add egg and yeast; mix well. Add enough remaining flour to make soft dough; mix well. Turn onto lightly floured surface. Knead for about 8 minutes or until smooth and elastic. Place in greased bowl, turning to grease surface. Cover. Let rise in warm place for 1 1/2 hours or until doubled in bulk. Punch down. Let rise until doubled in bulk. Punch down. Let rest for 10 minutes. Roll on lightly floured surface into 12 x 9-inch rectangle. Cut dough in half crosswise. Cut each half into 12 strips. Roll each strip to 10 inches long; twist. Place crullers on baking sheet. Cover. Let rise in warm place for 45 minutes or until almost doubled in bulk. Fry in deep fat at

375 degrees for about 2 minutes, turning once. Drain on paper towels. Brush with confectioners' sugar icing if desired. Yleld: 2 dozen.

Frances Irving
Raleigh, North Carolina

GLAZED YEAST DOUGHNUTS

    2 pkg. yeast
    4 c. lukewarm milk
    2 tbsp. shortening
    1 c. margarine
    4 eggs, beaten
    1 c. sugar
    1 tbsp. salt
    2 1/2 tsp. vanilla extract
    10 c. sifted flour
    1 lb. confectioners' sugar

Dissolve yeast in milk in large bowl. Melt shortening and margarine together in saucepan. Cool slightly. Stir into yeast mixture. Stir in eggs, sugar, salt and 1 1/2 teaspoons vanilla; mix well. Work in flour gradually. Place in greased bowl, turning to grease surface. Cover. Let rise in warm place until doubled in bulk. Roll on floured board to 1/4-inch thickness. Cut with doughnut cutter. Place on baking sheet. Let rise in warm place until doubled in bulk. Fry in 350-degree deep fat until brown. Drain on paper towels. Mix confectioners' sugar, 1/2 cup hot water and remaining vanilla in small bowl to smooth paste. Dip doughnuts into glaze. Drain on rack. Yield: 60 doughnuts.

Louise Paxton
Greenfield, Oklahoma

ORANGE-GLAZED DOUGHNUTS

    1/4 c. shortening
    3/4 c. milk
    1 pkg. yeast
    1 egg, beaten
    1/4 c. sugar
    1 tsp. salt
    1/4 tsp. nutmeg
    3 1/4 to 3 3/4 c. all-purpose flour
    2 c. confectioners' sugar
    1/4 c. orange juice

Heat shortening and milk in saucepan. Soften yeast in 1/4 cup warm water. Combine egg, sugar, salt, nutmeg and milk mixture in large bowl. Cool to lukewarm. Add yeast; mix well. Add flour gradually to make soft dough. Turn onto floured surface. Knead for 1 minute. Place in greased bowl, turning to grease surface; cover. Let rise in warm place until doubled in

bulk. Roll on lightly floured board to 1/2-inch thickness. Cut into desired shapes. Place 2 inches apart on cookie sheet. Let rise in warm place until light. Fry in deep fat at 365 degrees until brown on both sides. Drain on absorbent paper. Combine confectioners' sugar and orange juice in small bowl; mix well. Drizzle over hot doughnuts.

Sister Angela Marie Becker
Green Bay, Wisconsin

POTATO DOUGHNUTS

    3/4 c. mashed potatoes
    1 1/2 tsp. salt
    1/3 c. sugar
    2 tbsp. each shortening, butter
    2 pkg. dry yeast
    1 c. milk, scalded
    2 eggs, beaten
    4 1/2 c. flour

Force potatoes through ricer into large bowl. Add salt; mix well. Cream next 3 ingredients in bowl. Add to potatoes. Crumble yeast into cooled milk. Add eggs to potato mixture; mix well. Add yeast mixture; mix well. Stir in flour gradually. Place dough in greased bowl, turning to grease surface. Cover with damp cloth. Let rise in warm place until doubled in bulk. Punch dough down. Shape into doughnuts. Place on floured board. Cover with dry cloth. Let rise until light. Fry in deep fat at 350 degrees. Drain on paper towels. Roll in sugar if desired. Yield: 40 doughnuts.

Mrs. Doris Larke
Peoria, Illinois

RAISED DOUGHNUTS

    2 cakes yeast
    Sugar
    1 c. milk, scalded
    1/2 c. shortening
    2 tsp. salt
    2 eggs, well beaten
    5 c. flour

Dissolve yeast and 1 teaspoon sugar in 1/4 cup lukewarm water in small bowl. Pour milk over shortening, 1/2 cup sugar and salt in large bowl. Mix until shortening is dissolved. Cool to lukewarm. Add eggs and yeast mixture; mix well. Stir in flour to make stiff dough. Roll on floured surface to 1/2-inch thickness. Cut into doughnut shapes. Place on baking sheet; cover. Let rise in warm place until very light. Fry in deep fat at 375 degrees until brown.

Mrs. Vivian Steinbauer
Bronson, Michigan

FILLED DOUGHNUTS

2 pkg. dry yeast
3/4 c. milk, scalded
1/3 c. shortening
1/2 c. sugar
1 tsp. salt
2 eggs, beaten
4 1/2 to 5 c. sifted flour
18 prunes

Dissolve yeast in 1/2 cup warm water. Combine milk, shortening, 1/4 cup sugar and salt in bowl. Stir until shortening is dissolved. Cool to lukewarm. Add yeast, eggs and 2 cups flour; beat well. Add enough remaining flour to make soft dough. Turn onto lightly floured surface. Knead for about 8 minutes or until smooth and elastic. Place in greased bowl; turn to grease surface. Cover. Let rise in warm place for about 50 minutes or until doubled in bulk. Cook prunes in remaining sugar according to package directions. Drain; cool. Cut prunes in half; remove pits. Cut dough in half. Roll on floured surface to 3/8-inch thickness. Cut with 2 1/2-inch biscuit cutter. Place prune half on each round. Fold dough over prune. Seal edges. Cover. Let rise in warm place for 20 minutes or until doubled in bulk. Fry in deep fat at 375 degrees for about 1 minute on each side or until golden brown. Drain on paper towels. Roll in additional sugar. Yield: 3 dozen.

Dorothy Pfieffer
Atlanta, Georgia

WALNUT KOLACHE

1 pkg. dry yeast
1/4 c. shortening
3 tbsp. sugar
1 1/2 tsp. salt
3/4 c. milk, scalded
1 egg, beaten
3 c. sifted all-purpose flour
3/4 c. chopped walnuts
Melted butter
12 cooked dried apricots
1 c. sifted confectioners' sugar
1/4 tsp. vanilla extract

Soften yeast in 1/4 cup warm water. Add shortening, sugar and salt to milk in large bowl. Stir until shortening melts and sugar dissolves. Cool to lukewarm. Add egg and yeast; mix well. Stir in half the flour; beat until smooth. Add 1/2 cup walnuts. Blend in remaining flour gradually. Drop by heaping tablespoonfuls onto lightly greased baking sheets. Brush with butter. Let rise for 1 hour or until doubled in bulk. Dip

apricots into remaining walnuts. Press 1 apricot into center of each roll. Bake at 350 degrees for about 25 minutes or until brown. Combine confectioners' sugar, 1 tablespoon water and vanilla in bowl. Spread over warm buns. Yield: 1 dozen.

Photograph for this recipe on opposite page.

BROWN YEAST BREAD

2 pkg. yeast
1 c. quick-cooking rolled oats
Margarine
1/2 c. dark sorghum molasses
1 tbsp. salt
4 to 6 c. flour

Dissolve yeast in 1/2 cup warm water. Cook oats using package directions in 1 1/2 cups boiling water. Combine oats, 1/2 cup margarine, molasses, salt and yeast in large mixer bowl. Add 2 cups flour. Beat with electric mixer. Add enough flour to make stiff dough. Turn onto floured surface. Knead for 5 to 10 minutes, adding flour, until dough is smooth and elastic. Place in bowl. Brush with margarine; cover. Let rise in warm place until doubled in bulk. Punch down. Shape into 2 loaves. Place in greased loaf pans. Brush with margarine. Let rise until doubled in bulk. Bake at 375 degrees for 15 minutes. Reduce temperature to 350 degrees. Bake for 1 hour longer or until bread tests done. Yield: 2 loaves.

Martha Miller
Chalmers, Indiana

ANADAMA BREAD

1 tsp. salt
1/3 c. yellow cornmeal
1/3 c. molasses
1 1/2 tsp. shortening
1 pkg. dry yeast
4 to 4 1/2 c. sifted flour

Bring 1 1/2 cups water and salt to a boil in saucepan. Stir in cornmeal. Return to boiling point, stirring constantly. Pour into large mixing bowl. Stir in molasses and shortening. Cool to lukewarm. Dissolve yeast in 1/4 cup lukewarm water. Add to cornmeal mixture; mix well. Stir in half the flour. Add enough remaining flour to make stiff dough. Turn onto lightly floured board. Knead until smooth and elastic. Let rise in warm place until doubled in bulk. Place in greased 9 x 5 x 3-inch loaf pan; pat into loaf shape. Let rise again until doubled in bulk. Bake at 375 degrees for 40 to 45 minutes.

Mrs. Lana Giehl
Groveport, Ohio

BUTTERMILK BREAD

3 tbsp. sugar
2 1/2 tsp. salt
1/3 c. shortening
1 c. buttermilk, scalded
1 pkg. yeast
5 1/2 to 5 3/4 c. flour
1/4 tsp. soda

Combine sugar, salt and shortening with buttermilk in saucepan; stir until dissolved. Cool to lukewarm. Dissolve yeast in 1 cup warm water in large bowl. Stir in buttermilk mixture. Add 3 cups flour and soda; beat until smooth. Add enough additional flour to make stiff dough. Turn onto lightly floured board. Knead for 10 minutes, or until smooth and elastic. Place in greased bowl; cover with cloth. Let rise in warm place for 1 hour or until doubled in bulk. Punch down. Turn onto lightly floured surface. Let rest for 15 minutes. Cut in half; place in 2 greased loaf pans. Let rise, covered, in warm place for about 1 hour or until doubled in bulk. Bake at 400 degrees for 45 minutes.

Mrs. R. A. Aldridge
Gretna, Virginia

BUTTERCRUST BREAD

1 c. buttermilk
Butter
2 1/4 tsp. salt
1/4 c. sugar
1 cake yeast
1/2 tsp. soda
6 c. flour

Heat buttermilk in saucepan. Add 1/3 cup butter, salt and sugar. Stir until butter melts. Cool. Dissolve yeast in 1 cup warm water in bowl. Add buttermilk mixture; mix well. Mix soda with 1 cup flour. Stir into yeast mixture. Add 4 cups flour, 1 cup at a time, beating well after each addition. Spread remaining flour on board. Turn dough onto board. Knead for 10 minutes or until smooth and elastic. Place dough in greased bowl, turning to grease surface. Cover. Let rise in warm place until doubled in bulk. Punch down. Turn onto floured board. Shape into 2 loaves. Place in greased 9 x 5 x 3-inch loaf pans. Brush tops with melted butter. Let rise until doubled in bulk. Bake at 350 degrees for 35 minutes or until bread tests done. Brush with melted butter. Yield: 2 loaves.

Lynne Anders
Belmont, California

CASSEROLE BREAD

Milk
4 1/2 tbsp. sugar
1 1/2 tbsp. salt
2 tbsp. oil
3 pkg. yeast
3 eggs, beaten
1/2 c. powdered milk
6 3/4 c. all-purpose flour
1 tbsp. sesame seed

Scald 1 1/2 cups milk in saucepan. Combine with sugar, salt and oil in large bowl; mix well. Dissolve yeast in 1 1/2 cups warm water in small bowl. Add eggs and yeast to milk mixture; mix well. Add powdered milk and flour. Beat until well blended. Cover with towel. Place in cold oven over pan of boiling water. Close oven. Let rise for 40 minutes or until doubled in bulk. Remove from oven. Stir batter down. Beat vigorously for 30 seconds. Turn onto lightly floured surface. Knead for 4 minutes. Place in greased 8 x 4-inch baking dish. Brush top with 2 tablespoons milk. Sprinkle with sesame seed. Bake in 400-degree oven for 40 to 50 minutes or until bread tests done. Remove from oven. Cool for 5 minutes. Remove from pan. Cool on rack. Yield: 1 large loaf.

Mrs. Lloyd W. Brauer
Las Vegas, Nevada

CASSEROLE PUMPERNICKEL BREAD

3 pkg. dry yeast
1/2 c. dark molasses
2 tbsp. caraway seed
1 tbsp. salt
2 tbsp. shortening
2 1/4 to 2 3/4 c. sifted all-purpose
*   flour*
2 3/4 c. rye flour
Cornmeal

Dissolve yeast in 1 1/2 cups warm water in large bowl. Add next 4 ingredients, 1 cup all-purpose flour and rye flour; beat until smooth. Add enough all-purpose flour to make stiff dough. Turn onto lightly floured surface. Knead for 8 to 10 minutes or until smooth and elastic. Place in greased bowl, turning to grease surface. Cover. Let rise in warm place for 1 1/2 hours or until doubled in bulk. Stir down; beat for about 30 seconds. Divide dough into 2 greased casseroles. Sprinkle with cornmeal. Cover; let rise in warm place for 1/2 hour or until doubled in

bulk. Bake at 375 degrees for 30 to 35 minutes or until well browned.

Natalie Preer
Wilmington, Delaware

CHEDDAR CHEESE BREAD

Sugar
1 1/2 tsp. salt
1 pkg. dry yeast
1 egg, well beaten
1/2 lb. grated Cheddar cheese
3 to 4 c. sifted all-purpose flour
Oil

Mix 1 cup hot water, 1/4 cup sugar and salt in large bowl; cool to lukewarm. Stir 1 teaspoon sugar into 2 tablespoons lukewarm water. Add yeast. Let stand for 5 to 10 minutes or until thoroughly dissolved. Stir; add to cooled mixture. Blend in egg, cheese and enough flour to make stiff dough. Turn onto lightly floured board. Knead for about 5 minutes or until smooth and elastic. Shape into loaf. Place in greased 10 x 5 x 3-inch loaf pan. Brush with oil. Cover with damp towel. Let rise in warm place until doubled in bulk. Bake in 375-degree oven for 45 minutes or until bread tests done. Remove from pan. Brush with oil. Yield: 1 loaf.

Mrs. Mary Schafer
Waupaca, Wisconsin

REFRIGERATOR CHEESE BREAD

7 to 8 c. all-purpose flour
2 pkg. dry yeast
1/4 c. sugar
1 tbsp. salt
1 c. milk
3 c. shredded Cheddar cheese
Butter, melted

Combine 3 cups flour, yeast, sugar and salt in bowl; mix well. Heat 2 cups water and milk in saucepan to 120 degrees. Add to dry ingredients gradually. Beat for 2 minutes at medium speed of electric mixer, scraping bowl occasionally. Add 1 cup flour; beat at high speed for 2 minutes. Stir in cheese and enough flour to make soft dough. Turn onto well-floured surface. Knead for 5 to 10 minutes or until smooth and elastic. Cover with towel. Let rest for 20 minutes. Punch down. Divide in half. Roll each half into 14 x 9-inch rectangle. Roll as for jelly roll from short side, sealing edges after each turn. Seal ends; fold under. Place, seam side down, in 2 buttered 9 x 5 x 3-inch loaf pans. Brush loaves with melted butter. Cover loosely with plastic wrap. Refrigerate for 2 to 24 hours. Remove from refrigerator. Let stand at room temperature for 10 minutes. Bake in 375-degree oven for 35 to 40 minutes or until bread tests done. Remove from pans. Cool on wire rack.

Photograph for this recipe on page 15.

CHEESE CASSEROLE BREAD

1 pkg. dry yeast
1/4 c. milk, scalded
1 1/2 c. sifted flour
1 tbsp. sugar
1/2 tsp. salt
Butter
1 egg, beaten
1/2 c. grated Parmesan cheese
2 tbsp. chopped parsley

Dissolve yeast in 1/4 cup warm water. Cool milk to lukewarm. Sift flour, sugar and salt into mixing bowl. Cut in 1/3 cup butter until crumbly. Add egg, yeast and milk; beat well. Stir in cheese and parsley; mix well. Turn into greased casserole. Cover with damp cloth. Let rise for 40 minutes or until doubled in bulk. Dot with additional butter. Bake in 375-degree oven for 20 to 25 minutes or until bread tests done. Cut into pie-shaped wedges to serve. Yield: 8 servings.

Mrs. Jere Lyn Heitkamp
Normangee, Texas

EASY CHEESE BREAD

2 pkg. dry yeast
1 11-oz. can Cheddar cheese soup
1 pkg. dry Italian salad dressing mix
3 1/2 to 3 3/4 c. flour

Soften yeast in 1/2 cup warm water in large bowl. Add soup and salad dressing mix. Add flour gradually to make stiff dough, beating well. Knead dough on floured surface for about 5 minutes until smooth and elastic. Place in greased bowl, turning to grease surface. Cover. Let rise in warm place for 30 minutes or until doubled in bulk. Shape dough into four 10-inch loaves. Place on greased cookie sheets. Cover. Let rise for 30 minutes or until doubled in bulk. Bake at 400 degrees for 30 to 40 minutes.

Remove from pans immediately; cool on wire racks.

Ruby Carver
Oklahoma City, Oklahoma

HERB CHEESE BREAD

2 pkg. yeast
1 c. milk, scalded
3 tbsp. sugar
1 tbsp. shortening
1 tbsp. salt
1 c. shredded Cheddar cheese
4 1/2 c. sifted flour
1/2 tsp. ground sage

Dissolve yeast in 1 cup warm water. Pour milk into large bowl. Add sugar, shortening and salt; stir to melt shortening. Cool to lukewarm. Add yeast, cheese, flour and sage; mix well. Cover. Let rise for 1 hour or until doubled in bulk. Stir batter down; beat vigorously. Turn batter into greased 9 x 5 x 3-inch pan. Bake at 375 degrees for 55 minutes or until bread tests done. Yield: 8 servings.

Mrs. Ella Adair
Tropic, Utah

EGG BRAIDS

2 pkg. dry yeast
3 eggs
1 3/4 c. milk
2 tbsp. sugar
1 tbsp. salt
3 tbsp. margarine
6 3/4 to 7 1/4 c. flour
Oil

Sprinkle yeast over 1/2 cup warm water in large bowl. Separate 1 egg; reserve white. Add yolk, remaining eggs, milk, sugar, salt and margarine to yeast mixture. Stir in 2 cups flour. Beat until smooth. Add enough flour to make soft dough. Knead on lightly floured board until smooth and elastic. Cover. Let rest for 20 minutes. Punch down. Divide into 10 equal portions. Roll each part on lightly floured surface into 18-inch roll. Braid 3 rolls together. Twist 2 rolls together. Place over braid, pinching ends to seal. Repeat with remaining 5 rolls. Brush with oil; cover. Refrigerate for 2 to 24 hours. Let stand at room temperature for 10 minutes. Brush with reserved slightly beaten egg white. Bake at 375 degrees for 25 to 30 minutes. Yield: 2 braids.

Mrs. Glenda B. Thornhill
Groveland, Florida

COOL-RISE YEAST BREAD

2 pkg. dry yeast
1 3/4 c. warm milk
2 tbsp. sugar
1 tbsp. salt
Margarine
5 1/2 to 6 1/2 c. flour

Dissolve yeast in 1/2 cup warm water in large bowl. Add milk, sugar, salt and 3 tablespoons margarine. Add 2 cups flour. Beat for 1 minute. Add 1 cup flour. Beat vigorously for 150 strokes. Add remaining flour to make soft dough. Stir until dough leaves side of bowl. Turn onto lightly floured board. Knead until smooth and elastic. Cover with plastic wrap and towel. Let rest for 20 minutes. Divide dough in half. Roll each half to 8 x 12-inch rectangle. Roll as for jelly roll from short side. Seal ends. Fold ends under. Place in greased loaf pans. Brush with oil. Place waxed paper over top. Cover with plastic wrap. Refrigerate for 2 to 24 hours. Remove from refrigerator. Let rest for 10 minutes. Bake at 400 degrees for 30 to 40 minutes or until bread tests done. Remove from pans. Brush with melted margarine.

Mrs. Henry H. English
Detroit, Michigan

COUNTY FAIR EGG BREAD

2 pkg. yeast
1 1/2 c. scalded milk
1/2 c. butter
2 tsp. salt
1/2 c. sugar
2 eggs, beaten
9 c. sifted flour

Dissolve yeast in 1/2 cup warm water. Combine milk, butter, salt and sugar in large bowl. Stir to dissolve butter. Cool to lukewarm. Add yeast, eggs and about 3 cups flour. Beat until smooth. Work in enough remaining flour to make soft dough. Turn dough onto floured surface. Knead until smooth and elastic. Place dough in greased bowl, turning to grease surface. Cover. Let rise for 1 1/2 hours or until doubled in bulk. Punch dough down. Shape into 3 loaves. Place in greased bread pans. Let rise until almost doubled in bulk. Bake at 425 degrees for 10 minutes. Reduce temperature to 350 degrees. Bake for 40 minutes longer.

Mrs. T. L. Reagan
Ludlow, Massachusetts

HERB BREAD

2 c. milk
2 tsp. French's Herb Seasoning
4 tsp. caraway seed
1 tsp. aniseed
1/4 c. sugar
2 pkg. dry yeast
7 to 7 1/2 c. sifted all-purpose flour
1 tbsp. salt
1/3 c. shortening
5 eggs
Butter, melted

Combine milk, herb seasoning, caraway seed and aniseed in saucepan. Heat to boiling point. Pour into mixing bowl. Stir in sugar; cool to lukewarm. Soften yeast in 1/4 cup warm water. Add to milk. Add 3 cups flour; beat thoroughly. Add salt and shortening. Add 3 eggs one at a time, beating well after each addition. Beat in as much remaining flour as possible. Stir until dough leaves side of bowl. Turn onto floured surface. Knead until smooth and elastic. Place in greased bowl, turing to grease surface; cover. Let rise in warm place until doubled in bulk. Divide in half. Divide each half into 3 equal portions. Roll each piece into rope 14 inches long, tapering ends. Place 2 ropes on greased baking sheet in X shape. Place remaining rope across top. Braid from center to ends on both sides. Seal ends; tuck under. Brush with melted butter. Let rise until doubled in bulk. Beat 1 egg. Brush over tops of loaves. Sprinkle with additional caraway seed if desired. Bake at 375 degrees for 40 to 50 minutes or until bread tests done. Divide remaining 1/2 dough into 2 portions. Roll each into 20-inch long rope. Coil 1 rope in center of deep round baking dish or on greased cookie sheet. Coil remaining rope around first. Tuck ends under. Brush top with melted butter. Let rise until doubled in bulk. Brush with remaining beaten egg. Sprinkle with additional 1 teaspoon of aniseed or caraway seed. Bake at 375 degrees for 40 to 50 minutes or until bread tests done. Yield: 2 loaves.

Photograph for this recipe on page 2.

FRENCH BREAD WITH CORNSTARCH GLAZE

1 pkg. dry yeast
1 1/2 tsp. salt
1 tbsp. shortening
1 tbsp. sugar
3 1/2 c. flour

1 tsp. cornstarch
1/4 c. yellow cornmeal

Dissolve yeast in 1 1/4 cups warm water in large bowl. Add salt, shortening and sugar. Stir in flour. Turn onto lightly floured board. Knead for 8 to 10 minutes or until smooth and elastic. Place in greased bowl turning to grease surface; cover. Let rise in warm place until doubled in bulk. Punch dough down; let rise again until almost doubled in bulk, about 1/2 hour. Combine cornstarch and 1 teaspoon cold water with 1/2 cup boiling water in saucepan. Cook until smooth, stirring constantly. Cool slightly. Punch dough down; turn onto floured board. Cut dough into 2 equal portions. Roll each half into 8 x 10-inch rectangle. Roll as for jelly roll from long side; seal ends. Shape into long tapered loaves. Place on greased baking sheet, sprinkled lightly with yellow cornmeal. Brush loaves with cornstarch glaze. Let rise, uncovered, for 1 1/2 hours. Brush again with cornstarch glaze. Make 1/4-inch slashes in dough at 2-inch intervals with sharp knife. Brush again with cornstarch glaze. Bake at 400 degrees for 10 minutes. Reduce temperature to 350 degrees. Bake for 30 minutes longer or until bread tests done.

Mrs. William T. Schmidt
Fort Wolters, Texas

HERB BATTER BREAD

1 pkg. dry yeast
2 tbsp. shortening
2 tsp. salt
2 tbsp. sugar
3 c. sifted flour
1/2 tsp. nutmeg
1 tsp. sage
2 tsp. caraway seed
Butter, melted

Dissolve yeast in 1 1/4 cups warm water in mixer bowl. Add shortening, salt, sugar and half the flour. Beat for 2 minutes at medium speed of electric mixer, scraping bowl frequently. Add remaining flour and nutmeg, sage and caraway seed. Blend until smooth. Scrape side of bowl. Cover. Let rise in warm place for about 1/2 hour or until doubled in bulk. Stir down, beating for 25 strokes. Spread evenly in greased 9 x 5 x 3-inch loaf pan. Shape top of loaf with hand. Let rise for 40 minutes or until within 1 inch of top of pan. Bake at 375 degrees for 45 to 50 minutes or until brown. Remove from pan immediately. Brush top with butter. Cool on rack. Yield: 6 servings.

Linda Hepburn
San Diego, California

HERB AND BUTTER BREAD

1/2 c. butter
1/3 c. (firmly packed) brown sugar
2 c. scalded milk
1 tbsp. salt
1/2 tsp. each sweet basil, thyme
1 tsp. caraway seed
2 pkg. dry yeast
7 1/2 to 8 c. all-purpose flour

Brown butter in saucepan. Stir in next 6 ingredients. Cool to lukewarm. Dissolve yeast in 1/2 cup warm water. Add to milk mixture. Add enough flour gradually to make stiff dough. Turn onto floured surface. Knead for 5 to 8 minutes or until smooth and elastic. Place in greased bowl, turning to grease surface. Cover. Let rise in warm place for about 1 1/2 hours or until doubled in bulk. Punch dough down. Let rise for 1/2 hour longer. Shape into 2 loaves. Place in 9 x 5 x 3-inch pans. Cover. Let rise in warm place for 45 minutes or until doubled in bulk. Bake at 375 degrees for 35 to 40 minutes.

Lana Jean Frank
Portland, Oregon

LAZY LADY BREAD

1/2 c. milk, scalded
4 1/2 tsp. sugar
1 1/2 tbsp. margarine
1 pkg. dry yeast
4 c. flour, sifted
2 tsp. salt

Combine 1 cup boiling water and milk in bowl. Add 3 teaspoons sugar and margarine; mix well. Dissolve yeast in 1/4 cup warm water. Add to milk mixture; mix well. Set aside. Sift flour, salt and 1 1/2 teaspoons sugar together into large bowl. Make well in center. Pour liquid ingredients into flour mixture; mix thoroughly. Cover with waxed paper. Let rise until doubled in bulk. Divide in half. Shape into 2 loaves. Place in greased loaf pans. Let rise until doubled in bulk. Bake at 400 degrees for 15 minutes. Reduce temperature to 350 degrees. Bake for 40 to 45 minutes longer or until golden brown. Yield: 2 loaves.

Mrs. Paul Martin
Richmond, Virginia

GARLIC CASSEROLE BREAD

1 c. milk, scalded
3 tbsp. sugar
2 tsp. salt
2 tbsp. butter
2 pkg. yeast
1/2 tsp. garlic powder
4 c. flour

Mix milk, sugar, salt and butter in bowl. Cool to lukewarm. Dissolve yeast in 1 cup warm water. Stir into milk mixture. Add garlic powder and flour. Beat until blended. Cover. Let rise in warm place for 40 minutes or until doubled in bulk. Stir down. Beat for 30 seconds. Turn into greased 1 1/2-quart casserole. Bake in 375-degree oven for 1 hour or until bread tests done.

Mrs. E. N. Harding
Jackson, Mississippi

MIXED GRITS BREAD

1 pkg. dry yeast
4 c. flour
1 c. cooked grits, cooled
1/4 c. shortening
2 tbsp. sugar
2 tsp. salt
Soft butter

Dissolve yeast in 1 cup lukewarm water in bowl. Combine next 5 ingredients in large bowl. Stir in yeast. Turn onto floured surface. Knead until smooth and elastic. Place in greased loaf pan; brush top with butter. Let rise in warm place until doubled in bulk. Bake at 400 degrees for 45 to 50 minutes or until light brown. Remove from pan; place loaf on oven rack. Bake until golden brown. Remove from oven; brush top of loaf with butter.

Mrs. B. W. Crouch
McCormick, South Carolina

NEVER-FAIL WHITE BREAD

3 pkg. yeast
3/4 c. sugar
2 1/2 tbsp. salt
1 qt. milk, scalded
1/2 c. shortening
25 c. (about) sifted flour

Dissolve yeast in 1/3 cup lukewarm water. Combine next 4 ingredients with 1 quart boiling water in large bowl; mix well. Cool to lukewarm. Add dissolved yeast and half the flour; beat until smooth. Work in enough remaining flour to make soft dough. Turn onto floured board. Knead until smooth and elastic. Place dough in bowl. Cover. Let rise in warm place until doubled in bulk. Punch dough down. Shape into 8 loaves. Place in greased loaf pans. Cover. Let rise in warm place until doubled in bulk. Bake in 400-degree oven for 1/2 hour or until bread tests done. Freezes well.

Mrs. Louella R. Pence
Macon, Illinois

NO-KNEAD WHITE BREAD

1 pkg. yeast
3 tbsp. margarine
3/4 c. powdered milk
1 tbsp. salt
2 tbsp. honey
3 c. instant flour

Dissolve yeast in 1/4 cup warm water. Mix 2 cups hot water, margarine and powdered milk in bowl. Add salt and honey; mix well. Stir in yeast mixture. Add 2 cups flour; mix lightly. Spread remaining flour on board. Knead dough until smooth and elastic. Place in large greased bowl, turning to grease surface; cover. Let rise in warm place for 1 hour. Punch dough down. Let rise for 15 minutes. Cut into 2 portions. Let rest for about 10 minutes. Roll out to remove air. Turn over and pat. Roll as for jelly roll. Seal ends. Place in greased loaf pans. Let rise for about 1 1/2 hours. Bake at 400 degrees for 1/2 hour.

Mrs. Charles J. Allen
Watertown, New York

OATMEAL BATTER BREAD

3/4 c. rolled oats
1/4 c. sorghum molasses
1 1/2 tsp. salt
Butter
1 pkg. yeast
4 c. sifted all-purpose flour

Pour 1 1/2 cups boiling water over oats in medium bowl. Stir in molasses, salt and 3 tablespoons butter. Dissolve yeast in 1/4 cup warm water in large mixer bowl. Stir in oatmeal mixture. Add 2 cups flour gradually. Beat for 2 minutes at medium speed of electric mixer. Blend in remaining flour by hand. Cover with towel. Let rise in warm place for about 1/2 hour. Beat batter vigorously by hand for 25 strokes. Spread in greased 9 x 5 x 3-inch pan; cover. Let rise for 5 minutes. Bake in 425-degree oven for 40 to 50 minutes. Brush top with melted butter.

Mrs. Nina D. Erickson
Lafayette, Indiana

OLD-FASHIONED HONEY BREAD

2 1/4 c. milk, scalded
2 1/2 tsp. salt
1/4 c. shortening
3/4 c. honey
2 pkg. dry yeast
1 egg, beaten
7 c. sifted flour
1 c. yellow cornmeal

Combine milk, salt, shortening and honey. Cool to lukewarm. Dissolve yeast in 1/4 cup warm water in large bowl. Add milk mixture and egg; mix well. Sift flour and cornmeal together. Stir half the dry ingredients into liquid ingredients. Beat until smooth. Stir in remaining flour mixture. Turn onto lightly floured board. Knead until smooth and elastic. Place in greased bowl, turning to grease surface; cover. Let rise in warm place for 1 1/2 hours or until doubled in bulk. Punch down. Divide dough into thirds. Shape into 3 loaves. Place in 3 greased 9 x 5 x 3-inch pans; cover. Let rise in warm place for about 1 hour or until doubled in bulk. Bake at 375 degrees for about 40 minutes or until bread tests done.

Mrs. George E. Allen
Fort Stewart, Georgia

ONE-RISE BREAD

1 pkg. dry yeast
2 1/3 c. flour
2 tbsp. sugar
1 tsp. salt
1/4 tsp. soda
1 c. sour cream
1 egg

Dissolve yeast in 1/4 cup warm water in large mixer bowl. Add 1 1/3 cups flour and remaining ingredients. Beat at low speed of electric mixer for 30 seconds. Beat at high speed for 2 minutes. Stir in remaining flour. Beat at low speed until blended. Place in greased loaf pan. Let rise in warm place until almost doubled in bulk. Bake in 350-degree oven for 25 to 30 minutes or until bread tests done. Cool on wire rack. Freezes well.

Mrs. Jane Markham
Houston, Texas

ONION BREAD

1 pkg. yeast
2 tsp. sugar
Salt
3 c. flour
3 tbsp. butter, melted

1/2 c. chopped onion
2 tsp. paprika

Sprinkle yeast in 1 cup warm water; stir until dissolved. Add sugar, 1 teaspoon salt and 2 cups flour, stirring to blend. Beat thoroughly. Stir in remaining flour. Knead until smooth. Shape dough into ball. Place in greased bowl, turning to grease surface; cover. Let rise in warm place until doubled in bulk. Punch down. Divide in half; let rest for 5 minutes. Place in greased baking pan. Brush tops with butter. Sprinkle onion evenly over tops. Press into surfaces with fingers. Let dough rise for 45 minutes or until doubled in bulk. Sprinkle lightly with salt and paprika. Bake in 450-degree oven for 20 to 25 minutes or until bread tests done.

Mrs. Martha Shaddock
Bearden, Arkansas

PEASANT BREAD

2 pkg. dry yeast
2 tsp. salt
2 tbsp. sugar
2 tbsp. margarine, melted
1 pkg. spaghetti sauce mix
6 c. flour

Dissolve yeast in 2 cups warm water in large bowl. Combine salt, sugar, margarine, sauce mix and half the flour in bowl. Add to yeast. Beat until smooth. Scrape side of bowl. Beat in remaining flour until blended. Cover. Let rise in warm place until doubled in bulk. Stir down. Beat for 25 seconds. Turn into greased 2-quart casserole. Bake in 375-degree oven for 1 hour. Cool on rack.

Catherine Downs
Jackson, Tennessee

QUICK YEAST BREAD

1 pkg. yeast
2 tbsp. oil
2 tbsp. sugar
2 tsp. salt
3 c. flour

Dissolve yeast in 1 1/4 cups warm water in large mixer bowl. Add oil, sugar, salt and 2 cups flour. Beat for 2 minutes at medium speed of electric mixer. Blend in remaining flour with spoon until smooth. Cover. Let rise in warm place for 1/2 hour or until doubled in bulk. Stir batter down for 25 strokes. Spread evenly in loaf pan. Bake at 375 degrees for 45 minutes.

Mrs. Melvin Gower
Norfolk, Virginia

SHREDDED WHEAT BREAD

1 cake yeast
1 c. warm milk
2 shredded wheat biscuits, crumbled
1 tsp. salt
1/3 c. sugar
1/3 c. molasses
3 tbsp. shortening
6 to 7 c. flour

Dissolve yeast in 1/2 cup lukewarm water. Combine 1 cup boiling water and warm milk in large bowl. Stir in shredded wheat. Add next 4 ingredients and dissolved yeast; mix well. Add enough flour to make stiff dough. Cover. Let rise in warm place until doubled in bulk. Punch dough down. Divide dough in half; shape into 2 loaves. Place in greased loaf pans; cover. Let rise until doubled in bulk. Bake at 400 degrees for 15 minutes. Reduce temperature to 350 degrees. Bake for 25 to 35 minutes longer or until bread tests done. Yield: 2 loaves.

Mrs. George C. Arnberg, Jr.
Montgomery, Alabama

SOUR CREAM BREAD

1/2 c. sour cream
2 c. milk, scalded
1 pkg. dry yeast
6 c. flour
2 tbsp. sugar
2 tsp. salt

Blend sour cream and milk in large mixing bowl. Cool to lukewarm. Add yeast; stir until dissolved. Add 2 cups flour; mix well. Blend sugar and salt; sprinkle over dough. Stir in gently. Cover with damp cloth. Let rise for 1/2 hour. Stir dough down; add enough flour to make stiff dough. Turn onto floured board. Knead in remaining flour until dough is smooth and elastic. Divide dough in half. Place in greased loaf pans. Brush tops with melted shortening. Let rise in warm place for 1 1/2 hours or until doubled in bulk. Bake at 400 degrees for 20 minutes. Reduce temperature to 325 degrees for 20 minutes longer or until bread leaves side of pan. Yield: 2 loaves.

Mrs. F. D. McCready, Jr.
Portsmouth, New Hampshire

SOURDOUGH BREAD

7 c. flour
5 tsp. sugar
1 pkg. dry yeast

2 tsp. salt
1/2 tsp. soda

Combine 1 cup flour, 1 cup water and 1 tablespoon sugar in large bowl; mix well. Cover. Let stand in warm place for 2 to 3 days or until fermented. Dissolve yeast in 1 1/2 cups warm water in large bowl. Add 1 cup Starter, 4 cups flour, salt and remaining sugar. Stir vigorously for 3 minutes. Cover. Let rise in warm place for 2 hours. Combine soda with 1 cup flour in bowl. Stir into dough. Turn onto floured surface. Knead in remaining flour to make stiff dough. Shape into 2 loaves. Place in baking pan; cover. Let rise in warm place until doubled in bulk. Brush tops of loaves with water; score diagonally. Bake in 400-degree oven for 45 to 50 minutes or until bread tests done.

Meg Noller
Castle Rock, Colorado

SALLY LUNN BREAD

1 cake yeast
1/2 c. sugar
1 1/4 sticks butter
2 tsp. salt
1 c. milk, scalded
3 or 4 eggs, well beaten
4 1/2 c. flour

Dissolve yeast in 1/2 cup warm water in large mixer bowl. Stir sugar, butter and salt into scalded milk; cool to lukewarm. Add to yeast mixture with eggs. Beat in flour gradually with electric mixer at low speed. Cover. Let rise in warm place for 2 hours or until doubled in bulk. Stir down. Place in well-greased bundt pan; cover. Let rise in warm place for 1/2 hour or until pan is almost full. Bake at 350 degrees for 45 to 50 minutes or until bread tests done. Cool in pan.

Mrs. Louise Barton
Herrin, Illinois

BASIC WHEAT BREAD

2 c. all-purpose flour
2 pkg. dry yeast
1 c. milk
1/4 c. each oil, honey
1 tbsp. salt
1 egg
4 to 4 1/2 c. whole wheat flour

Combine all-purpose flour and yeast in large mixing bowl. Combine milk, 1 cup water, oil, honey and salt in saucepan. Warm over low heat. Add milk mixture to flour mixture. Beat at medium speed of electric mixer for 3 minutes or until smooth. Add egg; mix well. Stir in enough whole wheat flour to make moderately stiff dough. Turn onto lightly floured surface. Cover with bowl. Let rest for 10 minutes. Knead for 5 to 10 minutes or until smooth and elastic. Cover. Let rest for 20 minutes. Divide dough in half. Shape into 2 loaves. Place in 2 greased loaf pans. Brush with additional oil. Let rise in warm place for 1 hour or until doubled in bulk. Bake in preheated 400-degree oven for 35 to 40 minutes or until bread tests done.

Martha C. Chastain
Cummings, Georgia

WHOLE WHEAT BREAD

2 pkg. yeast
1 tsp. sugar
1/4 tsp. ginger
4 tsp. salt
3/4 c. (firmly packed) brown sugar
4 c. all-purpose flour
1/2 c. butter
8 c. whole wheat flour

Combine yeast, sugar and ginger with 1/2 cup warm water in small bowl. Set aside. Combine 2 1/2 cups warm water, salt, brown sugar and 2 cups all-purpose flour in large bowl; mix well. Add yeast mixture; mix well. Cover. Let rise in warm place for 1 1/2 to 2 hours. Melt butter in 1 cup boiling water in bowl. Cool. Add whole wheat flour; mix well. Stir into yeast mixture. Stir in remaining all-purpose flour. Turn onto floured board. Knead. Place in greased bowl, turning to grease surface. Cover. Let rise in warm place for 45 minutes. Form into loaves. Place in 9 x 5-inch pans. Cover. Let rise for 1/2 hour. Bake at 375 degrees for 35 minutes. Yield: 3 loaves.

Mrs. William N. Boak
Hope Farm, New York

BUBBLE BREAD

1 pkg. yeast
1 1/2 c. plus 2 tsp. sugar
1 1/2 c. milk, scalded
1/2 c. shortening
1 tbsp. salt
6 c. sifted flour
2 eggs beaten
Butter, melted
2 tsp. cinnamon
1/2 c. nuts
1 sm. bottle maraschino cherries

Dissolve yeast and 2 teaspoons sugar in 1/2 cup warm water. Combine milk, shortening, 1/2 cup sugar and salt in large bowl. Cool. Add enough flour to make thick batter. Stir in yeast mixture and eggs; beat well. Add enough flour to make soft dough. Let stand for 10 minutes. Knead until smooth and elastic. Place in greased bowl, turning to grease surface. Cover. Let rise in warm place until doubled in bulk. Punch down. Let rest for 20 minutes. Roll on lightly floured surface to 1/2-inch thickness. Cut into 1-inch strips. Shape into balls. Dip into melted butter. Combine remaining sugar and cinnamon in small bowl. Roll dough in cinnamon mixture. Place in greased angel food cake pan. Sprinkle nuts and cherries between balls. Let rise for 30 minutes. Bake for 30 minutes at 350 degrees. Yield: 15 servings.

Mrs. Carol Stuart
Geneseo, Kansas

CHERRY TEA RING

4 to 4 1/4 c. flour
1/2 c. (firmly packed) brown sugar
1/2 c. chopped pecans
1 1/2 c. drained cherries
1 pkg. yeast
3/4 c. lukewarm milk
1/4 c. sugar
1 tsp. salt
1 egg, beaten
1/4 c. shortening, melted
Butter, melted

Combine 1/2 cup flour and next 3 ingredients in bowl; mix well. Set aside. Dissolve yeast in 1/4 cup warm water in large bowl. Add milk, sugar, salt, egg and shortening. Sift remaining flour. Stir 1 3/4 cups flour into milk mixture. Add enough remaining flour to make soft dough. Turn onto lightly floured board. Knead until smooth and elastic. Place in greased bowl. Cover. Let rise in warm place for 1 1/2 hours or until doubled in bulk. Punch dough down. Let rise until doubled in bulk. Roll into 9 x 15-inch rectangle. Spread with butter. Cover with cherry mixture. Roll as for jelly roll. Seal ends. Shape into ring on greased baking sheet, seam-side down. Pinch ends together. Slash at 1-inch intervals, cutting 2/3 of the way down. Turn each section on outward side. Let rise in warm place for 35 to 40 minutes or until doubled in bulk. Bake at 375 degrees for 25 minutes. Spread with powdered sugar icing if desired.

Mrs. Carolyn Lankford
Oakley, Idaho

CHOCOLATE CHIP COFFEE CAKE

3/4 c. margarine
2/3 c. sugar
1 tsp. salt
1/2 c. milk, scalded
2 pkg. dry yeast
2 eggs, beaten
3 1/2 c. flour
1 c. semisweet chocolate chips
1 1/2 tsp. cinnamon

Combine 1/2 cup margarine, 1/3 cup sugar and salt with milk in bowl; stir to dissolve. Cool to lukewarm. Dissolve yeast in 1/2 cup warm water in large bowl. Add milk mixture, eggs and 2 cups flour. Beat at medium speed of electric mixer until smooth. Blend in 1 cup flour and 1/2 cup chocolate chips with spoon. Spoon into well-greased 10-inch tube pan. Combine remaining ingredients in bowl; mix until crumbly. Sprinkle over coffee cake. Bake at 350 degrees for 30 minutes or until coffee cake tests done. Yield: 12-15 servings.

Emily T. Duley
Upper Marlboro, Maryland

COFFEE CAN BREAD

4 c. flour
1 pkg. dry yeast
1/4 c. sugar
1/2 c. margarine
1 tsp. salt
1/2 c. milk
2 eggs, slightly beaten
Cinnamon to taste
Raisins (opt.)
Chopped nuts (opt.)

Measure 2 cups flour into large mixing bowl. Sprinkle with yeast. Combine 1/2 cup water, sugar, margarine and salt in saucepan. Cook over low heat, stirring constantly, until margarine is melted. Stir in milk. Combine milk mixture, eggs and flour mixture, stirring until yeast is dissolved. Add enough flour to make medium dough. Turn onto lightly floured board. Knead until smooth and elastic. Divide dough in half. Pat each portion into 9 x 12-inch rectangle. Sprinkle each with cinnamon, raisins and nuts. Roll as for jelly roll. Place in oiled coffee cans. Cover with aluminum foil. Let rise until foil rises 1 inch from tops of cans. Bake at 400 degrees for 20 minutes. Remove foil. Bake for 10 to 15 minutes longer or until golden brown.

Cool for 15 minutes before removing from cans.

Mrs. Marian S. Holcombe
Oreland, Pennsylvania

COOL-RISE SWEET DOUGH

5 to 6 c. all-purpose flour
2 pkg. dry yeast
1/2 c. sugar
1 1/2 tsp. salt
Margarine, softened
2 eggs
Oil

Combine 2 cups flour, yeast, sugar and salt in large bowl; stir well. Add 1/2 cup margarine. Add 1 1/2 cups hot water. Beat at medium speed of electric mixer for 2 minutes. Add eggs and 1 cup flour. Beat at high speed for 1 minute or until thick and elastic. Stir in enough remaining flour gradually with wooden spoon to make soft dough. Turn onto floured board. Divide into 2 portions. Knead for 5 to 10 minutes or until smooth and elastic. Cover with plastic wrap and towel. Let rest on board for 15 to 20 minutes. Punch down. Shape into braid or rolls. Place on baking sheet. Brush with oil. Cover loosely. Refrigerate for 2 to 48 hours. Let stand, uncovered, for 10 minutes at room temperature. Puncture surface bubbles with oiled toothpick just before baking. Bake in preheated 375-degree oven for 30 to 35 minutes or until bread tests done. Remove from pan immediately. Cool on rack. Brush with margarine while warm. Frost and decorate as desired.

Mrs. Alene A. Cox
Smithfield, Virginia

CORNMEAL-RAISIN BREAD

2 pkg. dry yeast
1 1/3 c. milk, scalded
3/4 c. sugar
1 tbsp. salt
1/3 c. shortening, melted
2 eggs, beaten
1 1/2 c. cornmeal
6 c. all-purpose flour
1 1/2 c. raisins

Dissolve yeast in 1/2 cup warm water. Combine milk, sugar, salt and shortening in large bowl. Cool to lukewarm. Stir in eggs and cornmeal. Add yeast and 3 cups flour. Beat until smooth. Stir in remaining flour and raisins. Beat until blended. Cover. Let rise in warm place for 1 hour or until doubled in bulk. Stir down. Beat vigorously for 30 seconds. Place in 2 greased loaf pans. Cover. Let rise in warm place for 45 minutes or until almost doubled in bulk. Bake in 375-degree oven for 45 to 50 minutes. Remove from pans. Cool.

Mrs. Gustava Murks
Florence, Alabama

CREOLE CASSEROLE BREAD

1 c. milk, scalded
3 tbsp. dark brown sugar
1 tbsp. salt
2 tbsp. margarine, softened
2 pkg. dry yeast
1 tsp. cinnamon
1/4 tsp. nutmeg
4 c. unsifted flour

Mix milk, brown sugar, salt and margarine in large bowl. Cool to lukewarm. Dissolve yeast in 1 cup warm water. Stir into milk mixture. Add cinnamon, nutmeg and flour; stir until well blended. Cover. Let rise in warm place for 1 hour or until doubled in bulk. Stir down. Beat vigorously for 30 seconds. Turn into greased 1 1/2-quart casserole. Bake in 375-degree oven for 1 hour or until bread tests done.

Mrs. Besse Miller
Perryton, Texas

FRANK'S PETALS

1 pkg. dry yeast
Sugar
1 1/2 tsp. salt
2 1/2 to 3 c. flour
3 tbsp. oil
1/4 c. (firmly packed) brown sugar
2 tsp. cinnamon
3/4 c. chopped nuts
1/2 c. butter, melted
1/2 c. confectioners' sugar
1 to 2 tsp. milk

Dissolve yeast in 1 cup warm water in large bowl. Add 2 tablespoons sugar, salt and half the flour; beat thoroughly. Add oil and remaining flour. Turn onto floured surface. Knead until smooth and elastic. Let rise in warm place for 45 minutes to 1 hour or until doubled in bulk. Roll into strips, 6 inches long x 1/2 inch thick. Combine 3/4 cup sugar, brown sugar, cinnamon and nuts. Dip each strip into butter. Coat with cinnamon mixture. Wind strip into flat coil in center of baking pan. Continue adding strips, placing close together to make round, flat coffee cake. Cover. Let rise for 45 minutes to 1 hour or until doubled in bulk. Bake at 350 degrees for 25 to 30 minutes or until golden brown. Cool slightly. Combine confectioners' sugar and milk in bowl. Drizzle over top of coffee cake.

Mrs. Thomas E. Maxwell
Big Sandy, Montana

GEORGIA PEACH COFFEE CAKES

2 pkg. dry yeast
1 1/4 c. sugar
3/4 c. butter, softened
1/2 c. milk, scalded
2 tsp. salt
3 eggs, beaten
5 to 5 1/2 c. flour
1 c. peach preserves
2 tsp. cinnamon
1 c. chopped pecans
1 c. sifted confectioners' sugar
1 tsp. vanilla extract
3 tsp. cold milk

Dissolve yeast in 1/2 cup warm water. Combine 1/2 cup sugar, 1/2 cup butter, milk and salt in large bowl. Stir until butter is melted. Cool to lukewarm. Blend in eggs and yeast. Add enough flour to make stiff dough. Turn onto floured surface. Knead for 3 to 5 minutes or until dough is smooth and elastic. Place in greased bowl, turning to grease surface; cover. Let rise in warm place for 1 1/2 hours. Punch down. Divide dough in half. Roll each half on floured board to 20 x 10-inch rectangle. Spread with remaining butter. Spread 1/4 cup preserves on each half. Combine remaining sugar, cinnamon and pecans in small bowl; mix well. Sprinkle mixture over preserves on each half dough. Roll as for jelly roll from long side. Seal edges and ends. Form into circles on baking sheet. Slash center of circle lengthwise 1/3 of the way through to within 2 inches of ends. Let rise in warm place for 1/2 hour. Spoon 1/4 cup preserves down center of each circle. Bake at 350 degrees for 20 to 25 minutes. Combine remaining ingredients in bowl; mix well. Drizzle over coffee cakes.

Mrs. James Baker
Tulsa, Oklahoma

DAISY COFFEE CAKE

2 pkg. yeast
1 c. milk
1/2 c. sugar
1 1/2 tsp. salt
1/4 c. margarine, softened
2 eggs
5 to 6 c. sifted flour

Dissolve yeast in 2/3 cup warm water in large bowl; stir until dissolved. Add next 5 ingredients and 3 cups flour. Beat at low speed of electric mixer for 1 minute or until smooth. Beat at medium speed for 2 to 3 minutes or until thick and elastic. Add 2/3 cup flour. Stir until dough leaves side of bowl. Divide in half. Knead for 5 to 10 minutes or until smooth and elastic. Cover with plastic wrap and towel. Let rest for 20 minutes. Punch down. Roll on lightly floured board into 6 x 18-inch rectangle. Cut lengthwise into 3 strips. Braid strips together. Place in greased 9-inch round pan. Form circle. Brush with oil. Repeat process. Cover lightly with plastic wrap. Refrigerate for 2 to 48 hours. Remove from refrigerator. Uncover. Let stand for 10 minutes. Bake at 375 degrees for 25 to 30 minutes or until coffee cake tests done.

Marguerite Holloway
Petersburg, Illinois

GLORIOUS MORNING CAKE

1 pkg. dry yeast
1/2 c. oil
1 tsp. salt
Sugar
1 c. milk, scalded
2 eggs, beaten
6 c. (about) flour
1/4 c. butter, melted
3/4 c. crushed pineapple, drained
3/4 c. coconut
1/2 c. chopped nuts
2 tbsp. pineapple juice

Dissolve yeast in 1/2 cup warm water. Combine oil, salt, 2/3 cup sugar and milk in bowl; mix well. Cool to lukewarm. Add yeast and eggs; mix well. Add enough flour to make soft dough. Turn onto floured surface. Knead until smooth and elastic. Let rise in warm place until doubled in bulk. Punch dough down. Shape into 1-inch balls. Arrange layer of balls, touching, in well-greased 9-inch tube pan. Combine butter, 1/2 cup pineapple, 1/2 cup coconut, 1/4 cup sugar and nuts in bowl. Spoon half the mixture over balls. Add another layer of balls. Top with remaining filling, pushing firmly

between balls. Let rise in warm place until doubled in bulk. Bake at 350 degrees for 35 to 40 minutes. Combine remaining pineapple, pineapple juice, 1 cup sugar and remaining coconut. Spread over cake. Bake until topping is brown. Yield: 12 servings.

Darlene Ledgewood
Commerce City, Colorado

DOUBLE DARK BROWN BREAD

1 cake yeast
1 tsp. salt
3/4 c. sugar
2 c. warm milk
14 c. (about) all-purpose flour
1/2 c. shortening
3/4 c. molasses
2 c. graham flour
2 c. rye flour

Dissolve yeast, salt and sugar in 4 cups warm water in large bowl. Stir in milk and 6 cups all-purpose flour. Add shortening, molasses, graham flour and rye flour; mix until smooth. Knead in enough remaining all-purpose flour to make stiff dough. Let rise overnight. Divide dough in half. Knead each half until smooth and elastic. Shape each into 3 loaves. Place in greased bread pans. Let rise again until doubled in bulk. Bake at 350 degrees for about 1 hour. Yield: 6 loaves.

Sharon Cox
Bristol, Ohio

SAVARIN RING

1/2 c. milk, scalded
Sugar
1/2 tsp. salt
3 tbsp. shortening
1 pkg. dry yeast
2 eggs, beaten
3 c. sifted all-purpose flour
1/4 c. apple juice
3/4 c. (firmly packed) light brown sugar
3 tbsp. butter
5 c. canned apples
2 tsp. grated lemon rind
2 tbsp. lemon juice

Combine milk, 3 tablespoons sugar, salt and shortening in bowl; mix well. Cool to lukewarm. Dissolve yeast in 1/4 cup warm water in large bowl; stir well. Add milk mixture and eggs; mix well. Add enough flour to make stiff dough. Turn onto floured surface. Knead until smooth and elastic. Place in greased bowl, turning to grease surface; cover with towel. Let rise until doubled in bulk. Punch down. Place in greased 3-quart 11-inch ring mold. Cover. Let rise until doubled in bulk. Bake at 400 degrees for 25 minutes. Invert onto plate. Combine apple juice, brown sugar and butter in saucepan. Bring to a boil. Spoon over ring until all is absorbed. Cool. Combine apples, 2/3 cup sugar, lemon rind and lemon juice in bowl. Pour into shallow baking pan. Bake at 400 degrees for 25 minutes. Chill. Spoon into center of ring.

Photograph for this recipe on page 4.

APPLE-PRUNE BREAKFAST RING

  3/4 c. milk
  1/4 c. sugar
  1 tsp. salt
  1 pkg. dry yeast
  1 egg, slightly beaten
  1/4 c. shortening
  3 1/2 c. sifted flour
  2 tbsp. butter, melted
  3/4 c. chopped cooked prunes
  1 1/2 c. pared diced apples
  1 tbsp. lemon juice

  1/2 c. (firmly packed) brown sugar
  1 tsp. cinnamon
  3/4 c. chopped walnuts

Combine warm milk, sugar and salt in bowl. Dissolve yeast in 1/4 cup lukewarm water. Add yeast to milk mixture. Add egg and shortening; mix well. Stir in enough flour to make soft dough. Turn onto lightly floured surface. Knead for 5 minutes or until smooth and elastic. Place in greased bowl, turning to grease surface; cover. Let rise in warm place for 1 1/2 to 2 hours or until doubled in bulk. Punch down. Let rise for 30 to 45 minutes or until doubled in bulk. Roll dough into 9 x 18-inch rectangle. Spread with butter. Combine remaining ingredients. Spread over dough. Roll as for jelly roll. Place, seam side down, on greased baking sheet to form a ring. Seal ends together. Cut with scissors 2/3 through from outer edge at 1-inch intervals. Turn each slice slightly to side; cover. Let rise until doubled in bulk. Bake at 375 degrees for 25 minutes. Frost while warm with thin confectioners' sugar icing. Yield: 8 servings.

Photograph for this recipe below.

ORANGE MARMALADE SWIRL

1 pkg. dry yeast
1 c. milk, scalded
1/4 c. sugar
1 tsp. salt
1/2 c. shortening
3 1/4 c. sifted flour
1 egg, slightly beaten
1/2 tsp. vanilla extract
1 c. orange marmalade

Dissolve yeast in 1/4 cup warm water. Combine next 4 ingredients in bowl. Cool to lukewarm. Add 2 cups flour to milk mixture; beat well. Add yeast, egg and vanilla; beat well. Add remaining flour; beat until smooth. Cover. Let rise for 1 hour or until doubled in bulk. Punch dough down. Spread dough in 2 greased 9-inch pans. Shape depressions in batter with floured fingers in round swirl. Fill depressions with orange marmalade. Let dough rise until doubled in bulk. Bake at 350 degrees for 35 minutes. Yield: 16 servings.

Mrs. Jean Puckett
Klamath Falls, Oregon

SOFT PRETZELS

1 pkg. yeast
1 tbsp. sugar
2 tsp. salt
4 c. flour
1 egg yolk
Coarse salt

Dissolve yeast in 1 1/2 cups lukewarm water. Add sugar and salt; stir until dissolved. Add flour; mix well. Turn dough onto floured board. Knead for about 5 minutes. Roll into thin strips; shape into pretzels. Place on well-greased cookie sheet. Beat egg yolk with 1 tablespoon water; brush on pretzels. Sprinkle generously with coarse salt. Bake in 425-degree oven for 15 to 20 minutes.

Fran Banks
Freedom, Pennsylvania

BASIC REFRIGERATOR ROLLS

Sugar
2 tbsp. shortening
1 pkg. dry yeast
1 egg, beaten
2 1/2 tsp. salt
1/3 c. dry milk
7 c. flour

Cream 1/2 cup sugar with shortening in large mixing bowl. Combine 1/2 cup lukewarm water, 1 teaspoon sugar and yeast in bowl; stir well. Pour 1 cup boiling water over creamed mixture; stir until dissolved. Add 1 cup cold water and egg; mix well. Add yeast mixture; stir. Add salt, dry milk and 6 cups flour; mix well. Let rest for 5 minutes. Spread on remaining flour on board. Knead dough until smooth and elastic. Place in oiled bowl, turning to oil surface. Cover loosely. Place in refrigerator until needed. Shape dough into rolls. Place on greased baking pan. Let rise in warm place until doubled in bulk. Bake in 375-degree oven for 10 to 25 minutes. Yield: 24 rolls.

Ione Johnson
Bigelow, Arkansas

BLENDER BRIOCHES

1/2 c. milk
1 pkg. yeast
1/3 c. butter, softened
1/4 c. sugar
1 egg
2 egg yolks
1/4 tsp. salt
Grated rind of 1 lemon (opt.)
2 c. flour

Place lukewarm milk and yeast in blender container with next 6 ingredients. Process for 30 seconds. Add 1/2 cup flour; process for 10 seconds. Pour over remaining flour in 2-quart mixing bowl. Blend thoroughly. Cover. Let rise in warm place for 3 hours. Stir dough down. Cover. Refrigerate overnight. Drop dough from buttered spoon into buttered muffin cups, filling less than 1/2 full. Let rise in warm place until doubled in bulk. Bake at 375 degrees for 15 minutes. Yield: 18 brioches.

Dale Wilson
Rochester, New York

BOWKNOTS

1 1/2 c. buttermilk, scalded
2 pkg. dry yeast
1/2 c. shortening
1/2 c. sugar
1 tsp. salt
1 egg, beaten
1/2 tsp. soda
4 1/2 c. flour

Cool buttermilk to lukewarm. Combine with yeast in large bowl; stir until dissolved. Add next 4 ingredients; beat well. Combine soda and flour. Add to yeast mixture; mix well. Shape into ball. Place in greased bowl, turning to grease surface. Cover. Let rise in warm place until doubled in bulk. Roll a small amount of dough into rope 5 inches long. Tie in single knot. Repeat process until all dough is used. Place on greased baking sheets. Let rise in warm place until doubled in bulk. Bake at 375 degrees for 15 minutes. Yield: 3 dozen.

Eleanor Kyle
Des Moines, Iowa

BUTTERHORNS

1 pkg. dry yeast
1/2 c. sugar
1/2 c. shortening
1 tsp. salt
2 eggs, beaten
4 c. sifted flour
Butter, melted

Dissolve yeast in 3 tablespoons warm water. Combine next 4 ingredients with 1 cup warm water in large bowl; mix well. Stir in yeast and flour; mix well. Refrigerate overnight. Roll into circle. Brush with melted butter. Cut into 16 wedges. Roll up from wide end. Place on greased baking sheet. Let rise in warm place until doubled in bulk. Bake at 350 degrees until bread tests done. Yield: 16 rolls.

Mrs. Jeanette Crouse
O'Fallon, Illinois

BUTTER TWISTS

6 tbsp. margarine
1 tsp. salt
1/2 c. sugar
1 c. milk, scalded
1 pkg. yeast
2 eggs, beaten
6 c. flour

Combine margarine, salt and sugar with milk in bowl; mix well. Cool. Dissolve yeast in 1/2 cup warm water. Add milk mixture and yeast to eggs in large bowl; mix well. Add flour. Knead on lightly floured surface. Let rest for 20 minutes. Knead until smooth and elastic. Place in bowl. Let rise in warm place until doubled in bulk. Punch down. Shape into rolls. Let rise in baking pan. Bake at 350 degrees for 25 minutes. Yield: 1 1/2 dozen rolls.

Janet Younger
Kansas City, Missouri

CORNMEAL ROLLS

1 pkg. yeast
1 c. cornmeal
2 c. milk
1/2 c. shortening
1/2 c. sugar
1 tsp. salt
2 eggs, beaten
5 c. sifted flour
Butter, melted

Dissolve yeast in 1/4 cup lukewarm water. Combine next 5 ingredients in top of double boiler. Bring to a boil, stirring constantly. Cook over boiling water for 10 minutes, stirring constantly. Add eggs and half the flour. Add yeast; mix well. Add enough remaining flour to make soft dough. Turn onto floured board. Knead until smooth and elastic. Shape into ball. Place in greased bowl, turning to grease surface. Cover. Let rise in warm place until doubled in bulk. Punch down; cover. Let rise for 10 minutes. Shape into small balls. Dip into melted butter. Place 3 balls together in greased muffin cups. Let rise in warm place until doubled in bulk. Bake in 400-degree oven for 20 to 25 minutes. Yield: 2 1/2 dozen.

Lucille Cook
Hutchins, Texas

EASY REFRIGERATOR ROLLS

3/4 c. sugar
1 c. shortening
2 tsp. salt
2 eggs, beaten
1 pkg. yeast
6 c. flour
Melted butter

Place sugar, shortening and salt in large bowl. Pour 1 cup boiling water over sugar mixture; stir well. Cool to lukewarm. Stir in eggs; mix well. Sprinkle yeast over 1 cup lukewarm water; let stand for 5 minutes. Stir well; add to sugar mixture. Add flour gradually; mix well with wooden spoon. Cover with foil. Refrigerate for 2 hours or longer. Roll onto floured surface into rectangle. Brush with melted butter. Roll as for jelly roll; cut into 1-inch slices. Place in greased muffin cups. Let rise for 2 hours or until doubled in bulk. Bake in 400-degree oven for 15 minutes or until brown.

Mrs. Sue Stilley
Forestburg, Texas

HOT YEAST ROLLS

1/2 c. sugar
1 1/2 tsp. salt
2 pkg. yeast
1 egg
1/4 c. shortening
6 1/2 to 7 c. flour

Combine sugar and salt with 2 cups lukewarm water in large mixing bowl. Dissolve yeast in sugar mixture. Stir in egg. Add shortening. Add half the flour, stirring well. Add remaining flour gradually, stirring until dough leaves side of bowl. Place dough in greased bowl, turning to grease surface. Cover with damp towel. Place in refrigerator for 1 hour. Punch dough down. Shape into rolls. Place on baking sheet. Let rise in warm place for 2 hours. Bake at 400 degrees for 12 to 15 minutes. Yield: 3 1/2 dozen rolls.

Carla Montgomery
Amarillo, Texas

ICEBOX ROLLS

1 qt. milk, scalded
1 c. sugar
1 c. mashed potatoes
1 c. melted shortening
2 pkg. yeast
12 c. flour
1 tsp. each salt, soda
2 tsp. baking powder

Cool milk to lukewarm. Combine sugar and potatoes in large mixing bowl; mix well. Add milk and shortening; mix well. Stir in yeast. Sift 6 cups flour, salt, soda and baking powder together. Stir into yeast mixture. Cover. Let rise in warm place for 2 hours. Punch dough down. Knead in remaining flour. Cover. Refrigerate overnight. Shape dough into rolls. Place in greased baking pans. Let rise in warm place until almost doubled in bulk. Bake at 400 degrees for about 15 minutes or until brown.

Mrs. Betty Peters
Inkster, Michigan

LEMON PARTY ROLLS

2 tbsp. sugar
1/2 tsp. salt
Butter
1/2 c. milk, scalded
1 pkg. yeast
1 egg, well beaten
1/2 tsp. grated lemon rind
2 c. flour

Mix sugar, salt, 2 tablespoons butter and milk in large bowl. Cool. Dissolve yeast in 2 tablespoons lukewarm water. Add to milk mixture. Stir in egg, lemon rind and flour; mix well. Let rise in warm place for 45 minutes to 1 hour or until doubled in bulk. Punch down. Turn onto floured surface. Roll to 1/3-inch thickness. Cut with biscuit cutter. Brush rolls with melted butter. Fold in half. Place on greased baking sheet. Cover. Let rise until doubled in bulk. Bake at 375 degrees for 8 to 10 minutes. Brush tops with melted butter. Yield: 2 dozen rolls.

Virginia Claypool
Marshall, Illinois

NEVER-FAIL ROLLS

1 pkg. dry yeast
1/3 c. sugar
1 tsp. salt
1/3 c. shortening
1 egg, well beaten
2 1/4 c. sifted flour
Butter, melted

Combine yeast, sugar, salt and shortening in large bowl. Add 1 cup warm water; mix well. Add egg. Add flour slowly. Beat for 25 strokes. Cover. Let rise in warm place for 2 hours. Punch down. Turn onto well-floured surface. Knead gently for 1 minute. Roll out to 1/3-inch thickness. Cut into desired shapes. Brush with butter. Let rise in warm place for 2 hours. Bake at 375 degrees for 15 minutes. Increase temperature to 425 degrees. Bake for 10 minutes. Yield: 3 1/2 dozen.

Julie Rogers
Tucson, Arizona

ONION ROLLS

1 pkg. yeast
1 c. milk, scalded
2 tbsp. sugar
1 1/2 tsp. salt
1/2 c. margarine
3 1/2 c. sifted flour
4 med. onions, sliced
1 egg, beaten
1/4 c. sour cream
1 tbsp. poppy seed

Soften yeast in 1/4 cup warm water. Combine milk, sugar, 1 teaspoon salt and 1/4 cup margarine in large bowl. Stir to melt margarine. Cool to lukewarm. Add yeast and 2 1/2 cups flour;

beat until smooth. Add remaining flour; blend well. Cover. Let rise in warm place for 1 hour or until doubled in bulk. Saute onions in remaining margarine in skillet until tender. Cool. Combine egg, sour cream and remaining salt in bowl; mix well. Turn dough onto floured surface. Knead lightly. Shape into 12-inch long roll. Cut into 12 parts. Shape each part into ball. Place on greased baking sheet; flatten each ball. Press onions into top of rolls; spread with sour cream mixture. Sprinkle with poppy seed. Let rise for about 45 minutes or until doubled in bulk. Bake at 375 degrees for 25 minutes or until brown.

Ellen F. Dow
Windsor, Vermont

POTATO ROLLS

1 c. milk
1/2 c. shortening
1/2 c. sugar
1 tsp. salt
1 pkg. yeast
4 1/2 to 4 3/4 c. flour
1 c. mashed potatoes
2 eggs, beaten
Butter, melted

Scald milk, shortening, sugar and salt in saucepan. Cool. Dissolve yeast in a small amount of warm water. Combine with milk mixture in large bowl; mix well. Add 2 cups flour and mashed potatoes; beat until smooth. Add eggs and remaining flour; mix well. Cover. Refrigerate until 2 1/2 hours before serving time. Shape into rolls. Cover. Let rise in warm place for 2 hours or until doubled in bulk. Bake at 425 degrees for 20 minutes. Brush with melted butter. Refrigerated dough will keep 1 week. Yield: 3 dozen rolls.

Sarah Smith
Groton, Connecticut

REFRIGERATOR BUNS

1 pkg. yeast
1 tsp. salt
5 c. flour
1 c. shortening
1 c. sugar
2 eggs, beaten

Dissolve yeast in 2 cups warm water. Add salt and enough flour to make thin batter. Beat until smooth. Let rise in warm place for 2 hours. Cream shortening and sugar in large bowl. Beat in eggs. Add yeast mixture and 1

cup cold water. Add enough remaining flour to make soft dough. Chill thoroughly. Shape into buns. Place in greased baking pans. Let rise for 1/2 hour. Bake at 375 degrees until lightly browned.

Peggy Frost
Esbon, Kansas

RYE ROLLS

2 c. milk
1 cake yeast
1/2 c. (firmly packed) brown sugar
2 tsp. each salt, caraway seed
2 eggs, beaten
1/2 c. melted shortening
3 c. each pure rye flour, wheat flour

Heat milk in saucepan; cool to lukewarm. Dissolve yeast in milk in large bowl. Stir in brown sugar, salt, caraway seed and eggs, mixing well. Let stand for 20 minutes or until bubbly. Add shortening and combined flours to make stiff dough. Work with hands to mix well. Turn onto floured surface. Knead until smooth and elastic. Shape into rolls. Place on baking pan. Let rise in warm place until doubled in bulk. Bake in 425-degree oven until brown.

Mrs. Lillian Wilkins
Vale, Oregon

SOUR CREAM AND CHIVE BUNS

3/4 c. sour cream
2 tbsp. sugar
1 tsp. salt
2 tbsp. shortening
1 pkg. dry yeast
2 1/4 c. flour
1 egg
1 1/2 tbsp. chopped chives

Bring sour cream, sugar, salt and shortening to a boil in saucepan. Cool to lukewarm. Dissolve yeast in 1/4 cup warm water in mixing bowl. Stir in sour cream mixture and half the flour. Beat until smooth. Add remaining flour, egg and chives; beat until smooth. Scrape side of bowl. Cover with cloth. Let rise in warm place for about 30 minutes or until doubled in bulk. Stir batter down. Fill 12 greased muffin cups 1/2 full with batter. Let rise in warm place for 20 to 30 minutes or until dough reaches tops of muffin cups. Bake in 400-degree oven for 15 to 20 minutes. Yield: 12 buns.

Debra Jason
Boise, Idaho

TENDER-CRUST ROLLS

3 tbsp. butter
1/4 c. sugar
1/2 tsp. salt
1 c. milk, scalded
1 cake yeast
3 1/2 to 4 c. flour
2 eggs

Add butter, sugar and salt to milk in bowl; mix well. Cool to lukewarm. Crumble yeast into milk mixture; stir until dissolved. Add 1 cup flour; beat with rotary beater until well blended. Add eggs; beat until smooth. Mix in remaining flour until thoroughly blended. Turn onto floured surface; cover. Let rest for 5 minutes. Knead for 10 minutes or until smooth and elastic. Place in greased bowl, turning to grease surface; cover. Let rise in warm place until doubled in bulk. Turn onto floured surface. Knead slightly. Shape dough as desired. Place on baking sheets. Cover with damp cloth. Let rise in warm place until light. Bake in 425-degree oven for 8 to 10 minutes. Yield: 3 dozen rolls.

Wilma J. Howell
Claridge, Pennsylvania

THREE-DAY YEAST ROLLS

2 pkg. yeast
1 c. margarine
3/4 c. sugar
2 eggs, beaten
7 c. sifted flour
2 tsp. salt

Dissolve yeast in 1/4 cup warm water. Melt margarine in 1 cup boiling water in saucepan. Add sugar, 1 cup cold water and eggs, mixing well. Stir yeast into margarine mixture. Combine flour and salt in large mixing bowl. Add yeast mixture; stir well. Turn dough into large greased bowl; cover. Place in refrigerator until ready to use. May be kept for 3 days. Remove from refrigerator. Turn onto lightly floured board. Knead dough until smooth and elastic. Shape into rolls. Place on greased baking sheet. Let rise until doubled in bulk. Bake in 425-degree oven for 25 minutes or until brown.

Mrs. Joy Barkowsky
Hereford, Texas

BUTTERSCOTCH PECAN ROLLS

2 pkg. yeast
1/4 c. sugar

1 1/4 tsp. salt
1 egg
3 c. flour
2 tbsp. shortening, melted
Brown sugar
Butter, melted
Pecans

Dissolve yeast in 1 1/4 cups warm water in large mixing bowl. Blend in sugar, salt and egg. Add flour gradually. Beat with electric mixer at medium speed. Add shortening; beat well. Place 1 1/2 teaspoons brown sugar, 1/2 teaspoon butter and 3 or 4 pecans in each muffin cup. Spoon batter into muffin cups, filling 1/3 full. Let rise for 25 minutes. Bake at 375 degrees for 20 minutes. Remove from pan immediately. Cool on racks. Serve warm. Yield: 2 dozen rolls.

Sister M. Eleanora
Fort Wayne, Indiana

BUTTER ROLLS

4 c. flour
Sugar
1/2 tsp. salt
1 c. shortening
1 cake yeast
1 c. milk
2 eggs, beaten
Butter, softened
Chopped nuts (opt.)

Sift flour, 1/2 cup sugar and salt into large bowl. Cut in shortening until crumbly. Soften yeast with 1 tablespoon warm water in small bowl. Add milk, yeast mixture and eggs to flour mixture; mix well. Refrigerate overnight. Divide into 4 or 5 portions. Roll each portion into 1/2-inch thick circles. Spread with butter. Cut into 8 wedges. Roll each wedge from wide end. Place in baking pan. Let rise for about 1 hour. Sprinkle with sugar and chopped nuts. Bake at 375 degrees for 10 to 15 minutes.

Mrs. William Flynn
Ankara, Turkey

OATMEAL YEAST ROLLS

1/3 c. shortening
1/3 c. (firmly packed) brown sugar
1 tsp. salt
1 c. rolled oats
1 egg, beaten
1 cake yeast, crumbled
3/4 c. nonfat dry milk
4 c. sifted all-purpose flour

Combine 1 1/2 cups boiling water and first 4 ingredients in 5-quart bowl. Cool to lukewarm. Add egg and yeast; mix well. Sift dry milk with 2 cups flour. Add to oat mixture; beat until smooth. Add enough flour to make soft dough. Turn onto floured surface. Knead until smooth and elastic. Place in greased bowl, turning to grease surface. Cover with waxed paper and towel. Let rise in warm place for 1 hour or until doubled in bulk. Punch down. Let rest for 10 minutes. Shape into 32 balls, 1 1/2 inches in diameter. Place 1 inch apart in 2 well-greased 8 x 8-inch pans. Cover. Let rise for 1 hour or until doubled in bulk. Bake in 375-degree oven until brown.

Photograph for this recipe above.

FROSTED PINEAPPLE SQUARES

Sugar
3 tbsp. cornstarch
1/4 tsp. salt
5 egg yolks
1 1-lb. 14-oz. can crushed pineapple
2/3 c. milk, scalded
1 pkg. yeast
1 c. margarine
4 c. flour

Combine 1/2 cup sugar, cornstarch and salt in saucepan; mix well. Stir in 1 egg yolk and pineapple. Cook until thick, stirring constantly. Cool. Combine milk and 1 teaspoon sugar in small bowl. Dissolve yeast in 1/4 cup warm water. Stir in remaining egg yolks. Cut margarine into flour until crumbly. Add milk mixture and yeast mixture; blend thoroughly. Divide dough into halves. Roll each half on floured surface to fit 16 x 10-inch pan. Place half the dough in bottom of pan; spread pineapple mixture over top. Place remaining dough over pineapple mixture; seal edges. Snip top of dough. Cover. Let rise in warm place until doubled in bulk. Bake at 375 degrees for 35 to 40 minutes or until golden. Frost with confectioners' sugar icing. Serve warm.

Mrs. Jerome Hegna
Echo, Minnesota

ORANGE ROLLS WITH GLAZE

2 cakes yeast
Sugar
1 c. milk, scalded
6 tbsp. shortening
1 tsp. salt
3 eggs, beaten
7 c. flour
7 tbsp. grated orange rind
1/2 c. corn syrup
1/4 c. orange juice

Dissolve yeast and 1 tablespoon sugar in 1 cup warm water. Combine cooled milk with shortening, 1/2 cup sugar, salt, eggs and 2 cups flour in large bowl; beat well. Add yeast mixture. Add remaining flour gradually, beating well after each addition. Turn onto lightly floured surface. Knead until smooth and elastic. Place in greased bowl, turning to grease surface; cover. Let rise in warm place until doubled in bulk. Turn onto lightly floured board. Roll into rectangle. Mix 3/4 cup sugar and 6 tablespoons orange rind in small bowl. Spread over dough. Roll as for jelly roll from long side; cut into slices. Place on greased baking sheet. Let rise in warm place. Bake in 350-degree oven for 20 minutes or until brown. Combine syrup, 1 cup sugar, orange juice and remaining orange rind in saucepan; bring to a boil. Spread on warm rolls. Yield: 3 dozen rolls.

Patsy Jean Walters
Kelliher, Minnesota

PULL-APART

1 1/2 c. sugar
1 c. butter, softened
1 tsp. vanilla extract
3 eggs, beaten
1 pkg. dry yeast
1/2 c. lukewarm milk
1/2 c. sour cream
4 c. flour
3 egg whites
1 c. chopped nuts
2 tsp. cinnamon

Cream 1/2 cup sugar, butter and vanilla in bowl; stir in eggs. Mix well. Dissolve yeast in milk. Stir into creamed mixture; mix well. Add sour cream alternately with flour, beating well after each addition. Refrigerate overnight. Let stand at room temperature for 1 hour. Turn onto floured surface. Roll into 1/8-inch thick rectangle. Beat egg whites in bowl until soft peaks form; add 1/2 cup sugar gradually, beating until stiff. Spread over dough. Sprinkle with nuts, cinnamon and remaining sugar. Roll

as for jelly roll. Slice into 6 pieces. Place in large greased tube pan. Let rise in warm place for 2 hours. Bake at 350 degrees for 30 to 40 minutes or until brown.

Geraldine Pace
St. Augustine, Florida

QUICK PRALINE ROLLS

1 pkg. dry yeast
2 1/4 c. sifted flour
2 tbsp. sugar
2 tsp. baking powder
1/2 tsp. salt
2/3 c. butter
1/3 c. milk, scalded
1 egg
3/4 c. (firmly packed) brown sugar
1/2 c. chopped nuts

Soften yeast in 1/4 cup warm water. Sift next 4 ingredients together into mixing bowl. Cut in 1/3 cup butter until crumbly. Stir in cooled milk, egg and yeast; beat well. Refrigerate overnight. Place dough on floured surface, turning to flour all sides. Roll to 15 x 10-inch rectangle. Mix brown sugar and remaining butter in bowl. Spread half the brown sugar mixture over dough. Sprinkle with chopped nuts. Roll as for jelly roll. Cut into 1-inch slices. Place on greased cookie sheets. Flatten. Spread with remaining brown sugar mixture. Let rise in warm place for 45 minutes. Bake at 425 degrees for 10 to 12 minutes.

Mrs. W. L. Burns
Fuchu AS, Japan

RICH YEAST CRESCENTS

3 1/2 c. flour
2 tbsp. sugar
1 tsp. salt
1 c. shortening
1 cake yeast
1/2 c. milk, scalded
2 eggs, slightly beaten
Confectioners' sugar
Jam
2 egg whites, beaten

Sift dry ingredients into large bowl. Cut shortening and yeast in until crumbly. Add cooled milk and eggs; mix well. Chill for 2 hours or overnight. Divide dough into 5 equal portions. Roll each portion into 10-inch circle on surface sprinkled with confectioners' sugar. Cut each circle into 8 wedges; spread each with jam. Roll up; shape into crescents. Place on greased baking sheet; brush with beaten egg whites. Bake at 400 degrees for 15 minutes.

Mrs. Louella R. Pence
Macon, Illinois

QUICK

DERBY BEATEN BISCUITS

2 c. sifted self-rising flour
1 tsp. sugar
1/4 c. shortening
1/3 to 2/3 c. milk

Sift flour and sugar together into bowl. Cut in shortening until crumbly. Blend in enough milk to make stiff dough. Force dough through coarse blades of food chopper 6 times, or beat 300 strokes with rolling pin. Dough should be slightly blistered, elastic and smooth. Turn onto floured surface; roll to 1/4-inch thickness. Cut with floured biscuit cutter. Prick tops with fork. Bake at 300 degrees for 45 to 55 minutes. Yield: 12 biscuits.

Mrs. Chelsea Merritt
Tollesboro, Kentucky

KENTUCKY BEATEN BISCUITS

4 c. sifted flour
1 tsp. salt
2 tbsp. sugar
1 tsp. baking powder
1 c. shortening
1 c. cold milk

Sift first 4 ingredients together in bowl. Cut in shortening until crumbly. Combine milk and 1/4 cup ice water. Add all at once to flour mixture; mix well. Knead on floured board about 5 minutes or roll through biscuit kneader about 25 times or until mixture pops and is soft and velvety. Keep kneader well floured with additional flour to keep dough from sticking to rollers or board. Fold dough each time it is put through kneader. Roll out 1/4 to 1/2 inch thick; cut with small biscuit cutter. Prick through dough with fork. Bake in 350-degree oven for about 40 minutes. Beat dough with heavy rolling pin and work until of smooth, waxy consistency and popping if biscuit kneader is not available.

Shirley Edmondson
Montgomery, Alabama

BUTTERMILK BISCUITS

2 c. flour
4 tsp. baking powder
1/2 tsp. each soda, salt
1 c. buttermilk
1/3 c. oil

Sift dry ingredients together into bowl. Add buttermilk and oil; blend well. Knead on floured surface. Pat out to 3/4-inch thickness. Cut with biscuit cutter. Place on greased baking pan. Bake at 450 degrees until lightly browned.

Freddie Brown Perkins
Los Angeles, California

COUNTRY BUTTERMILK BISCUITS

2 c. sifted all-purpose flour
1/2 tsp. salt
1/2 tsp. soda
3 tsp. baking powder
2 tbsp. shortening
1 c. buttermilk
1/4 c. melted butter

Combine first 4 ingredients in bowl. Cut in shortening until crumbly. Add buttermilk; blend well. Turn onto floured surface. Knead gently several times. Pat out to 1/4-inch thickness. Spread with half the butter; fold over to form 2 layers. Brush top with remaining butter. Cut with biscuit cutter. Place 1/2 inch apart in greased 9-inch baking pan. Bake at 400 degrees for 12 to 15 minutes.

Carnell Barnes
Winnie, Texas

BUTTERSCOTCH-PECAN BISCUITS

1/4 c. butter, melted
1/2 c. (firmly packed) brown sugar
Pecan halves
2 c. all-purpose flour
2 tbsp. sugar
3 tsp. baking powder
1 tsp. salt
1/3 c. shortening
3/4 c. milk

Combine butter, brown sugar and 1 tablespoon water in large bowl. Place 2 teaspoons mixture in each of 12 muffin cups; arrange pecan halves on top. Add flour, sugar, baking powder and salt to remaining brown sugar mixture; blend well. Cut in shortening; add milk, stirring until flour is moistened. Turn onto lightly floured board; knead gently for 20 seconds. Roll to 1/2-inch thickness. Cut with floured biscuit cutter. Place in muffin cups. Bake at 425 degrees for 15 to 18 minutes. Turn out of pan immediately. Yield: 1 dozen.

Ruth G. Seitz
Pittsburgh, Pennsylvania

BUTTER STICKS

1/2 c. margarine
2 c. self-rising flour
2 tsp. sugar
2/3 c. plus 1 tbsp. milk
Poppy seed

Melt margarine in rectangular baking dish. Combine flour, sugar and milk. Stir until dough leaves side of bowl. Knead several times on floured board. Roll into 3-inch wide rectangle. Cut in half lengthwise. Cut crosswise into strips. Place over melted margarine in baking dish. Sprinkle with poppy seed. Bake in 425-degree oven for 15 minutes or until brown.

Mrs. Cecile Poling
Houston, Texas

CAMP BISCUITS

2 c. sifted flour
3 3/4 tsp. baking powder
1 tsp. salt
6 tbsp. shortening
3/4 c. milk

Sift dry ingredients into bowl. Cut in shortening until crumbly. Stir in milk. Knead on lightly floured surface. Roll to 1/4-inch thickness. Cut with floured biscuit cutter. Cook in lightly greased hot skillet over very low heat until brown on underside and about 1 inch thick. Turn; brown on other side. Yield: 18 biscuits.

Frances Amy Prez
Sarasota, Florida

CHEESE BISCUITS

2 c. sifted flour
3 tsp. baking powder
1/2 tsp. salt
1/2 c. grated American cheese
4 tbsp. cold shortening
3/4 c. milk

Sift dry ingredients together into bowl. Add cheese; mix well. Cut in shortening until crumbly. Add milk; mix well. Turn onto floured board. Knead lightly, using as little flour as possible. Roll out 1/2 inch thick; cut with floured biscuit cutter. Place on greased baking sheet. Bake in 450-degree oven for about 12 minutes. Yield: 14 biscuits.

Dawn Perkins
Baton Rouge, Louisiana

CLOUD BISCUITS

2 c. sifted all-purpose flour
1 tbsp. sugar
4 tsp. baking powder
1/2 tsp. salt
1/2 c. shortening
1 egg, beaten
2/3 c. milk

Sift dry ingredients together into bowl. Cut in shortening until crumbly. Combine egg and milk in small bowl; add to flour mixture all at once. Stir until dough leaves side of bowl. Turn onto floured surface; knead gently about 20 strokes. Roll to 3/4-inch thickness. Cut with biscuit cutter. Place on ungreased baking sheet. Bake at 450 degrees for 10 to 14 minutes. Yield: 24 biscuits.

Mrs. Harriet Okino
Hilo, Hawaii

COUNTRY-STYLE BISCUITS

2 c. sifted flour
4 tsp. baking powder
1 tsp. salt
1 to 1 1/4 c. whipping cream

Sift dry ingredients together into bowl. Add cream gradually, stirring until mixture holds together. Turn onto lightly floured surface. Knead 8 to 10 times. Roll to 1/2-inch thickness. Cut with biscuit cutter. Place 3/4 inch apart on ungreased cookie sheet. Bake at 425 degrees for 10 minutes or until lightly browned.

Karen Mae Jones
Newton, Kansas

DOWN EAST BISCUITS

2 c. flour
1 tsp. (rounded) soda
2 tsp. (rounded) cream of tartar
1 tsp. salt
Shortening
1 c. milk

Combine first 4 ingredients in bowl; mix well. Cut in 1/4 cup shortening until crumbly. Add milk gradually; mix until dough clings together. Turn onto floured surface. Knead lightly. Pat out; cut with biscuit cutter. Melt a small amount of additional shortening in 8-inch pan. Dip top of biscuit in shortening; turn and place in pan. Bake at 425 degrees for 12 minutes or until golden brown.

Mrs. Polly Webster
Lincoln, Maine

EASY DROP BISCUITS

2 c. self-rising flour
1/2 c. mayonnaise
1/2 c. milk

Combine all ingredients in bowl; mix well. Drop by tablespoons into greased muffin cups. Bake at 375 degrees for 12 to 15 minutes. Yield: 1 dozen.

Mrs. Nancy D. Stubblefield
McMinnville, Tennessee

MINIATURE DROP BISCUITS

1/4 c. butter
1 c. self-rising flour
1/2 c. sour cream

Cut butter into self-rising flour until crumbly. Add sour cream. Stir until mixture forms stiff dough. Fill 2 x 1-inch muffin cups full. Bake at 450 degrees for 12 to 15 minutes or until brown. Serve immediately. Yield: 12 biscuits.

Mrs. Darrell Ritter
South Weymouth, Massachusetts

ORANGE TEA BISCUITS

Grated rind of 2 oranges
1 recipe biscuit dough
Sugar cubes, halved
Orange juice

Stir orange rind into biscuit dough. Roll on floured surface. Cut with biscuit cutter. Place on baking sheet. Dip sugar cubes into orange juice. Place on biscuits. Bake at 450 degrees for 10 minutes or until brown.

L. B. Noel
Batavia, New York

ROLLED BAKING POWDER BISCUITS

2 c. sifted flour
3 tsp. baking powder
1/2 tsp. salt
4 tbsp. shortening
2/3 to 3/4 c. milk

Sift dry ingredients together in bowl. Cut in shortening until crumbly. Make well in flour mixture; pour in milk. Mix lightly to form soft dough. Place on floured surface. Knead several times. Roll out to 1/2-inch thickness. Cut with biscuit cutter. Place on ungreased baking sheet. Bake at 425 degrees for 10 to 12 minutes. Yield: 10-12 servings.

Mrs. Zelota M. Yates
Raleigh, North Carolina

CHEESE BRAMBLES

1/2 c. butter, softened
1 3-oz. package cream cheese, softened
1 c. flour
1/4 tsp. salt
Dash of cayenne pepper
American cheese, cubed

Blend butter and cream cheese together in bowl. Cut in flour, salt and cayenne pepper until crumbly. Blend until dough leaves side of bowl. Refrigerate until chilled. Turn onto floured surface. Roll to 1/8-inch thickness. Cut into 2-inch rounds. Place cheese cube on half of each round. Fold in half. Seal edges. Place on baking sheet. Chill until baking time. Bake at 450 degrees for 8 to 10 minutes. Yield: 36-40 brambles.

Nancy M. Riley
Waterford, Ohio

CHEESE STRAWS

1 1/2 c. flour
1 tsp. each baking powder, salt
1/4 tsp. pepper
2 c. grated cheese
1/2 stick butter, softened

Sift dry ingredients together into mixing bowl. Add cheese; mix well. Cut in butter until crumbly. Add enough cold water to make stiff dough. Turn onto floured surface. Roll to 1/4-inch thickness. Cut into strips. Place on baking sheet. Bake at 375 degrees until lightly browned.

Mrs. Velm T. Stickland
Laurel, Mississippi

APPLE COFFEE CAKE

Sugar
1/2 tsp. salt
2 tbsp. butter, softened
1 egg, beaten
3/4 c. milk
Cake flour
2 tsp. baking powder
1 tsp. vanilla extract
5 or 6 apples, peeled, sliced
2 tbsp. flour

Blend 2 tablespoons sugar, salt and 1 tablespoon butter in bowl. Add egg and milk; mix well. Blend in 2 cups flour, baking powder and vanilla; mix well. Spread in greased 6 x 10 x 2-inch baking pan. Arrange apples in rows over dough. Combine 1/2 cup sugar, 2 tablespoons flour and 1 tablespoon butter in bowl. Mix until crumbly. Sprinkle over apples. Bake at 350 degrees for 1/2 hour or until apples are tender and golden brown. Yield: 8-10 servings.

Mrs. Helen Goska
West Bend, Wisconsin

DUTCH APPLE BREAKFAST CAKE

7 c. sifted flour
1/4 c. baking powder
1 1/2 tsp. salt
Sugar
1 c. shortening
3 eggs, beaten
1 No. 2 1/2 can finely chopped apples,
*   drained*
3 tbsp. butter, melted
4 1/2 tsp. cinnamon

Mix flour, baking powder, salt and 6 tablespoons sugar in bowl. Cut in shortening until crumbly. Add eggs and 2 1/4 cups water. Mix to form soft dough. Spread evenly in bottoms of 2 greased 9 x 13-inch baking pans. Combine apples, butter, cinnamon and 1 2/3 cups sugar in bowl. Spread evenly over batter. Bake at 400 degrees for 25 minutes. Yield: 25 servings.

Mrs. Ethel Reese
Salido, Colorado

QUICK APPLE COFFEE CAKE

3 c. flour
1 1/2 tsp. each soda, baking powder
3/4 tsp. salt
3/4 c. butter
2 c. sugar
1 1/2 tsp. vanilla extract
3 eggs
1 1/2 c. sour cream
1 can apple pie filling
2/3 c. (firmly packed) brown sugar
1 1/2 tsp. cinnamon
1 1/2 c. chopped walnuts

Sift together first 4 ingredients; set aside. Cream together butter, 1 1/2 cups sugar and vanilla in bowl. Add eggs, one at a time, beating well after each addition. Add flour mixture to creamed mixture alternately with sour cream, beating well after each addition. Spread half the batter in greased 13 x 9 x 2-inch baking pan. Spoon half the apple pie filling over batter. Repeat layers. Combine remaining ingredients in bowl; mix well. Sprinkle over coffee cake. Bake at 350 degrees for 1 hour.

Irene E. Krause
Shawano, Wisconsin

BLUEBERRY COFFEE CAKE

Sugar
1/4 c. shortening
1 egg
1 tsp. vanilla extract
3/4 c. milk
1 3/4 c. flour
3 tbsp. baking powder
1/2 tsp. salt
1 1/2 c. blueberries, drained
1/2 tsp. cinnamon

Cream 3/4 cup sugar, shortening, egg and vanilla in large bowl. Add milk; blend well. Add next 3 ingredients; mix well. Spread half the batter in greased 9-inch square baking pan. Cover with blueberries. Sprinkle with 2 tablespoons sugar. Spread remaining batter over top. Combine cinnamon and 4 tablespoons sugar. Sprinkle over batter. Bake at 375 degrees for 35 minutes. Yield: 9 servings.

Judy Daniels
Panama City, Florida

CRANBERRY COFFEE CAKE

1/2 c. shortening
1 c. sugar
2 eggs
1 c. applesauce
Salt
1 1/2 c. flour
3/4 tsp. soda
1 tsp. cinnamon
1/2 tsp. cloves
1/4 tsp. nutmeg
1 c. rolled oats
3/4 c. whole cranberry sauce
1 1/2 c. confectioners' sugar
1/2 c. syrup

Cream shortening in large bowl. Add sugar and eggs, mixing well. Add applesauce; blend thoroughly. Batter will be lumpy. Sift 1/2 teaspoon salt and next 5 ingredients together. Add to creamed mixture; blend thoroughly. Stir in oats and cranberry sauce. Pour batter into greased 9-inch square baking pan. Bake at 350 degrees for 50 to 55 minutes. Cool. Combine confectioners' sugar, syrup and 1/4 teaspoon salt in bowl. Beat until blended. Spread on cake. Yield: 9 servings.

Lois B. Jenkins
Franklin, Pennsylvania

BLUEBERRY TEA CAKE

1 tbsp. shortening
1 c. sugar
1 egg
1 1/4 c. sifted flour
2 tsp. baking powder
1/3 c. milk
1/2 c. blueberries

Cream shortening, sugar and egg in bowl. Sift together flour and baking powder. Add to creamed mixture alternately with milk, mixing well after each addition. Fold in blueberries. Spoon into greased and floured layer cake pan. Bake at 375 degrees for 20 to 25 minutes. Yield: 8 servings.

Mrs. Beatrice Birchard
Hackettstown, New Jersey

QUICK CHOCOLATE COFFEE CAKE

1 1/4 c. sugar
4 tbsp. butter
1 egg, beaten
2 c. all-purpose flour
1/2 tsp. soda
2 tsp. baking powder
Pinch of salt
1 c. chocolate milk
1/2 tsp. cinnamon

Cream together 1 cup sugar and 2 tablespoons butter in large bowl. Add egg; mix well. Sift together next 4 ingredients. Add to creamed mixture alternately with chocolate milk, beating well after each addition. Pour into buttered 8-inch square baking pan. Melt remaining butter in saucepan. Pour over batter. Combine cinnamon and remaining sugar. Sprinkle over batter. Bake at 350 degrees for 25 to 35 minutes or until coffee cake tests done. Yield: 8 servings.

Mrs. Janet Latham
Buhl, Idaho

COWBOY COFFEE CAKE

2 1/2 c. sifted flour
1/2 tsp. salt
2 c. (firmly packed) brown sugar
2/3 c. shortening
2 tsp. baking powder
1/2 tsp. each soda, nutmeg and cinnamon
1 c. sour milk
2 eggs, well beaten
Chopped nuts (opt.)
Cinnamon to taste (opt.)

Combine flour, salt and brown sugar in bowl. Cut in shortening until crumbly. Reserve 1/2 cup mixture. Add baking powder, soda and spices to flour mixture; mix well. Add sour milk and eggs; mix well. Pour into 2 waxed paper-lined 8 x 8 x 2-inch baking pans. Sprinkle with reserved flour mixture. Sprinkle nuts and cinnamon over top. Bake at 375 degrees for 25 to 30 minutes. Yield: 10 servings.

Jessie Thomas
Elida, New Mexico

FRENCH COFFEE CAKE

2 1/2 c. flour
1/2 tsp. each baking powder, salt
1 tsp. soda
1 1/4 c. sugar
1 c. shortening
3 eggs
1 c. sour cream
1 1/2 tsp. vanilla extract
2 tbsp. cinnamon
1/2 c. chopped nuts

Sift first 4 ingredients together. Cream 1 cup sugar and shortening in bowl. Add eggs one at a time, beating well after each addition. Beat sour cream and vanilla in bowl. Add to creamed mixture alternately with dry ingredients, mixing well after each addition. Combine 4 tablespoons sugar, cinnamon and nuts in bowl. Sprinkle 1/3 of the mixture in bottom of 8-inch tube pan. Pour 1/3 of the batter over nut mixture. Alternate layers until all ingredients are used. Bake at 350 degrees for 50 minutes. Yield: 10-12 servings.

Mrs. Nicole MacDonald
Perth, New Brunswick, Canada

GERMAN PEACH-CREAM KUCHEN

2 c. sifted flour
3/4 c. sugar
1/4 tsp. baking powder
1 tsp. salt
1/2 c. butter
1 No. 2 1/2 can peach slices, drained
1 tsp. cinnamon
2 egg yolks, beaten
1 c. sour cream

Sift flour, 1/4 cup sugar, baking powder and salt together into bowl. Cut in butter until crumbly. Press mixture firmly into bottom and side of lightly greased 9-inch springform pan. Arrange peaches evenly over crumbs. Combine remaining sugar and cinnamon in bowl; mix well. Sprinkle over peaches. Bake at 400 degrees for 15 minutes. Blend egg yolks and sour cream in bowl. Spoon over peaches. Bake for 20 minutes longer or until golden brown. Serve warm or chilled. Yield: 8 servings.

Mrs. Victor Kendall
Norfolk, Virginia

JEWISH COFFEE CAKE

1 1/2 c. sugar
1/4 c. each shortening, butter
2 eggs
1 c. sour cream
1 tsp. vanilla extract
2 c. flour
1 1/2 tsp. baking powder
1/2 tsp. soda
Pinch of salt
2 tsp. cinnamon
1 c. nuts, finely chopped

Cream 1 cup sugar, shortening and butter in bowl. Add next 7 ingredients; beat until smooth. Pour half the batter into greased tube pan. Combine 1/2 cup sugar, cinnamon and nuts. Sprinkle half the cinnamon mixture over batter. Add remaining batter. Top with remaining cinnamon mixture. Bake at 350 degrees for 1 hour.

Mrs. Velma G. Mahood
Milwaukee, Wisconsin

SNICKERDOUGH

1/2 c. butter
1 c. sugar
2 eggs
1/2 tsp. salt
2 tsp. baking powder
1 tsp. soda
2 c. all-purpose flour
1 c. buttermilk
1 tsp. lemon juice
2/3 c. confectioners' sugar
1 tsp. cinnamon

Cream butter and sugar in bowl. Add eggs one at a time, beating well after each addition. Sift next 4 ingredients together. Combine buttermilk and lemon juice. Add to creamed mixture alternately with dry ingredients, beating well after each addition. Pour batter into 2 greased and floured 9-inch layer pans. Sprinkle with confectioners' sugar and cinnamon. Bake at 375 degrees for 25 to 30 minutes. Cool for 10 minutes. Turn onto serving plates. Yield: 12 servings.

Jewell Carver
Amarillo, Texas

SOUR CREAM COFFEE CAKE

1/2 lb. margarine
1 1/2 c. sugar
3 eggs
2 1/2 c. flour
2 tsp. baking powder
1 tsp. soda
1 c. sour cream
1 tsp. vanilla extract
1 tsp. lemon extract
Few drops of almond extract
1 tsp. cinnamon
1 c. chopped pecans

Cream margarine and 1 cup sugar together in large bowl. Add eggs, one at a time, beating well. Sift flour, baking powder and soda. Add alternately with sour cream to creamed mixture, beating well after each addition. Add flavorings. Pour half the batter into greased and floured loaf pan. Combine remaining ingredients in bowl; mix well. Sprinkle half the topping over batter. Swirl slightly. Add remaining batter; spread on remaining topping. Swirl slightly. Bake at 350 degrees for 35 to 40 minutes. Cool in pan. Yield: 18 servings.

Elizabeth Johnston
Murfreesboro, Tennessee

SPICY COFFEE CAKE

1 1/2 c. sifted flour
1 tsp. each baking powder, cinnamon
1/2 tsp. each soda, salt
1/2 c. butter, softened
1 c. sugar
2 eggs
1 c. sour cream
1 c. corn flake crumbs
1/2 c. (firmly packed) brown sugar
1/2 c. chopped pecans

Sift dry ingredients together. Cream butter and sugar in bowl. Add eggs; beat well. Add dry ingredients to creamed mixture alternately with sour cream, mixing after each addition. Stir in 1/2 cup corn flake crumbs. Combine remaining corn flake crumbs, brown sugar and pecans. Spoon half the batter into greased 9 x 9 x 2-inch pan. Sprinkle with half the crumb mixture. Repeat with remaining batter and crumb mixture. Bake at 350 degrees for 40 minutes or until cake tests done. Serve warm with whipped cream.

Marthanne Limehouse
Yonges Island, South Carolina

STREUSEL-TOPPED ORANGE COFFEE CAKE

2 1/8 c. sifted flour
1 c. sugar
1 1/2 tsp. cinnamon
1 1/2 tsp. baking powder
1/8 tsp. soda
1/2 tsp. salt
1/2 tsp. nutmeg
1/3 c. shortening
2 tbsp. grated orange rind
1/3 c. chopped nuts
1 egg, well beaten
1/2 c. milk
2 tbsp. butter, melted

Sift 2 cups flour, 1/2 cup sugar, 1 teaspoon cinnamon and next 4 ingredients together into bowl. Cut in shortening with pastry blender until crumbly. Add orange rind and nuts. Blend egg and milk in small bowl. Add to flour mixture, stirring until just mixed. Spread batter in greased 9-inch square baking pan. Combine remaining flour, sugar, cinnamon and butter in bowl; mix well. Sprinkle over batter. Bake at 375 degrees for 25 minutes. Cut into squares to serve. Yield: 9 servings.

Mrs. Requa K. Spears
Pikeville, Kentucky

DOUBLE CORN BREAD

1 No. 2 can cream-style corn
1/2 c. (scant) oil
1 c. self-rising cornmeal
2 eggs, beaten
1 sm. carton sour cream

Combine all ingredients in mixing bowl; mix well. Pour into baking dish. Bake in 425-degree oven for 1/2 hour or until bread tests done.

Emily Rickman
Danville, Virginia

EAST TEXAS CORN BREAD

1 c. cornmeal
1 c. buttermilk
3/4 tsp. soda
2 eggs, beaten
1/2 tsp. bacon drippings
1/2 tsp. salt
1 1/2 green peppers, grated
1 med. onion, grated
1 lg. can whole kernel corn, drained
1/2 lb. longhorn cheese, grated

Combine first 6 ingredients in large bowl; mix well. Pour half the mixture into skillet. Sprinkle with half the green peppers, onion and corn. Pour remaining batter over vegetables. Sprinkle cheese over top. Cover with remaining vegetables. Bake at 350 degrees for 1 hour. Yield: 4 servings.

Mrs. Bobbi Mowrey
Merna, Nebraska

GOLDEN CORN BREAD

1 c. cornmeal
1 c. sifted flour
1/4 c. sugar
1/2 tsp. salt
4 tsp. baking powder
1 egg
1 c. milk
1/4 c. shortening

Sift dry ingredients into bowl. Add egg, milk and shortening. Beat with egg beater until smooth. Pour into greased 8-inch baking pan. Bake at 425 degrees for 20 to 25 minutes. Yield: 6 servings.

Mrs. William Hamlet
Chattanooga, Tennessee

MEXICAN CORN BREAD

1 1/2 c. yellow cornmeal
3 tsp. baking powder
1 tsp. salt
2 eggs
2/3 c. oil
1 c. buttermilk
3 jalapeno peppers, chopped
1 No. 303 can cream-style corn
1 c. grated longhorn cheese

Combine first 3 ingredients in bowl. Add eggs and oil; mix well. Blend in buttermilk. Add jalapeno peppers and corn; mix well. Pour half the batter into greased baking dish. Top with half the cheese. Repeat layers. Bake at 350 degrees for 45 minutes or until bread tests done. Yield: 12-14 servings.

Mrs. Walton Gay
Moultrie, Georgia

JALAPENO CORN BREAD

2 c. yellow cornmeal
1 tsp. salt
2 tbsp. sugar
1/2 tsp. soda
1 c. milk
2 eggs

2 tbsp. garlic salt
1 c. chopped onion
1/4 c. chopped pimento
4 jalapeno peppers, minced
1 c. whole kernel corn
4 slices crisp-cooked bacon, crumbled
2 tbsp. bacon drippings
1/2 lb. Cheddar cheese, grated

Combine first 4 ingredients in large bowl. Add milk and eggs; mix well. Add next 6 ingredients; beat for 1 minute. Pour half the cornmeal mixture into 10-inch iron skillet greased with bacon drippings. Top with half the cheese. Repeat layers. Bake in 350-degree oven for 35 minutes. Yield: 8 servings.

Carla Sue Park
Dayton, Texas

SOUR CREAM CORN BREAD

1 1/2 c. yellow cornmeal
3 tsp. baking powder
1/2 tsp. salt
3 eggs
1 c. sour cream
1 c. grated Cheddar cheese
1 sm. can cream-style corn
1/2 c. seeded, chopped jalapeno peppers
1/2 c. corn oil

Sift first 3 ingredients together into bowl. Add remaining ingredients; stir until just mixed. Pour into greased baking pan. Bake in 450-degree oven for 30 to 40 minutes or until bread tests done.

Linda Jaramillo
Tierra Amarillo, New Mexico

HUSH PUPPIES

1 1/2 c. white cornmeal
1/2 c. sifted flour
2 tsp. baking powder
1 tbsp. sugar
1/2 tsp. salt
1 sm. onion, finely chopped
1 egg, beaten
3/4 c. milk
Oil for deep frying

Sift dry ingredients together into large bowl. Add onion, egg and milk. Stir until just mixed. Drop by spoonfuls into hot deep fat. Fry until golden brown. Drain on absorbent paper. Serve hot. Yield: 2 dozen.

Mrs. Carolyn G. Chance
Goochland, Virginia

SQUASH PUPPIES

1 c. self-rising cornmeal
1/2 c. self-rising flour
1/2 c. chopped onion
1 c. grated squash
1 egg, beaten
2 tbsp. milk
Oil for deep frying

Combine cornmeal and flour in bowl. Add onion and squash; mix well. Stir in egg and enough milk to make stiff batter. Drop by spoonfuls into hot deep fat. Fry until brown on all sides. Drain. Yield: 4-6 servings.

Jo Nell Hollingsworth
Fayette, Alabama

CREOLE CORN MUFFINS

2 eggs, beaten
1 1/2 c. milk
3/4 c. melted shortening
2 1/2 c. sifted flour
1 tsp. salt
2 tbsp. baking powder
4 tbsp. (heaping) sugar
4 1/2 tbsp. (heaping) cornmeal
2 tbsp. each chopped green pepper, onion
* and pimento*
3/4 c. grated American cheese

Blend eggs, milk and shortening together in bowl. Combine dry ingredients in large bowl. Add remaining ingredients; mix well. Pour milk mixture into cornmeal mixture, stirring until just mixed. Fill hot greased muffin tins 1/2 full. Bake at 400 degrees for 25 to 30 minutes. Yield: 2 dozen.

Thelma McClain
Bremond, Texas

GRITS-MEAL MUFFINS

1 c. milk
1 egg
1 c. cooked grits
1 tbsp. melted shortening
1/2 tsp. salt
2 tsp. baking powder
1 1/4 c. cornmeal

Combine milk, egg and grits in bowl; blend well. Add remaining ingredients; mix well. Place in well-greased muffin cups. Bake at 425 degrees for 25 minutes. Yield: 12 muffins.

Mrs. Bill Jones
Americus, Georgia

HERBED CORN GEMS

2 c. self-rising cornmeal
1/2 tsp. salt
1/4 tsp. thyme
1/2 tsp. celery seed
1 egg, lightly beaten
2 tsp. grated onion
1/2 c. sour cream
2 tbsp. melted shortening

Sift first 3 ingredients together into bowl. Add next 4 ingredients; mix well. Stir in shortening. Place in lightly greased muffin cups. Bake at 450 degrees for 20 minutes. Serve hot.

Mrs. J. O. Honeycutt
Gardendale, Alabama

CRISPY SPOON BREAD

3 c. milk
1 1/4 c. white cornmeal
3 lg. eggs, beaten
1 3/4 tsp. baking powder
1 tsp. salt
2 tbsp. butter, melted

Bring milk to a boil in saucepan. Stir in cornmeal. Cook until thick, stirring constantly. Remove from heat. Cool until batter is stiff. Add remaining ingredients. Beat for 15 to 20 minutes with electric mixer. Pour into greased casserole. Bake at 375 degrees for 30 to 35 minutes. Yield: 6 servings.

Mrs. Estelle B. Nickell
West Liberty, Kentucky

OLD-FASHIONED SPOON BREAD

1 c. cornmeal
1/2 tsp. salt
2 tbsp. margarine
4 eggs, beaten
1 c. milk

Stir cornmeal and salt into 2 cups boiling water in saucepan. Stir for 1 minute. Remove from heat. Add margarine; beat well. Add eggs. Beat in milk. Beat until well blended. Pour into buttered baking dish. Bake in 450-degree oven for 25 minutes. Serve in baking dish. Yield: 8 servings.

Janice Hamblin
Jeff, Kentucky

SOUTHERN SPOON BREAD

2 c. milk
Butter

1 1/4 c. white cornmeal
1 tsp. each baking powder, salt
2 eggs, well beaten

Heat milk and 4 tablespoons butter in saucepan. Stir until butter melts. Mix cornmeal, baking powder and salt in bowl. Blend in half the milk mixture and eggs; mix well. Stir in remaining milk mixture. Pour into baking pan. Dot with butter. Bake in 450-degree oven for 20 to 25 minutes or until bread tests done. Yield: 8 servings.

Katharine Rigby
Union Furnace, Ohio

CORN STICKS

1 1/2 c. cornmeal
1/2 c. sifted all-purpose flour
1 tsp. each soda, salt and baking powder
2 tsp. sugar
2 eggs, well beaten
2 c. buttermilk
3 tbsp. butter, melted

Sift dry ingredients together. Combine eggs, buttermilk and butter in large bowl; beat well. Add dry ingredients; beat thoroughly. Fill well-greased corn stick pans 2/3 full. Bake in 425-degree oven for 20 to 25 minutes. Yield: 12 servings.

Photograph for this recipe on page 53.

BUTTERMILK DOUGHNUTS

4 1/2 c. sifted flour
1 tbsp. baking powder
1 tsp. each salt, cinnamon
1/2 tsp. each soda, nutmeg
2 eggs
1 c. sugar
2 tbsp. melted shortening
1 c. buttermilk
Oil for deep frying

Sift 4 cups flour with next 5 ingredients into bowl. Beat eggs until thick in large bowl. Add sugar gradually; beat thoroughly. Add shortening; mix well. Add dry ingredients alternately with buttermilk; blend well. Add enough remaining flour to make soft dough. Chill for 1 hour. Turn onto floured surface. Roll to 1/2-inch thickness. Cut with floured doughnut cutter. Fry in deep fat at 365 degrees for 2 to 3 minutes or until light brown, turning doughnuts when they rise to surface. Drain on absorbent paper. Roll in confectioners' sugar. Yield: 24 doughnuts.

Linda J. McCraw
Gaffney, South Carolina

DROP DOUGHNUTS

Sugar
2 c. flour
3 tsp. baking powder
1 tsp. each salt, nutmeg
1/4 c. oil
1 egg, beaten
3/4 c. milk
Oil for deep frying
Cinnamon

Combine 1/4 cup sugar with next 4 ingredients in bowl; mix well. Add oil, egg and milk. Stir until just mixed. Drop by spoonfuls into deep fat at 375 degrees. Fry until brown, turning doughnuts when they rise to surface. Drain on absorbent paper. Roll in additional sugar and cinnamon. Yield: 8 doughnuts.

Felicia Allison
Dellcrest, Tennessee

EASY DOUGHNUTS

1/3 c. sugar
1/2 c. milk
1 egg, beaten
2 tbsp. shortening, melted
1 1/2 c. sifted flour
2 tsp. baking powder
1/2 tsp. salt
Oil for deep frying
Confectioners' sugar to taste

Combine first 4 ingredients in bowl. Blend flour, baking powder and salt. Add to milk mixture. Stir until just mixed. Drop by teaspoonfuls into 365-degree fat. Fry for 3 to 4 minutes, turning to brown both sides. Drain on paper towels. Sprinkle with confectioners' sugar. Yield: 8 servings.

Mrs. Gayle C. Johns
Millerstown, Pennsylvania

GOLDEN PUFFS

2 1/2 c. flour
1/2 c. sugar
3 tsp. baking powder
1/2 tsp. salt
1 tsp. nutmeg
1/4 c. oil
3/4 c. milk
1 egg
Oil for deep frying

Sift dry ingredients together into bowl. Add next 3 ingredients. Stir until thoroughly mixed. Drop by teaspoonfuls into deep fat at 375 degrees. Fry for 3 minutes or until golden brown. Drain on absorbent paper. Warm puffs may be rolled in cinnamon-sugar mixture or dipped into thin confectioners' sugar icing. Yield: 20 servings.

Mrs. Nadine Kaiser
Hydro, Oklahoma

ORANGE DROP DOUGHNUTS

1/2 c. sugar
2 tbsp. shortening
2 eggs
2 c. flour
2 tsp. baking powder
1/4 tsp. salt
1/2 c. orange juice
1/4 tsp. orange extract
2 tbsp. grated orange rind (opt.)
Oil for deep frying
Confectioners' sugar

Cream sugar and shortening in bowl. Add eggs; beat well. Sift flour, baking powder and salt together. Add to creamed mixture alternately with orange juice and orange flavoring, beating well after each addition. Stir in orange rind. Drop by spoonfuls into hot deep fat. Fry until evenly browned. Sprinkle doughnuts with confectioners' sugar or dip into chocolate frosting. Yield: 3 dozen.

Mrs. Darlene Haws
McFarland, California

SWEET CREAM GREBBLES

Sugar
1/2 tsp. salt
1/4 tsp. soda
2 tsp. baking powder
4 c. flour
1 c. each cream, buttermilk
3 eggs, well beaten

Combine 2 tablespoons sugar and next 4 ingredients in large bowl. Add cream, buttermilk and eggs; stir until dough leaves side of bowl. Refrigerate for 3 hours. Turn onto floured surface. Roll to 1/2-inch thickness. Cut in desired shapes. Fry in hot deep fat until brown. Drain on absorbent paper. Roll in sugar while still warm. Yield: 12 servings.

Mrs. James Waller
Oklahoma City, Oklahoma

SWEET PASTRY KNOTS

3 eggs
2 tsp. sugar
1/4 tsp. salt
1/2 tsp. vanilla extract
2 c. (about) flour
1 1/2 tsp. baking powder
2 tbsp. butter, softened
Oil for deep frying
Confectioners' sugar

Combine first 4 ingredients with 1 tablespoon water in bowl; beat well. Sift flour and baking powder into bowl. Add to egg mixture gradually; beat well. Stir in butter until blended. Add enough additional flour to make stiff dough. Turn onto floured surface. Knead until smooth and elastic. Cover. Let rest for 1 hour. Divide dough in half. Roll halves into rectangles. Cut dough into 1 x 5-inch strips. Tie into knots. Set aside for 10 minutes. Fry knots in deep oil at 375 degrees until golden brown. Sprinkle with confectioners' sugar. Serve with whipped cream. Yield: 8 servings.

Mrs. David Richmond
Coolville, Ohio

EASY DROP DUMPLINGS

1 c. sifted flour
1 1/2 tsp. baking powder
1/2 tsp. salt
1 tbsp. shortening
1/2 c. milk

Sift flour, baking powder and salt into bowl. Cut in shortening until crumbly. Add milk; stir until just mixed. Drop by teaspoonfuls into boiling stew. Cover. Cook for 12 minutes without removing cover. Yield: 4-6 servings.

Mrs. William C. Westcoat
Bremerhaven, Germany

CLOUD-LIGHT DROP DUMPLINGS

1 c. sifted flour
2 tsp. baking powder
1/2 tsp. salt
1/2 c. milk
Sprig of parsley, minced

Sift dry ingredients together into small bowl. Add milk and parsley; mix well. Drop by spoonfuls into boiling stew. Cover. Cook for 20

minutes. Do not raise lid while cooking. Reduce heat. Boil gently until dumplings test done.

Mrs. Harry L. Gans
Washington, D. C.

WHOLE WHEAT FLAT BREAD

1/2 c. sugar
1/2 c. shortening
1 qt. buttermilk
1 tsp. salt
3 c. whole wheat flour
3 c. flour
2 tsp. baking powder
2 tsp. soda

Cream sugar and shortening in bowl. Add buttermilk gradually; mix well. Add salt and whole wheat flour; blend thoroughly. Sift remaining dry ingredients together. Add all at once, stirring until dough leaves side of bowl. Roll onto pastry cloth until nearly paper thin. Lift onto cookie sheets. Bake in 375-degree oven for 12 minutes or until brown and crisp.

Ruth Radcliffe
Billings, Montana

APRICOT BREAD

2 c. sifted flour
1 c. sugar
2 1/2 tsp. baking powder
3/4 tsp. salt
1/2 c. chopped dried apricots
3/4 c. crunchy nut-like cereal nuggets
1 1/4 c. milk
1 egg, well beaten
2 tbsp. melted shortening

Sift flour with sugar, baking powder and salt in bowl. Stir in apricots and cereal nuggets. Blend milk with egg and shortening in small bowl. Add flour mixture; stir just until flour is moistened. Pour into greased 9 x 5-inch loaf pan. Bake at 350 degrees for 1 hour and 15 minutes or until bread tests done. Cool in pan for 10 minutes. Remove from pan; cool on rack. Wrap bread in foil. Store overnight for easier slicing.

Fannie L. Price
Spartanburg, South Carolina

APRICOT-NUT BREAD

1 can apricot nectar
1 1/2 c. chopped dates
1/3 c. chopped dried apricots
1 tbsp. grated orange rind

2 3/4 c. flour
2 tsp. soda
1 tsp. salt
1 tbsp. shortening, softened
1 c. sugar
1 egg
1/3 c. cream
1/2 c. chopped nuts

Combine first 3 ingredients in saucepan. Simmer for 4 minutes. Add orange rind. Sift flour, soda and salt together into large bowl. Blend in shortening and sugar. Add hot mixture; blend well. Add egg, cream and nuts; mix well. Pour into 4 greased and floured Number 2 cans, filling cans 2/3 full. Bake at 350 degrees for 50 minutes or until bread tests done. Remove from cans immediately; cool. Slice thin to serve.

Mrs. Edith Blasi
Odessa, Texas

HARVEST APRICOT LOAF

3/4 c. chopped dried apricots
1/2 c. chopped walnuts
1/4 c. flour
1 17-oz. package pound cake mix
1/4 c. milk
1/4 c. orange juice
3 eggs
1 1/4 tsp. grated orange rind
1/2 c. butter, softened

Stir apricots and walnuts in flour until coated in small bowl; set aside. Pour cake mix into mixer bowl. Add milk and orange juice. Blend until dry ingredients are moistened. Beat for 1 minute with electric mixer at medium-low speed. Blend in eggs and 1 teaspoon orange rind. Beat for 2 minutes at medium-low speed. Fold in apricot mixture. Pour batter into well-greased 9 x 5 x 3-inch loaf pan. Bake in 325-degree oven for about 1 hour and 15 minutes or until bread tests done. Cool in pan for 30 minutes. Turn onto rack. Cool. Blend 1/4 teaspoon orange rind with butter in bowl. Serve with apricot loaf.

Photograph for this recipe on page 39.

APPLESAUCE-NUT BREAD

1 egg, beaten
1 c. applesauce
2 tbsp. melted butter
2 c. flour
3/4 c. sugar
1 tsp. each cinnamon, salt
3 tsp. baking powder
1/2 tsp. soda
3/4 c. chopped nuts

Mix egg, applesauce and butter in large bowl. Sift dry ingredients together. Add to egg mixture; mix well. Add nuts. Pour into well-greased loaf pan. Bake at 350 degrees for 45 minutes.

Mrs. Rosetta Haire
Crescent City, Illinois

AVOCADO-NUT BREAD

2 c. flour
1/2 tsp. each soda, baking powder
3/4 c. sugar
1/4 tsp. salt
1 egg, slightly beaten
1/2 c. sour milk
1/2 c. mashed avocado
1 c. chopped nuts

Sift first 5 ingredients together in large bowl. Add egg and sour milk; mix well. Stir in avocado and nuts. Pour into greased 9 x 5 x 3-inch loaf pan. Bake at 350 degrees for 1 hour.

Mrs. F. T. Black
El Paso, Texas

APRICOT-BANANA TEA BREAD

1/2 c. chopped dried apricots
All-purpose flour
2/3 c. shortening
1 c. sugar
2 eggs
1 1/2 c. mashed bananas
1 tbsp. lemon juice
1 tsp. soda
1 tsp. salt
Confectioners' sugar

Combine apricots with 1 tablespoon flour; set aside. Cream shortening and sugar in large bowl. Add eggs one at a time, beating well after each addition. Blend in bananas and lemon juice. Combine 1 3/4 cups flour, soda and salt. Blend into banana mixture. Stir in apricots. Turn into greased and floured 9 x 5 x 3-inch loaf pan. Bake in 325-degree oven for 1 hour and 10 minutes or until bread tests done. Remove from pan. Cool. Sift confectioners' sugar over top. Yield: 1 loaf.

Photograph for this recipe on cover.

BANANA TEA LOAF

    1 3/4 c. sifted flour
    3/4 tsp. soda
    1 1/4 tsp. cream of tartar
    1/2 tsp. salt
    1/2 c. nuts
    2 eggs
    1/2 c. butter, softened
    2 sm. ripe bananas, sliced
    3/4 c. sugar

Sift first 4 ingredients into bowl; add nuts. Place remaining ingredients in blender container. Process on high speed for 20 seconds. Pour over dry ingredients; stir until just mixed. Turn into greased loaf pan. Bake in preheated 375-degree oven for 45 minutes. Yield: 8 servings.

Janice M. Mountz
Topton, Pennsylvania

BANANA-NUT BREAD

    1/2 c. butter
    1 c. sugar
    2 eggs
    1/2 tsp. salt
    1 tsp. vanilla extract
    1 tsp. soda
    2 c. flour
    3 bananas, mashed
    1/2 c. chopped nuts

Cream butter and sugar in bowl. Beat in eggs, salt and vanilla; mix well. Sift together soda and flour. Add to creamed mixture. Add bananas and nuts; mix well. Pour into greased loaf pan. Bake at 300 degrees for 1 hour or until bread tests done.

Mrs. Betty G. Brant
Shanksville, Pennsylvania

BASIC BANANA BREAD

    1/2 c. butter, softened
    1 tsp. vanilla extract
    1 c. sugar
    2 eggs
    1 1/3 c. mashed bananas
    1 tbsp. milk
    2 c. all-purpose flour
    1 tsp. soda
    1/4 tsp. salt
    1/2 c. chopped nuts

Cream butter, vanilla and sugar in large bowl until light and fluffy. Beat in eggs. Combine bananas and milk in bowl. Mix flour, soda and salt. Add dry ingredients to creamed mixture alternately with banana mixture, beating well after each addition. Stir in nuts. Pour into greased 9 x 5 x 3-inch loaf pan. Bake in 350-degree oven for 1 hour and 10 minutes, or until bread tests done. Cool for 10 minutes in pan. Turn out of pan; cool completely. Yield: 1 loaf.

Photograph for this recipe on cover.

TEXAS BANANA-NUT BREAD

    1/3 c. shortening
    3/4 c. sugar
    1 egg, beaten
    2/3 c. mashed bananas
    2 c. flour
    1/2 tsp. baking powder
    1/4 tsp. soda
    3 tsp. salt
    1/3 c. milk
    1/2 c. nuts

Cream shortening and sugar in bowl. Add egg and bananas; mix well. Sift dry ingredients together. Add to creamed mixture alternately with milk, beating well after each addition. Fold in nuts. Place in greased loaf pan. Bake at 350 degrees for 1 hour. Yield: 1 loaf.

Mrs. Betty Ambrose
Midland, Texas

CHERRY-BANANA BREAD

    1 stick margarine
    1 c. sugar
    3 eggs
    3 or 4 bananas, mashed
    1 tsp. vanilla extract
    2 c. flour
    1 tsp. salt
    1/2 tsp. soda
    1/2 c. pecans
    1 c. raisins
    1/3 c. maraschino cherries

Cream margarine and sugar in large bowl until fluffy. Add eggs, one at a time, beating well after each addition. Add bananas and vanilla; beat well. Combine 1 cup flour, salt and soda. Add flour mixture to batter; blend well. Combine pecans and raisins with remaining flour. Blend pecan mixture and cherries into batter. Pour into waxed paper-lined loaf pan. Bake at

325 degrees for 35 minutes or until bread tests done. Yield: 12 servings.

Joyce Weaver
Leonard, Texas

CRUNCHY BANANA BREAD

1/2 c. butter, softened
1/2 c. (firmly packed) light brown sugar
2 eggs
1 c. whole wheat flour
1 c. oats
1 tsp. soda
1/2 tsp. salt
1 1/2 c. mashed ripe bananas
1/4 c. milk
1/2 c. chopped peanuts

Cream butter and brown sugar in large bowl. Add eggs, one at a time, beating well after each addition. Mix whole wheat flour, oats, soda and salt. Add to creamed mixture with bananas and milk. Blend until just mixed. Stir in peanuts. Pour into greased 9 x 5 x 3-inch loaf pan. Bake in 350-degree oven for 1 hour, or until bread tests done. Cool for 10 minutes in pan. Turn out of pan. Serve warm or cool. Yield: 1 loaf.

Photograph for this recipe on cover.

BUTTERMILK-NUT BREAD

1 1/4 c. sifted all-purpose flour
3/4 tsp. each salt, soda
1 1/2 tsp. baking powder
1 c. whole wheat flour
1 c. chopped walnuts
2 eggs, well beaten
1/2 c. sugar
2 tbsp. butter, melted
1/3 c. molasses
1 c. buttermilk

Sift first 4 ingredients together in large bowl. Add whole wheat flour and walnuts. Blend remaining ingredients together in medium bowl. Stir into dry ingredients; beat until smooth. Pour into buttered 9 x 4 x 3-inch loaf pan. Bake in 350-degree oven for 50 to 60 minutes or until bread tests done. Yield: One 9 x 4-inch loaf.

Photograph for this recipe below.

YANKEE BANANA BREAD

2 c. whole wheat flour
1 c. yellow cornmeal
3/4 tsp. salt
1 tsp. soda
1 c. mashed bananas
1 c. buttermilk
3/4 c. molasses
3/4 c. snipped pitted dates

Mix whole wheat flour, cornmeal, salt and soda in large bowl. Stir in bananas and remaining ingredients. Turn into 3 greased and floured 1-pound cans. Bake in 350-degree oven for 45 minutes, or until bread tests done. Cool for 10 minutes in cans. Turn out of cans. Serve warm with butter. Loaves may be frozen. Yield: 3 loaves.

Photograph for this recipe on cover.

SPICY CARROT BREAD

1 c. sugar
3/4 c. oil
2 eggs
1/4 tsp. salt
1 1/2 c. grated carrots
1/2 c. chopped English walnuts
1 tsp. soda
1 1/2 c. flour
1/2 tsp. each cinnamon, nutmeg

Blend sugar and oil together in large bowl. Add eggs and salt; mix well. Stir in carrots and walnuts. Sift dry ingredients. Add to carrot mixture; blend well. Pour into greased 9 x 3-inch loaf pan. Bake at 350 degrees for 1 hour.

Mrs. De Vonna Hyde
Welcome, Minnesota

CHEDDAR-BRAN LOAF

1 1/2 c. sifted flour
1 1/2 tsp. baking powder
1/4 tsp. soda
1/2 tsp. salt
3 tbsp. butter
1/3 c. sugar
1 egg, well beaten
1 c. buttermilk
1 c. shredded Cheddar cheese
1 c. crushed 100% bran cereal

Sift first 4 ingredients together. Cream butter and sugar in bowl. Add egg; blend well. Add flour mixture alternately with buttermilk, beating well after each addition. Fold in cheese and

cereal. Spoon into well-greased 8 x 4-inch loaf pan. Bake in 350-degree oven for 1 hour. Remove from pan; cool.

Mrs. M. A. Berns
Norfolk, Virginia

CHEESE-NUT BREAD

2 c. sifted flour
1 tbsp. baking powder
3/4 tsp. salt
1/2 tsp. sugar
1 c. grated American cheese
1/4 c. chopped pecans
1 egg, beaten
3/4 c. milk
2 tbsp. butter, melted

Sift flour twice with baking powder, salt and sugar into bowl. Add cheese and pecans; mix thoroughly. Combine egg, milk and butter in small bowl; mix well. Pour into dry ingredients. Stir until just mixed. Pour into buttered 8 x 4 x 3-inch loaf pan. Let stand for 15 minutes. Bake in 350-degree oven for 1 hour or until bread tests done. Invert loaf onto wire rack. Cool before slicing. Yield: 1 loaf.

Magdalene Beehler
Crookston, Minnesota

BOSTON BROWN BREAD

4 c. sour milk
3 tsp. soda
3/4 c. sugar
1 c. molasses
1 tsp. salt
5 c. graham flour
1/2 c. flour
1 1/2 tsp. baking powder

Mix first 5 ingredients in large bowl. Add remaining ingredients; mix well. Pour into 3 greased loaf pans. Bake at 425 degrees for 10 minutes. Reduce temperature to 350 degrees. Bake for 45 minutes longer or until bread tests done.

Lynnie E. Oakes
Clermont, Florida

FRUITED CARROT BREAD

2 c. flour
2 tsp. each soda, cinnamon

1/2 tsp. salt
1 1/4 c. sugar
1/2 c. each chopped raisins, nuts
1/2 c. coconut
1 c. oil
2 tsp. vanilla extract
2 c. grated carrots
3 eggs, beaten

Combine first 5 ingredients in mixing bowl; blend lightly. Add raisins, nuts and coconut; mix well. Stir in remaining ingredients; blend well. Turn into 3 greased 1-pound coffee cans. Let stand for 20 minutes. Bake at 350 degrees for 1 hour. Cool slightly; remove from cans.

Barbara Newton
Hudson Falls, New York

CHEERY CHERRY BREAD

2 eggs
1 c. sugar
1 6-oz. jar maraschino cherries
3/4 c. chopped nuts
1 1/4 tsp. salt
1 1/2 c. all-purpose flour
1 1/2 tsp. baking powder

Beat eggs and sugar together in large bowl. Drain cherries, reserving juice. Add nuts and cherries to egg mixture. Combine remaining ingredients in bowl. Add dry ingredients to egg mixture alternately with reserved cherry juice, beating well after each addition. Pour into greased loaf pan. Bake at 350 degrees for 45 minutes. Yield: 12 servings.

Mrs. Louise H. Griner
Columbus, Georgia

CHERRY BREAD

1 c. sugar
2 c. flour
2 tsp. baking powder
1/2 tsp. salt
1 8-oz. jar cherries
1/4 c. chopped walnuts
1 egg, well beaten
4 tbsp. oil

Sift dry ingredients together into large bowl. Drain cherries, reserving juice. Add enough water to juice to measure 1 cup. Cut cherries in half. Add walnuts and cherries to flour mixture; mix well. Make well in center of mixture. Pour in egg and cherry juice; stir lightly. Blend in oil, stirring until just mixed. Pour into greased loaf

pan. Bake at 325 degrees for 1 hour and 15 minutes.

Mrs. Adeline Tanasichuk
Alberta, Canada

CINNAMON CRUNCH LOAF

1 1/2 c. coarsely chopped walnuts
1 tbsp. butter, melted
1 c. sugar
2 tsp. cinnamon
3 c. sifted all-purpose flour
4 1/2 tsp. baking powder
1 1/2 tsp. salt
1/4 c. shortening
1 egg, beaten
1 1/4 c. milk

Combine walnuts with butter in medium bowl. Add 1/4 cup sugar and cinnamon; mix until walnuts are well coated. Set aside. Sift flour, remaining sugar, baking powder and salt together in large bowl. Cut in shortening until crumbly. Combine egg and milk in small bowl. Stir into dry mixture until just mixed. Reserve 1/4 cup spiced walnuts. Add remaining walnut mixture to batter; mix lightly. Spoon into greased loaf pan. Sprinkle with reserved walnut mixture. Let stand for 15 minutes. Bake at 350 degrees for 1 hour or until loaf tests done. Cool in pan for 10 minutes. Turn onto wire rack.

Joan Metcalf
Yuma, Arizona

CRANBERRY-ORANGE LOAF

2 1/2 c. sifted flour
3/4 c. sugar
3 tsp. baking powder
1 tsp. each salt, cinnamon
1/2 tsp. soda
1/2 c. milk
1 egg, beaten
2 tbsp. melted shortening
1 1/2 c. ground cranberries
1/2 c. chopped nuts
1 tbsp. grated orange rind
1/4 c. orange juice

Sift first 6 ingredients together in bowl. Combine milk, egg and shortening in bowl; mix well. Add remaining ingredients and flour mixture, stirring until just mixed. Pour into loaf pan. Bake at 350 degrees for 40 minutes. Yield: 1 loaf.

Mrs. Judith Anderson
Tuscola, Illinois

CRANBERRY-COCOA BREAD

1 1-lb. can whole cranberry sauce
1 1/2 c. raisins
Grated rind of 1 orange
3 tbsp. butter, softened
1 c. sugar
1 egg, beaten
1/3 c. milk
3 c. sifted all-purpose flour
2 tsp. soda
1 tsp. each salt, cinnamon
1/4 c. cocoa
1/2 tsp. nutmeg
1 c. chopped walnuts
1 8-oz. package cream cheese, softened
1/4 c. cranberry juice

Combine first 3 ingredients in saucepan. Cook over low heat, stirring constantly, for 5 minutes. Cool. Cream butter and sugar in large bowl until light and fluffy. Combine egg and milk in small bowl. Stir into butter mixture, blending well. Sift dry ingredients together. Add to creamed mixture alternately with cranberry mixture, blending well after each addition. Fold in walnuts; blend well. Pour into greased and floured 9 x 5 x 3-inch baking pan. Bake at 350 degrees for 45 minutes. Remove from oven. Place tent of foil over top. Bake for 35 minutes longer or until bread tests done. Cool completely. Blend cream cheese and cranberry juice together in bowl. Spread on sliced bread.

Mrs. Nicole Riddle
Montgomery, Alabama

CRANBERRY RELISH BREAD

2 c. sifted flour
1 tsp. each soda, salt
3/4 c. sugar
1 egg, beaten
1/3 c. orange juice
1 tsp. grated orange rind
1/4 c. melted shortening
3 tbsp. white vinegar
1 c. coarsely chopped cranberries
1 c. chopped nuts

Sift first 4 dry ingredients into bowl. Combine next 4 ingredients in large bowl. Combine vinegar with enough water to measure 2/3 cup. Add to liquid ingredients; mix well. Add dry ingredients all at once. Stir until just mixed. Blend in cranberries and nuts. Pour into greased loaf pan. Bake at 350 degrees for 1 hour or until bread tests done. Remove from pan. Cool for several hours before slicing.

Mary M. Coopy
Champlain, New York

FAVORITE DATE-NUT BREAD

1 box dates, chopped
1 1/2 tsp. soda
1 tbsp. butter, softened
1 c. sugar
3/4 tsp. salt
1 egg, beaten
1 3/4 c. flour
3 tsp. baking powder
1 tsp. vanilla
1 c. chopped pecans

Combine dates and soda in bowl. Stir in 1 cup boiling water. Drain, reserving liquid. Blend next 4 ingredients in large bowl. Sift flour and baking powder together in bowl. Add to sugar mixture alternately with reserved liquid, beating well after each addition. Stir in dates, vanilla and pecans; turn into greased loaf pan. Bake at 350 degrees for 1 hour.

Mrs. Sammie Lee Pounds
New Site, Mississippi

FRUIT BREAD

1 c. butter
2 c. sugar
4 eggs
1 tsp. soda
1 c. buttermilk
3 1/2 c. flour
1/2 tsp. salt
6 1/4 oz. dates
1 c. chopped nuts
1 c. coconut
4 tbsp. grated orange rind
2 c. confectioners' sugar
1 c. orange juice

Cream butter and sugar in large bowl until light and fluffy. Add eggs; beat well. Dissolve soda in buttermilk. Sift flour and salt in bowl. Add alternately with buttermilk to egg mixture, beating well after each addition. Fold in next 3 ingredients and 2 tablespoons orange rind; mix well. Pour into 2 loaf pans. Bake at 350 degrees for 1 hour. Remove from pans. Combine confectioners' sugar, orange juice and remaining orange rind in saucepan. Bring to a boil. Pour syrup over bread; punch holes to allow syrup to saturate bread. Yield: 40 servings.

Mrs. Mary S. Dean
Rowlesburg, West Virginia

GINGER HEALTH BREAD

1/2 c. shortening
1/2 c. strained honey
1/2 c. (firmly packed) brown sugar
2 eggs
1 c. cottage cheese
1/4 c. unsweetened apple butter
1/2 tsp. ginger
1/4 tsp. each cinnamon, salt
3/4 tsp. soda
2 c. flour
2 tsp. baking powder
1/2 c. raisins

Cream shortening, honey and brown sugar in large bowl. Add eggs; beat well. Blend in next 5 ingredients. Sift soda, flour and baking powder together; add to batter. Blend until smooth. Add raisins. Pour into deep baking dish. Bake at 375 degrees for 45 minutes. Yield: 12 servings.

Maryetta Bowyer
Miller City, Ohio

GRAPE NUTS BREAD

1 c. Grape Nuts
2 c. buttermilk
2 eggs
2 c. sugar
4 c. flour
2 tsp. baking powder
1 tsp. each soda, salt

Soak Grape Nuts in buttermilk in small bowl for 1 hour. Combine eggs and sugar in large bowl; blend well. Add buttermilk mixture; mix well. Add remaining ingredients; mix thoroughly. Pour into 2 greased loaf pans. Bake at 350 degrees for 45 minutes or until bread tests done.

Mrs. Oliver G. Stutzman
Memphis, Tennessee

HEALTH BREAD

1 c. raisins
1 c. oatmeal
1 c. each graham flour, bran buds
1 tsp. salt
3/4 c. sugar
1 tsp. soda
1 c. sour milk

Combine raisins and 1 cup water in saucepan. Bring to a boil; boil for 5 minutes. Combine remaining ingredients in large bowl. Add raisins;

mix well. Turn into loaf pan. Bake at 350 degrees for 1 hour.

Mrs. Carl Ruff
Oak Harbor, Ohio

LEMON BREAD

2 tbsp. shortening
2 eggs
1 tbsp. ground lemon rind
1 1/2 c. flour
1 1/2 tsp. baking powder
1/2 tsp. salt
1/2 c. milk
1/2 c. chopped nuts
1 1/2 c. sugar
3 tbsp. lemon juice

Combine first 8 ingredients and 1 cup sugar together in large bowl; beat until smooth. Pour into well-greased and floured 9 x 5 x 3-inch loaf pan. Bake at 325 degrees for 1 hour. Remove from oven. Cool for 5 minutes. Combine lemon juice and 1/2 cup sugar in bowl; spread over bread.

Mrs. Margaret Redman
Marquette, Michigan

LEMON-NUT TEA BREAD

2 3/4 c. flour
3 tsp. baking powder
1/2 tsp. soda
3/4 tsp. salt
1/2 c. chopped nuts
1/4 c. shortening
2 1/4 c. sugar
5 eggs
2 1/2 tsp. finely grated lemon rind
7 tbsp. lemon juice
3/4 c. milk
1 1/2 c. bran flakes
Butter

Sift first 3 ingredients and 1/2 teaspoon salt together into bowl. Add nuts; mix well. Cream shortening and 1 1/4 cups sugar in bowl. Add 2 eggs and 1 1/2 teaspoons lemon rind; beat well. Stir in 4 tablespoons lemon juice and milk; mix well. Stir in bran flakes. Add dry ingredients; stir until just mixed. Spread in greased loaf pan. Bake at 350 degrees for 50 minutes. Cool. Slice. Beat remaining eggs slightly. Combine remaining salt, sugar, lemon rind, lemon juice and eggs in top of double boiler. Cook over boiling water until thick, stirring constantly. Stir in a small amount of butter. Cool. Store in refrigerator. Spread on bread slices.

Mrs. May Donna Gilmore
Rio, Wisconsin

LETTUCE LOAF

1 1/2 c. sifted flour
2 tsp. baking powder
1/2 tsp. each soda, salt
1/8 tsp. each ground mace, ginger
1 c. sugar
1/2 c. oil
1 1/2 tsp. grated lemon rind
1 c. finely chopped lettuce
2 eggs
1/2 c. chopped nuts

Sift first 6 ingredients together. Combine sugar, oil and lemon rind in large bowl. Add flour mixture and lettuce; mix well. Add eggs, one at a time, beating well after each addition. Stir in nuts. Turn into greased and floured loaf pan. Bake at 350 degrees for 55 minutes. Cool for 15 minutes. Remove from pan; cool on wire rack.

Mrs. Montie Rae Carpenter
Brightwood, Virginia

NUTMEG BREAD

1/2 c. shortening
1 c. sugar
1 egg
2 c. sifted flour
1/2 tsp. each baking powder, salt and
*   soda*
2 tsp. nutmeg
1 c. sour milk

Cream shortening and sugar in large bowl. Add egg; mix well. Sift dry ingredients together. Add to creamed mixture alternately with sour milk, blending well after each addition. Pour into greased loaf pan. Let stand for 20 minutes before baking. Bake at 350 degrees for 1 hour or until bread tests done. Cool for 5 minutes before removing from pan.

Estelle Cherry
Grandburg, Texas

OLIVE BREAD

2 1/4 c. sifted flour
4 tsp. baking powder
3/4 c. sliced pimento-stuffed olives
1/4 c. sugar
1 egg, beaten
1 1/4 c. milk
2 tbsp. melted butter

Sift flour and baking powder together in mixing bowl; add olives and sugar. Combine egg, milk and butter in bowl; mix well. Add to dry ingre-dients; stir just enough to moisten flour. Place in greased loaf pan. Bake at 375 degrees for 1 hour or until bread tests done.

Mrs. Myrtle S. VonCannon
Greensboro, North Carolina

ORANGE ROUND BREAD

2 1/2 c. flour
1/2 c. sugar
1/2 tsp. salt
3 1/2 tsp. baking powder
1/4 c. grated orange rind
1 egg
1 tbsp. melted shortening
1/2 c. each milk, orange juice

Sift dry ingredients together into large bowl. Add orange rind. Combine remaining ingredients in bowl; mix well. Add to dry ingredients; stir just until blended. Fill greased and floured baking powder cans 2/3 full. Bake at 350 degrees for 45 minutes or until bread tests done. Yield: 10-12 servings.

Mrs. Ella Mae Korthals
Huron, South Dakota

PINEAPPLE-DATE LOAF

1/4 c. soft butter
1/2 c. sugar
1 egg
1/4 tsp. lemon extract
1 8 1/2-oz. can crushed pineapple
1/4 c. chopped nuts
2 1/2 c. sifted flour
2 1/2 tsp. baking powder
1/4 tsp. soda
1 tsp. salt
1/2 c. finely chopped dates
1/4 c. chopped maraschino cherries,
*   drained*

Cream butter and sugar in large bowl; add egg and lemon extract. Drain pineapple, reserving liquid. Mix reserved pineapple juice and 1/4 cup water. Add pineapple and nuts to creamed mixture; mix well. Sift dry ingredients together; add dates. Mix well, separating date pieces. Stir into creamed mixture alternately with reserved juice. Fold in cherries; pour into greased loaf pan. Bake at 375 degrees for 55 minutes. Cool in pan for 10 minutes; remove from pan. Let stand overnight before serving. Yield: 10 servings.

Mrs. Winnie C. Perry
Lockport, Illinois

PINEAPPLE BREAD

1 3/4 c. flour
2 1/2 tsp. baking powder
1 tsp. salt
3/4 tsp. cinnamon
1/4 tsp. nutmeg
1/8 tsp. allspice
2/3 c. (firmly packed) light brown sugar
1/4 c. chopped nuts
2 eggs, beaten
1 8 1/2-oz. can crushed pineapple
1/3 c. milk
2 tbsp. molasses
1/4 c. melted shortening
1 1/2 c. whole wheat flakes

Combine first 6 ingredients in large bowl. Stir in brown sugar and nuts. Blend next 5 ingredients in bowl. Add to flour mixture. Stir until just mixed. Stir in wheat flakes gently. Pour into well-greased 5-cup ring mold. Bake at 350 degrees for 35 minutes or until bread tests done. Cool in pan for 10 minutes; turn onto rack. Wrap in foil.

Karen Thompson
Des Moines, Iowa

PINEAPPLE LOAF

1 lg. can crushed pineapple
2 1/2 c. sugar
4 tbsp. cornstarch
1 pt. applesauce
1 c. shortening
1 egg
1 egg, separated
3 c. flour
1 tsp. each baking powder, soda
Pinch of salt
1/2 c. milk
2 tsp. vanilla extract
1 tsp. evaporated milk

Combine pineapple, 1 cup sugar, cornstarch and applesauce in saucepan. Cook over medium heat until thick, stirring constantly. Remove from heat; let cool. Combine 1 cup sugar, shortening, egg and egg white in large bowl; mix well. Add flour, baking powder, soda and salt; blend until smooth. Add milk and vanilla; stir to blend. Cut dough in half. Roll half to fit bottom of greased 10 x 13-inch pan. Pour in pineapple filling; spread to within 1 inch from edge. Roll out remaining dough. Place over pineapple. Seal dough around edges of pan. Mix

egg yolk, evaporated milk and remaining sugar in bowl. Sprinkle over top of cake. Bake at 350 degrees for 45 minutes or until brown. Cool; cut into squares.

Pauline Thorndike
Milford, Connecticut

PUMPKIN BREAD WITH TOPPING

3 c. sugar
1 c. oil
4 eggs
2 c. mashed pumpkin
3 1/2 c. flour
2 tsp. soda
1 1/2 tsp. salt
1 tsp. each cinnamon, nutmeg
1 c. nuts (opt.)
1 pkg. Dream Whip
1 c. drained crushed pineapple

Beat first 4 ingredients with 2/3 cup water in large bowl. Sift dry ingredients together. Add to egg mixture; mix well. Stir in nuts. Pour into 2 small greased and floured loaf pans. Bake in 350-degree oven for 1 hour. Cool. Prepare Dream Whip according to package directions; stir in pineapple. Serve bread slices with pineapple topping.

Mrs. Patsy Evans
Bridge City, Texas

PUMPKIN SPICE BREAD

3 1/4 c. flour
2 tsp. soda
1 1/2 tsp. salt
1 tsp. each cinnamon, nutmeg
3 c. sugar
4 eggs, well beaten
1 c. oil
1 c. each pumpkin, mincemeat

Sift dry ingredients together. Combine eggs with remaining ingredients and 2/3 cup water in large bowl; mix well. Add dry ingredients all at once; stir until just mixed. Pour into 4 greased and floured loaf pans. Bake at 350 degrees for 50 minutes or until bread tests done. Cool on rack for 10 minutes; remove from pan. Let stand for several hours before slicing. Yield: 4 small loaves.

Mrs. Alma Wells
Salem, Oregon

EASY PUMPKIN BREAD

1 1/2 c. each sugar, (firmly packed)
   brown sugar
4 eggs
1 c. oil
5 tsp. cinnamon
2 tsp. each cloves, soda
1 tsp. each nutmeg, salt
3 c. flour
2 c. pumpkin

Combine sugars in large mixing bowl. Beat in eggs, oil and 2/3 cup water; mix well. Add next 5 ingredients. Add flour gradually, stirring until well blended. Add pumpkin; mix well. Pour into 4 greased coffee cans, filling 1/2 full. Bake at 350 degrees for 1 1/2 hours. Cool. Cover with plastic lids to store. May be frozen.

Mrs. Georgia Watson
Blossom, Texas

QUICK SALLY LUNN BREAD

1/2 c. shortening, softened
1/2 c. sugar
3 eggs
2 c. sifted flour
3 tsp. baking powder
3/4 tsp. salt
1 c. milk

Cream shortening and sugar in bowl. Add eggs one at a time, beating well after each addition. Sift dry ingredients in medium bowl. Add to creamed mixture alternately with milk, beating well after each addition. Place in greased 9 x 12-inch baking pan. Bake at 425 degrees for 1/2 hour or until brown. Cut into squares. Yield: 6 servings.

Mrs. W. C. Lumpkin
Tuskegee, Alabama

CARAWAY-RAISIN BREAD

5 c. sifted flour
1 c. sugar
1 tbsp. baking powder
1 1/2 tsp. salt
1 tsp. soda
1/2 c. butter
2 1/2 c. white seedless raisins,
   washed, dried
3 tbsp. caraway seed
2 1/2 c. buttermilk
1 egg, slightly beaten

Sift first 5 ingredients together into bowl. Cut in butter until crumbly. Stir in raisins and caraway seed. Add buttermilk and egg, stirring until just mixed. Mixture will appear lumpy. Turn into well-greased 11 x 3/4-inch heavy cast iron skillet. Bake at 350 degrees for 1 hour or until firm and brown.

Betty Bell
Montgomery, Alabama

MOLASSES-BRAN BROWN BREAD

1 c. bran cereal
1/2 c. seedless raisins
2 tbsp. shortening
1/2 c. molasses
1 egg
1 c. sifted flour
1 tsp. soda
1/2 tsp. each salt, cinnamon

Combine first 4 ingredients in large bowl. Stir in 3/4 cup boiling water until shortening is melted. Beat in egg. Sift remaining ingredients together. Add to bran mixture. Stir until just mixed. Pour into greased loaf pan. Bake at 350 degrees for 35 minutes. Yield: 10 servings.

Mrs. Ruth K. Ockman
Maplewood, New Jersey

STRAWBERRY BREAD

1 c. butter
1 1/2 c. sugar
1 tsp. vanilla extract
1 tsp. salt
1 tsp. lemon juice
4 eggs
1/2 tsp. soda
1/2 c. sour cream
3 c. flour
1/2 c. chopped nuts
1 c. strawberry preserves
1 tbsp. red food coloring

Blend first 5 ingredients in large bowl. Beat in eggs one at a time, beating well after each addition. Dissolve soda in sour cream; add to egg mixture. Fold in remaining ingredients; mix well. Pour batter into 2 large greased loaf pans. Bake at 350 degrees for 35 to 40 minutes or until bread tests done.

Marjorie Stuart
Rochester, New York

APPLE MUFFINS

2 1/4 c. sifted cake flour
3 1/2 tsp. baking powder
1/2 tsp. each salt, cinnamon and nutmeg
4 tbsp. shortening
Sugar
1 egg, beaten
1 c. milk
1 c. finely chopped pared apples

Sift flour together with baking powder, salt, 1/4 teaspoon cinnamon and 1/4 teaspoon nutmeg. Cream shortening and 1/2 cup sugar in bowl. Stir in egg. Add flour mixture to creamed mixture alternately with milk, mixing well after each addition. Fold in apples. Fill greased muffin tins 2/3 full. Mix 2 tablespoons sugar, cinnamon and nutmeg. Sprinkle over muffins. Bake at 425 degrees for 20 to 25 minutes. Yield: 6 servings.

Carolyn Stevens
Delaplaine, Arkansas

CINNAMON-APPLE MUFFINS

2 c. sifted flour
1/3 c. sugar
1 tbsp. baking powder
1 tsp. salt
2 tsp. cinnamon
1 egg, beaten
3/4 c. milk
3 tbsp. melted shortening
1 c. grated umpeeled apple
1/2 c. chopped pecans
2 tbsp. brown sugar

Sift first 4 ingredients with 1 1/2 teaspoons cinnamon into large bowl. Combine egg, milk, shortening and apple in bowl; mix well. Add to dry ingredients; stir until just mixed. Fill greased muffin cups 2/3 full. Mix pecans, brown sugar and remaining cinnamon. Sprinkle over tops of muffins. Bake at 300 degrees for 25 to 30 minutes. May be frozen. Yield: 1 dozen.

Mrs. Ronald Goolsbey
Appleton, Wisconsin

APRICOT MUFFINS

2 1/2 c. sifted flour
1 tsp. soda
1/4 tsp. salt
1 tsp. each nutmeg, allspice and
    cinnamon

2 tsp. baking powder
3 eggs, beaten
1 1/2 c. sugar
1/2 c. oil
1 c. buttermilk
1 1/2-lb. package dried apricots,
    cooked, mashed
1/2 c. nuts (opt.)

Combine first 7 ingredients in bowl; mix well. Combine eggs, sugar and oil in bowl; mix well. Add dry ingredients to sugar mixture alternately with buttermilk, mixing well after each addition. Fold in apricots and nuts. Fill greased muffin cups 2/3 full. Bake at 350 degrees for 25 minutes or until muffins test done. Yield: 8 servings.

Mrs. Margarette Rathke
Harlingen, Texas

BANANA MUFFIN SURPRISE

1/2 c. uncooked oats
1/2 c. milk
1 c. all-purpose flour
1/4 c. sugar
2 1/2 tsp. baking powder
1/2 tsp. each soda, salt and cinnamon
1/4 tsp. nutmeg
1/4 c. butter, melted
1 egg, beaten
1 c. mashed bananas
1/2 c. sunflower seed

Combine oats and milk in medium bowl. Set aside until milk is absorbed. Mix next 7 ingredients in medium bowl. Add butter, egg and bananas to oat mixture; mix well. Add to dry ingredients; stir until just mixed. Stir in sunflower seed. Fill greased 2 1/2-inch muffin cups 2/3 full. Bake in 425-degree oven for 15 minutes or until muffins test done. Yield: 12 to 14 muffins.

Photograph for this recipe on cover.

EASY BLUEBERRY MUFFINS

1 1/2 c. self-rising flour
2 c. vanilla ice cream, melted
1 1/2 c. fresh blueberries

Combine flour and ice cream in bowl; mix well. Fold in blueberries gently. Fill greased muffin cups 2/3 full. Bake at 350 degrees for 15 minutes. Yield: 12 muffins.

Mrs. Martha A. Stewart
Garden City, Georgia

BLUEBERRY FEATHER MUFFINS

Sugar
1/2 c. butter, softened
1 egg
2 2/3 c. sifted all-purpose flour
4 tsp. baking powder
1/2 tsp. salt
1 c. milk
1 tsp. vanilla extract
1 1/2 c. blueberries, rinsed, drained
1/2 tsp. cinnamon

Cream 1/3 cup sugar and 1/4 cup butter in bowl. Add egg; beat well. Combine 2 1/3 cups flour, baking powder and salt. Add to creamed mixture alternately with milk, mixing well after each addition. Stir in vanilla; beat well. Fold in blueberries. Fill greased muffin cups 2/3 full. Combine 1/2 cup sugar, 1/3 cup flour, 1/4 cup butter and cinnamon in bowl; mix until crumbly. Sprinkle over muffins. Bake at 350 degrees for 20 to 25 minutes or until golden brown. Serve warm. Yield: 1 dozen.

Photograph for this recipe on page 62.

BLUEBERRY MUFFINS

1 egg, slightly beaten
1 c. milk
1/4 c. oil
1 1/2 c. sifted flour
1/2 c. sugar
2 tsp. baking powder
1/2 tsp. salt
3/4 c. drained canned blueberries

Combine egg, milk and oil in bowl. Sift flour, sugar, baking powder and salt together. Add to egg mixture. Stir until just mixed. Blend in blueberries. Batter should be lumpy. Fill greased muffin cups 2/3 full. Bake in 400-degree oven for 20 to 25 minutes. Yield: 12 muffins.

Elaine Murphy
Biloxi, Mississippi

MAYONNAISE MUFFINS

1 c. self-rising flour
1/2 c. milk
1 tbsp. (rounded) mayonnaise

Combine all ingredients in mixing bowl. Stir until smooth. Spoon into 8 greased muffin cups. Bake in 450-degree oven for 8 minutes. Yield: 8 servings.

Mrs. Wade H. Harris
Seagrove, North Carolina

SHAKER BRAN MUFFINS

6 c. whole bran cereal
3 c. sugar
1 c. shortening
3 c. ground raisins
1 qt. buttermilk
4 eggs
5 c. sifted flour
1 tsp. salt
5 tsp. soda

Pour 2 cups boiling water over 2 cups bran cereal; set aside. Cream sugar, shortening, raisins, buttermilk and eggs together in bowl. Fold flour, salt, soda and remaining cereal into creamed mixture. Add soaked cereal to batter. Stir until just mixed. Store in refrigerator. Do not stir when ready to use. Spoon into greased muffin cups, filling cups 2/3 full. Bake at 400 degrees for 20 minutes. Batter may be refrigerated 4 to 6 weeks. Yield: 1 gallon batter.

Mrs. C. B. Haas
Elgin, North Dakota

THIRTY-DAY BRAN MUFFIN MIX

2 c. 100% bran cereal
4 c. All-Bran flakes
1 qt. buttermilk
1 c. shortening
2 c. sugar
6 eggs
5 c. sifted flour
5 tsp. soda
1 tsp. salt
Nuts (opt.)

Combine 100% bran, All-Bran flakes and 2 cups boiling water in bowl. Let stand for several minutes. Stir in buttermilk. Cream shortening and sugar together in bowl. Add eggs one at a time, beating well after each addition. Add to bran mixture; mix well. Sift flour, soda and salt together. Stir into bran mixture until just mixed. Cover. Refrigerate until needed. Will keep up to 30 days. Bake muffins in 400-degree oven for 15 to 20 minutes or until muffins test done. Nuts may be added to batter before baking.

Rowa Lee
Las Vegas, Nevada

RAISIN-BRAN MUFFINS

1 c. bran buds
1 c. All-Bran flakes
1 c. quick-cooking rolled oats
1/2 c. oil
1 c. sugar
2 eggs
2 c. buttermilk
2 1/2 c. flour
1 tsp. salt
2 1/2 tsp. soda
1 c. raisins

Combine bran buds, All-Bran flakes and rolled oats in mixing bowl. Stir in 1 cup boiling water. Let cool for several minutes. Mix oil and sugar together in bowl. Add eggs one at a time, beating well after each addition. Stir in buttermilk. Sift flour, salt and soda together. Stir into buttermilk mixture until just mixed. Stir in raisins. Fill greased muffin tins 3/4 full. Bake in 400-degree oven for 15 minutes or until muffins test done. Batter may be stored in covered container in refrigerator up to 1 week. Do not stir mixture before spooning into muffin tins after refrigeration. Yield: 24 muffins.

Mrs. Joy Barkowsky
Hereford, Texas

REFRIGERATOR BRAN MUFFINS

1 c. 100% Bran
9 tbsp. shortening
1 1/2 c. sugar
2 eggs, beaten
2 c. buttermilk
2 c. All-Bran
2 1/2 c. flour
2 1/2 tsp. soda
1/2 tsp. salt
1 c. raisins (opt.)

Pour 1 cup boiling water over 100% Bran in bowl; set aside. Cream shortening and sugar together in bowl. Add eggs and buttermilk. Add All-Bran. Sift flour, soda and salt together. Add to creamed mixture; mix well. Fold into 100% Bran mixture. Add raisins. Fill greased muffin cups 2/3 full. Bake at 400 degrees for 15 to 18 minutes. May store, covered, in refrigerator for 6 to 7 weeks. Yield: 6 dozen.

Nancy M. Riley
Waterford, Ohio

DELICIOUS CHERRY MUFFINS

1/2 c. shortening
1/2 c. (firmly packed) brown sugar
1/4 c. sugar
2 eggs, separated
1 c. flour
1/2 tsp. baking powder
1/4 tsp. salt
1 tsp. vanilla extract
1 tbsp. cherry juice
Pecans, coarsely chopped
1   4-oz. bottle cherries, drained

Cream shortening and sugars together in bowl. Add egg yolks; mix well. Sift dry ingredients together. Add to creamed mixture; blend well. Add vanilla and cherry juice. Beat egg whites until stiff peaks form. Fold into batter. Place several pecans in bottom of greased muffin cups. Spoon a small amount of batter over pecans. Add cherry to each. Cover with batter. Bake at 350 degrees for 25 minutes. Yield: 8 muffins.

Lucille Cook
Hutchins, Texas

COFFEE CAKE MUFFINS

1/2 c. (firmly packed) brown sugar
1/2 c. walnuts
Flour
2 tsp. cinnamon
2 tbsp. butter, melted
2 tsp. baking powder
1/2 tsp. salt
1/2 c. sugar
1/4 c. shortening
1 egg, beaten
1/2 c. milk

Combine brown sugar, walnuts, 2 tablespoons flour, cinnamon and butter in bowl. Mix until crumbly. Set aside. Sift remaining dry ingredients and 1 1/2 cups flour into bowl. Cut in shortening until crumbly. Combine egg and milk. Add to flour mixture. Stir until just mixed. Fill greased muffin cups 2/3 full with alternate layers of batter and walnut mixture, ending with walnut mixture. Bake at 375 degrees for 20 minutes or until muffins test done. Yield: 1 dozen.

Mrs. Douglas W. Sikes
Trent, Texas

COTTAGE CHEESE-CHIVE MUFFINS

2 c. all-purpose flour
3 tsp. baking powder
2 tbsp. sugar

2 tbsp. chopped chives
2 eggs, beaten
3/4 c. milk
3 tbsp. butter, melted
1 c. small-curd creamed cottage cheese

Sift flour, baking powder and sugar together in bowl. Stir in chives. Combine eggs, milk and butter in bowl; blend well. Stir in cottage cheese. Add to flour mixture. Stir until just mixed. Fill greased muffin cups 1/2 full. Bake in 425-degree oven for 15 to 20 minutes. Cool for several minutes in pan. Remove. Yield: 1 1/2 dozen.

Jessie K. Lannan
Sherrard, West Virginia

FRENCH BREAKFAST PUFFS

Butter
1 c. sugar
1 egg, beaten
1 1/2 c. flour
1 1/2 tsp. baking powder
1/2 tsp. salt
1/4 to 1/2 tsp. nutmeg
1/2 c. milk
1 tsp. cinnamon

Combine 1/3 cup butter, 1/2 cup sugar and egg in bowl; mix well. Sift next 4 ingredients together. Add to sugar mixture alternately with milk, beating well after each addition. Fill greased muffin cups 2/3 full. Bake in 350-degree oven for 20 to 25 minutes. Remove from pan. Melt 1/3 cup butter in small saucepan. Mix remaining sugar and cinnamon in bowl. Dip muffin tops in butter then sugar mixture. Serve hot. Yield: 1 dozen.

Mrs. Joan Moore
Alden, Iowa

MUSHROOM MUFFINS

1 4-oz. can mushroom stems and pieces
1 tsp. butter
2 c. flour
1/4 c. sugar
1 tsp. salt
3 tsp. baking powder
1 egg, beaten
3/4 c. milk
1/2 c. grated American cheese
1/4 c. melted shortening

Drain mushrooms, reserving 1/4 cup liquid. Saute mushrooms in butter in skillet for 3 min-

utes. Sift next 4 ingredients together in large bowl. Mix reserved mushroom liquid with mushrooms and remaining ingredients. Stir into flour mixture until just mixed. Fill greased muffin cups 2/3 full. Bake at 400 degrees for 20 to 25 minutes.

Mrs. Victor Kruppenbacher
Orlando, Florida

OATMEAL MUFFINS

1 c. sifted all-purpose flour
1/4 c. sugar
3 tsp. baking powder
1/2 tsp. salt
1 c. quick-cooking oats
1 egg, beaten
1 c. milk
3 tbsp. oil

Sift first 4 ingredients into bowl. Add oats; mix well. Add egg, milk and oil. Stir until just mixed. Fill greased muffin cups 2/3 full. Bake at 425 degrees for 15 minutes. Yield: 12 muffins.

Mrs. Elizabeth C. Ervin
Greenback, Tennessee

ORANGE MUFFINS

1/2 c. butter
1 1/2 c. sugar
2 eggs
2 c. flour
1 tsp. soda
1/4 tsp. salt
1 c. sour milk
Juice and grated rind of 1 orange
1 c. finely chopped pecans
1 c. seeded raisins

Cream butter and 1 cup sugar in bowl. Add eggs one at a time, beating well after each addition. Sift together flour, soda and salt. Add to creamed ingredients alternately with sour milk, mixing well after each addition. Stir in orange rind. Fold in pecans and raisins. Fill greased and floured muffin tins 2/3 full. Bake at 350 degrees for 20 to 30 minutes or until muffins test done. Combine 1/2 cup sugar and orange juice in saucepan. Heat until sugar dissolves. Dip muffins in orange mixture. Yield: 16-24 muffins.

Flora Fry
Coleman, Texas

PUMPKIN PUFFS

Sugar
2 tsp. baking powder
3/4 tsp. salt
1 1/2 c. sifted flour
1/2 tsp. each cinnamon, nutmeg
1/4 c. shortening
1 egg, beaten
1/2 c. cooked pumpkin
1/2 c. milk
1/2 c. raisins (opt.)

Sift 1/2 cup sugar and next 5 ingredients together into bowl. Cut in shortening until crumbly. Combine egg, pumpkin and milk in bowl. Add to flour mixture. Stir until just mixed. Fold in raisins. Fill greased muffin cups 2/3 full. Sprinkle each with 1/4 teaspoon sugar. Bake in 400-degree oven for 15 to 20 minutes or until muffins test done.

Mrs. Phyllis Larson
Glen Ellyn, Illinois

BUTTERMILK HOT CAKES

2 eggs, well beaten
2 c. buttermilk
1 tsp. soda
2 1/4 c. sifted flour
2 tsp. baking powder
1 tsp. salt
2 tsp. sugar
1/4 c. shortening, melted

Combine eggs, buttermilk and soda in bowl; mix well. Sift dry ingredients together. Add flour mixture and shortening to buttermilk mixture; mix well. Drop by spoonfuls onto hot griddle. Brown on both sides. Yield: 20 servings.

Patsy Savage Harris
Spring, Texas

KENTUCKY CORNMEAL PANCAKES

1 c. cornmeal
1/2 tsp. soda
2 1/2 tsp. salt
1 egg, beaten
1 to 1 1/4 c. buttermilk

Mix cornmeal, soda and salt in bowl; blend well. Add egg and buttermilk, beating until smooth. Drop by spoonfuls onto well-greased hot griddle. Bake until brown, turning once. Stir batter each time. Batter must be thin to produce lacy edges on pancakes. Yield: 6 servings.

Mrs. Mary Russell Cole
Calvert City, Kentucky

SASSY CINNAMON MUFFINS

1 1/2 c. flour
1/4 c. each sugar, (firmly packed) brown sugar
2 tsp. baking powder
1/2 tsp. each salt, cinnamon
1 egg, beaten
1/2 c. each oil, milk
1/2 c. chopped pecans

Sift together flour, sugars and next 3 ingredients into bowl. Combine egg, oil and milk in bowl; mix well. Add to dry ingredients; stir until just mixed. Fold in pecans. Fill greased muffin cups 2/3 full. Bake at 400 degrees for 20 to 25 minutes. Yield: 12 muffins.

Shari Bolander
Del Norte, Colorado

SOUTHERN PEANUT PANCAKES

1 3/4 c. milk
1 egg, beaten
3 tbsp. Planters Oil
1 1/2 c. flour
2 tbsp. sugar
2 tsp. baking powder
1/2 tsp. salt
1 1/4 c. whole kernel corn
1/4 c. chopped Planters cocktail peanuts

Blend together milk, egg and oil in large bowl. Add dry ingredients. Beat until smooth. Stir in corn and peanuts. Pour 3 tablespoons batter for each pancake onto hot greased griddle. Brown on both sides, turning once. Serve with maple syrup. Yield: 20 pancakes.

Photograph for this recipe on page 67.

PEANUT-BACON MUFFINS

1 egg, beaten
1 c. milk
2 tbsp. Fleischmann's margarine, softened
1/2 c. chopped Planters cocktail peanuts
6 slices crisp-cooked bacon, crumbled
1 3/4 c. flour
1/4 c. (firmly packed) light brown sugar
1 tbsp. baking powder

Combine egg, milk and margarine in large bowl; mix well. Add peanuts and bacon. Sift in remaining ingredients; stir until just mixed. Fill greased muffin cups 2/3 full. Bake at 400 degrees for 25 minutes or until golden brown. Cool on wire racks. Yield: 10 muffins.

Photograph for this recipe on page 67.

POPOVERS

1 c. flour
Pinch of salt
3 eggs, beaten
1 c. milk
1 tsp. melted shortening

Mix flour and salt in bowl. Combine eggs, milk and shortening in bowl. Add to flour gradually; mix well. Beat vigorously for 1 to 2 minutes. Fill hot buttered muffin cups 1/3 full. Bake at 450 degrees for 1/2 hour. Remove from pans immediately. Yield: 8 servings.

Mrs. Virginia McCarthy
Berryville, Arkansas

OATMEAL PANCAKES

2 c. milk
2 c. quick-cooking oats
1/3 c. sifted flour
2 1/2 tsp. baking powder
1 tsp. salt
2 eggs, separated
1/3 c. melted shortening

Heat milk; pour over oats in large bowl. Cool. Sift flour, baking powder and salt together. Add egg yolks and shortening to oats mixture; mix well. Stir in dry ingredients. Beat egg whites until stiff peaks form. Fold into oats mixture. Drop by spoonfuls onto hot griddle. Bake until covered with bubbles; turn. Brown remaining side. Oatmeal pancakes brown more slowly than plain pancakes. Serve with syrup and sausages. Yield: 4 servings.

Mrs. I. O. Freeman
Houston, Mississippi

PANCAKE MIX

6 c. sifted flour
1 tbsp. salt
2 tbsp. baking powder
1 c. shortening
1 egg, beaten
2/3 c. milk

Sift flour, salt and baking powder together twice into large bowl. Cut in shortening until crumbly. Store in tightly covered glass jar. Combine 1 cup Pancake Mix and egg in bowl. Stir in milk; mix well. Bake on hot griddle until underside is golden and bubbles appear on surface. Turn. Bake until golden.

Elsie Klassen
Tohigo, Alberta, Canada

RAISIN GRIDDLE CAKES

3 1/2 c. sifted flour
1 c. sugar
1 1/2 tsp. baking powder
1 tsp. each salt, nutmeg
1/2 tsp. soda
1 c. shortening
1 egg
1/2 c. milk
1 1/4 c. raisins

Sift dry ingredients together into bowl; cut in shortening until crumbly. Beat egg and milk in small bowl. Add egg mixture and raisins to flour mixture. Stir until all ingredients are moistened and dough holds together. Turn onto lightly floured surface. Roll 1/4 inch thick. Cut with 2-inch round cookie cutter. Bake cakes on hot greased griddle until underside is golden. Turn; brown other side. Yield: 4 dozen cakes.

Mrs. Juanita Willis
Carlsbad, New Mexico

CHEESE POPOVERS

1 c. flour
1/2 tsp. salt
2 eggs, slightly beaten
1 c. milk
1 c. grated cheese

Sift flour and salt together in bowl. Combine eggs and milk in small bowl; mix well. Add to dry ingredients. Beat until bubbly. Fill hot buttered muffin cups 1/3 full. Sprinkle with cheese. Add batter to fill 2/3 full. Bake at 425 degrees for 20 minutes. Reduce temperature to 350 degrees. Bake for 15 to 20 minutes longer. Yield: 6 servings.

Wanda Stacke
Marshfield, Wisconsin

APPLE ROLLS

2 c. flour
1/2 tsp. salt
4 tsp. baking powder
Sugar
3 tbsp. shortening
3/4 c. milk
4 or 5 apples, shredded
Cinnamon to taste

Sift flour, salt, baking powder and 2 tablespoons sugar in bowl. Cut in shortening until crumbly. Add milk gradually. Stir until dough leaves side of bowl. Turn onto floured surface.

Roll to 1/4-inch thickness. Sprinkle apples evenly over dough. Top with additional sugar and cinnamon. Roll as for jelly roll. Cut into 1-inch slices. Dissolve 2 cups sugar in 1/2 cup boiling water in baking pan. Place rolls in syrup. Bake at 350 degrees for 45 minutes. Serve with cream or ice cream. Yield: 15 servings.

Mrs. Renee R. Porter
American Fork, Utah

LEMON TWIRLY BUNS

2 c. sifted flour
2/3 c. sugar
3 tsp. baking powder
1/2 tsp. salt
1/2 c. shortening
1 egg, beaten
1/3 c. milk
2 tbsp. butter, melted
3/4 c. raisins
2 to 3 tsp. grated lemon rind
1/3 c. confectioners' sugar
2 tsp. lemon juice

Sift together flour, 1/3 cup sugar, baking powder and salt into bowl. Cut in shortening until crumbly. Combine egg and milk in small bowl. Add to dry ingredients, stirring until just mixed. Turn onto floured board. Knead lightly. Roll into 10 x 6-inch rectangle. Spread with melted butter. Combine remaining sugar, raisins and lemon rind; mix well. Spread evenly over dough. Roll as for jelly roll from long side. Seal edges. Slice into buns. Place in 9-inch cake pan. Bake in 425-degree oven for 20 minutes or until light brown. Combine remaining ingredients; mix well. Drizzle over buns. Yield: 10 servings.

Mrs. Jean G. Lawhorn
Roanoke, Virginia

OLD-FASHIONED VINEGAR ROLLS

3/4 c. cider vinegar
1 1/4 c. sugar
4 tsp. cinnamon
2 c. sifted flour
1 tbsp. baking powder
1 tsp. salt
1/3 c. shortening
3/4 c. milk
4 tbsp. butter
Cream

Combine vinegar, 1 1/2 cups water, 1 cup sugar and 2 teaspoons cinnamon in saucepan. Stir over low heat until sugar is dissolved. Cook over medium heat for 20 minutes. Sift flour, baking powder and salt together into bowl. Cut in shortening until crumbly. Stir in milk; mix well. Turn onto floured surface. Roll into 1/4-inch thick rectangle. Combine remaining sugar and cinnamon. Sprinkle over rectangle. Dot with 2 tablespoons butter. Roll as for jelly roll from long side. Cut into 1 1/4-inch slices. Place, cut-side up, close together in deep baking dish. Dot with remaining butter. Pour hot vinegar mixture over all. Bake at 375 degrees for 30 to 40 minutes. Serve hot with cream. Yield: 8 servings.

Mrs. A. C. Ross
Flomaton, Alabama

CHEESE WAFFLES

3 eggs, separated
2 c. milk
1/2 c. butter, melted
3 c. sifted flour
3 tbsp. sugar
1 1/2 tbsp. baking powder
Salt and pepper
1 1/4 c. grated cheese

Beat egg yolks in large bowl. Add milk. Add butter; mix well. Add next 3 ingredients and 1 teaspoon salt; blend well. Season to taste with salt and pepper. Add cheese, stirring until just mixed. Beat egg whites in bowl until stiff peaks form. Fold into cheese mixture. Bake in hot waffle iron until golden brown. Yield: 10-12 servings.

Mrs. Annie Wright
Blacksburg, Virginia

BROWNIE WAFFLES

1 1-oz. square unsweetened chocolate
1/3 c. shortening
2 eggs
1 3/4 c. sugar
1 c. sifted flour
1/2 tsp. vanilla extract
1/2 c. nuts (opt.)

Melt chocolate and shortening in small saucepan. Combine remaining ingredients in bowl; mix well. Add chocolate mixture; blend well. Bake in well-greased hot waffle iron. Serve with ice cream or whipped cream. Yield: 4-6 servings.

Mrs. Patsy Steffensen
Lake Norden, South Dakota

WALNUT PINWHEELS

Margarine, softened
1/2 c. (firmly packed) brown sugar
2 c. sifted flour
4 tbsp. baking powder
1/2 tsp. salt
3 tbsp. shortening
3/4 c. milk
1 1/2 tsp. cinnamon
3/4 c. chopped walnuts

Cream 4 tablespoons margarine and 1/4 cup brown sugar together in bowl. Place equal amounts of mixture in 12 muffin cups. Sift flour, baking powder and salt in bowl. Cut in shortening with pastry blender until crumbly. Add milk; blend with fork. Shape into ball. Turn onto floured surface. Roll into rectangle. Spread with 3 tablespoons margarine. Combine remaining brown sugar, cinnamon and walnuts in bowl; mix well. Sprinkle over margarine. Roll as for jelly roll. Cut into 12 slices. Place in muffin tins, cut side down. Bake at 425 degrees for 12 to 15 minutes. Yield: 12 muffins.

Mary Barbara Hardy
Farrell, Pennsylvania

CHOCOLATE WAFFLES

1 1/2 c. flour
3 tsp. baking powder
1/2 tsp. salt
6 tbsp. sugar
1 c. milk
2 eggs, beaten
2 tbsp. melted butter
2 sq. chocolate, melted
1/4 c. butter, softened
3/4 c. confectioners' sugar
1/2 tsp. vanilla extract

Sift first 4 ingredients together into bowl. Add next 4 ingredients all at once; mix well. Bake in well-greased hot waffle iron using waffle iron directions. Cream softened butter in small bowl. Add confectioners' sugar gradually, blending well. Add vanilla and 1 tablespoon hot water, a few drops at a time. Chill thoroughly. Top waffles with hard sauce.

Mrs. Gladys E. Meier
Detroit, Michigan

GINGERBREAD WAFFLES

2 c. sifted flour
3/4 tsp. soda
1/2 tsp. salt
2 tsp. ginger
2 eggs, separated
1 c. molasses
1/2 c. buttermilk
1/2 c. shortening, melted

Sift flour, soda, salt and ginger together into bowl. Set aside. Beat egg whites until soft peaks form. Beat egg yolks in separate bowl until thick. Add molasses, buttermilk and shortening; beat well. Make well in flour mixture. Stir in egg yolk mixture quickly until just mixed. Fold in egg whites with 8 to 10 strokes. Bake in greased hot waffle iron at slightly lower temperature for 1 to 2 minutes longer than for plain waffles.

Mrs. Mary Ann Sewalt
Bluegrove, Texas

STANDARD WAFFLES

2 c. sifted flour
3 tsp. baking powder
1 tsp. salt
2 tbsp. sugar
2 eggs, separated
1 1/2 c. milk
6 tbsp. shortening, melted

Sift first 4 ingredients together into large bowl. Combine egg yolks, milk and shortening in bowl; beat well. Add to flour mixture; stir until just mixed. Beat egg whites until stiff peaks form. Fold into batter. Pour a small amount of batter into moderately hot waffle baker. Bake for 4 to 5 minutes. Serve hot with butter and syrup. Yield: 6 waffles.

Mrs. Clemens J. Pantales
Mahopac, New York

SUNDAY NIGHT WAFFLES

2 eggs
3/4 c. oil
2 1/2 c. milk
2 1/2 c. flour
1 1/2 tbsp. sugar
3/4 tsp. salt
4 tsp. baking powder

Combine eggs, oil and milk in mixer bowl; beat well. Combine dry ingredients. Add to milk mixture. Beat at medium speed of electric mixer for 2 minutes. Bake in hot waffle iron using waffle iron directions. Yield: 6 servings.

Marthanne Limehouse
Yonges Island, South Carolina

SHORTCUT

GARLIC STICKS

1 can refrigerator biscuits
1/4 c. milk
1/2 c. crushed corn flakes
Garlic salt

Cut each biscuit in half. Roll into sticks 5 to 6 inches long. Dip each stick into milk. Roll in corn flakes. Sprinkle with garlic salt. Place on buttered baking sheet 1 inch apart. Bake in 450-degree oven for 7 to 10 minutes. Yield: 20 servings.

Clara Greer
Eden, North Carolina

HERB BREAD

1/4 c. margarine, melted
2 tsp. parsley flakes
2 tbsp. lemon juice
1/4 tsp. dillseed
2 cans refrigerator biscuits

Combine first 4 ingredients in small bowl. Dip biscuits into margarine mixture; stand on edge in greased 1-quart ring mold. Bake in 425-degree oven for 15 minutes or until golden brown. Yield: 10-12 servings.

Mrs. Imogene Spring
Seymour, Texas

MAGIC FRENCH BREAD

2 cans refrigerator biscuits
1 egg white, slightly beaten
Sesame seed

Open biscuits but do not separate. Place rows of biscuits, end to end, on cookie sheet. Press together lightly, shaping ends to form long loaf. Brush with egg white. Sprinkle with sesame seed. Bake in 350-degree oven for 30 minutes or until golden brown. Serve hot with butter. Yield: 1 loaf.

Marilyn Berousek
Maysville, Oklahoma

CRISPY ONION ROLLS

1/4 c. butter, melted
1/4 c. dry onion soup mix, finely crushed
1 can refrigerator biscuits

Combine butter and soup mix. Pour 1/2 of the butter mixture into 8-inch round baking pan. Arrange biscuits in pan. Pour remaining butter mixture over biscuits. Bake in 400-degree oven for 12 to 14 minutes until brown. Serve at once. Yield: 10 onion rolls.

Marcella Goodrich
Bakerstown, Ohio

ONION KUCHEN

2 med. onions, sliced
3 tbsp. butter
1 pkg. refrigerator biscuits
1 egg, slightly beaten
1 8-oz. carton sour cream
1/2 tsp. salt
1 tsp. poppy seed

Separate onions into rings. Saute in butter in skillet over low heat until transparent. Separate biscuits; place in 8-inch cake pan. Spoon onion mixture over top. Combine egg, sour cream and salt. Spoon over onion mixture. Sprinkle with poppy seed. Bake at 375 degrees for 1/2 hour or until topping is set. Slice into wedges. Serve warm. Yield: 6 servings.

Norma Gentry
Fieldale, Virginia

ROLL-UPS

1 pkg. refrigerator biscuits
10 2 x 1/4 x 1/2-in. strips cheese
Dry onion soup mix
Parsley flakes

Roll each biscuit into 4 x 3-inch rectangle. Place cheese strip in center. Sprinkle with onion soup mix. Roll as for jelly roll from long edge. Roll in parsley flakes. Bake using package directions. Yield: 3-4 servings.

Mrs. Phil Fulkerson
Belleville, Wisconsin

CINNAMON TWIST

1/2 c. sugar
2 tsp. ground cinnamon
1 pkg. refrigerator biscuits
1/4 c. melted margarine
2 tbsp. chopped walnuts (opt.)

Combine sugar and cinnamon. Roll each biscuit into 9-inch rope. Bring ends together; pinch to seal. Dip in margarine. Coat with sugar mixture. Twist into figure eight. Place on greased baking sheet. Sprinkle with walnuts. Bake in 400-degree oven for 10 to 12 minutes. Dough may be twisted into heart, shamrock or Christmas designs.

Joy N. Pool
Streator, Illinois

CINNAMON COFFEE CAKE

2 cans refrigerator biscuits
1/4 c. butter, melted
3/4 c. sugar
1 tbsp. cinnamon
1/4 c. chopped nuts

Separate biscuits. Dip into melted butter. Combine sugar and cinnamon; coat biscuits with sugar mixture. Overlap 15 biscuits around 9-inch layer pan. Overlap remaining 5 biscuits to fill inner circle. Drizzle with remaining butter. Sprinkle with nuts. Bake in 375-degree oven for 24 to 30 minutes. Let stand for 5 minutes. Turn onto rack. Invert onto serving plate. Yield: 10 servings.

Betty Jones
Cedarville, Michigan

QUICK COFFEE CAKE

2 pkg. flaky refrigerator biscuits
1 12-oz. jar peach preserves
1/2 c. chopped nuts
Maraschino cherries

Separate each biscuit into 3 layers. Arrange half the layers on baking sheet, overlaping to form 9-inch circle. Brush with preserves. Sprinkle with 1/4 cup nuts. Dip remaining biscuits into preserves; overlap on top. Bake at 400 degrees for 18 minutes. Brush with remaining preserves. Sprinkle with 1/4 cup nuts. Garnish with cherries. Yield: 6-8 servings.

Mrs. Mary Esther Rowe
Swartz Creek, Michigan

SPEEDY MARMALADE COFFEE CAKE

1/4 c. sugar
2 tbsp. chopped nuts
2 tsp. grated orange rind
1 pkg. refrigerator biscuits
2 tbsp. melted margarine

Combine sugar, nuts and orange rind in bowl. Dip biscuits into margarine; dip into sugar mixture. Arrange biscuits in overlapping circle in 9-inch pie pan. Bake at 400 degrees for 15 minutes or until golden. Yield: 8-10 servings.

Shirley Gumer
Portland, Oregon

DOUGHNUT DAISIES

Oil
1 can refrigerator buttermilk biscuits
Sugar
Jelly

Fill electric skillet 1/3 full with oil. Cut each biscuit almost to center in 5 equal sections. Pinch centers. Fry, 4 at a time, in 375-degree oil, turning to brown both sides. Drain on paper towels. Shake in bag containing sugar. Spoon a small amount of jelly into center of each daisy. Yield: 10 servings.

Kay Porters
Galion, Ohio

CARAMEL SCONES

1 can refrigerator biscuits
3/4 c. (firmly packed) brown sugar
1/4 c. butter
3 tbsp. cream

Arrange biscuits in 9-inch cake pan. Combine remaining ingredients in bowl; mix well. Pour over biscuits. Bake at 375 degrees for 15 minutes or until golden brown. Yield: 4-6 servings.

Mrs. Georgia Clark
Lamoni, Iowa

EASY SWEET ROLLS

1 tbsp. melted butter
1/4 c. maple syrup
1/4 c. chopped walnuts
1 10-count pkg. refrigerator biscuits
Cinnamon to taste

Combine butter and maple syrup in round 8-inch baking pan. Sprinkle in walnuts. Cut each biscuit into quarters. Place close together on syrup mixture. Sprinkle cinnamon over top. Bake in preheated 400-degree oven for 10 to 15 minutes or until biscuits are golden brown. Invert onto large plate. Serve warm.

June Dorothy Allan
Los Angeles, California

GOOEY CINNAMON ROLLS

1 pkg. refrigerator biscuits
1/3 c. sugar
2 tsp. cinnamon
3 tbsp. melted butter
1/2 c. miniature marshmallows

Separate and flatten biscuits. Combine sugar and cinnamon in bowl. Dip biscuits into butter then into sugar mixture. Place 4 marshmallows in center of each biscuit. Bring edges up to cover marshmallows. Seal tightly. Place in greased muffin cups, seam-side down. Bake in 400-degree oven for 10 to 12 minutes. Remove from pan immediately.

Margery Juk
Warren, Michigan

HONEY BUNS

2/3 c. butter
2/3 c. honey
1/2 c. sugar
1/2 c. chopped nuts
2 pkg. refrigerator biscuits

Combine butter, honey and sugar in saucepan. Bring to a boil over medium heat. Boil for 1 minute, stirring constantly. Pour into 9 x 13-inch baking dish. Sprinkle with nuts. Arrange biscuits over honey mixture. Bake at 425 degrees for 12 minutes. Invert on serving dish. Yield: 20 servings.

Pearl T. Aitken
Custer, South Dakota

KOFFEE KLATCH KUCHEN

2 tbsp. butter
1 pkg. refrigerator biscuits
1/4 c. orange marmalade
1/2 c. chopped pecans
1 egg, beaten
1/2 c. sour cream
1 tbsp. sugar
1/2 tsp. vanilla extract

Melt butter in 8-inch square pan. Roll each biscuit in melted butter, arranging in single layer in pan. Spoon marmalade into center of each biscuit; sprinkle with pecans. Bake at 450 degrees for 10 minutes. Combine remaining ingredients in small bowl; beat until smooth. Spoon over biscuits. Reduce temperature to 350 degrees. Bake for 20 minutes longer. Cut into squares. Serve warm. Yield: 9 servings.

Betty Berk
Othello, Washington

PECAN ROLLS

2 tbsp. melted butter
3 tbsp. corn syrup
1/2 c. (firmly packed) brown sugar
1/2 c. pecans
1 pkg. refrigerator biscuits

Brush muffin cups generously with melted butter. Pour a small amount of corn syrup over butter. Sprinkle with brown sugar. Place several pecans in each muffin cup. Top with biscuits. Brush with remaining butter. Bake at 425 degrees for 10 minutes. Yield: 8 servings.

Helen Keller Foster
Sewickley, Pennsylvania

PINEAPPLE UPSIDE-DOWN BREAKFAST ROLLS

1/2 c. (firmly packed) brown sugar
1/2 c. butter
3/4 c. crushed pineapple, drained
1 tsp. cinnamon
1 can refrigerator biscuits

Melt brown sugar and butter in 8-inch square cake pan. Add pineapple and cinnamon; mix well. Place biscuits over top. Bake in preheated 425-degree oven for 10 minutes. Invert onto serving plate. Yield: 10 rolls.

Mrs. Carolyn Saxe
Albion, Illinois

BLUE CHEESE ROLLS

1 pkg. refrigerator biscuits
1 4-oz. package blue cheese
1/4 c. butter or margarine
Paprika to taste

Preheat oven to 425 degrees. Remove biscuits from package; separate. Cut each biscuit into 4 pieces. Place biscuits 1/2 inch apart on large cookie sheet. Cream blue cheese and butter together; spread equally onto each biscuit. Sprinkle with paprika. Bake at 425 degrees for 8 minutes. Yield: 40 servings.

Nicky Beaulieu
Los Angeles, California

ORANGE-NUT BISCUITS

1 8-oz. package ready-to-bake biscuits
1/4 c. frozen Florida orange juice
concentrate, thawed
3 tbsp. chopped nuts
3 tbsp. brown sugar

Place biscuits in ungreased 9-inch round pan. Bake according to package directions. Combine orange juice concentrate, nuts and sugar in bowl. Spoon over biscuits. Bake for 4 to 5 minutes longer. Yield: 10 biscuits.

Photograph for this recipe on page 71.

ORANGE-CINNAMON TOAST

8 slices white bread, trimmed, cut in
half
2 tbsp. frozen Florida orange juice
concentrate, thawed
1/2 c. sugar
2 tsp. cinnamon
2 tbsp. melted butter

Place bread on baking sheet. Broil 2 inches from heat source until light brown. Combine remaining ingredients in bowl; mix well. Turn bread. Brush with orange mixture. Broil for 2 minutes longer or until light brown. Yield: 4 servings.

Photograph for this recipe on page 71.

GARLIC-BREAD STICKS

> 1 11-in. loaf unsliced sandwich bread
> 1/2 c. butter, melted
> 2 cloves of garlic, minced
> 1/4 c. sesame seed, toasted

Trim crusts from bread. Cut loaf in half crosswise, then in half lengthwise. Cut each piece crosswise into 4 sticks, 1 1/4 inches thick. Combine butter and garlic in bowl. Brush on all sides of bread sticks. Sprinkle with sesame seed. Arrange on baking sheet 2 inches apart. Toast at 400 degrees for 10 minutes. Yield: 16 sticks.

Janet McGhee
Winkelman, Arizona

HOT HERB BREAD

> 1 14-in. loaf French bread
> 1/2 c. butter, softened
> 1 tsp. parsley flakes
> 1/4 tsp. each oregano, dillweed
> 1/2 tsp. garlic salt
> Grated Parmesan cheese
> Parsley flakes

Cut bread diagonally into 1-inch slices. Blend next 5 ingredients together in bowl. Spread bread slices with butter mixture. Shape back into loaf. Wrap loaf in aluminum foil, boat fashion, twisting ends, leaving top open. Sprinkle with cheese and parsley flakes. Bake in 400-degree oven for 10 minutes. Yield: 1 loaf.

Darlene Smith
McFarland, California

QUICKIE TOAST

> 6 tbsp. butter
> 1 1/8 c. (firmly packed) light brown
>   sugar
> 1/4 c. evaporated milk
> 3/4 c. chopped pecans
> 10 slices day-old bread

Melt butter over low heat in saucepan. Stir in brown sugar, evaporated milk and pecans. Toast

bread on one side under broiler. Turn; spread pecan mixture on untoasted side. Broil for 1 to 2 minutes or until bubbly. Yield: 10 servings.

Sophia Campbell
Sugar Grove, Ohio

ONION BREAD

> 1 loaf French bread
> 5 scallions
> 1/2 c. butter, softened

Cut loaf in half lengthwise. Chop scallions. Mix with butter. Spread over bottom half loaf; add top half of bread. Wrap in aluminum foil. Place on baking sheet. Bake in 400-degree oven for 10 minutes. Yield: 4-6 servings.

LaVonne Geisler
Carlisle, Iowa

MAGIC FORMULA BISCUIT MIX

> 4 c. all-purpose pre-sifted flour
> 8 tsp. baking powder
> 1 tsp. salt
> 1/2 c. shortening
> 2/3 c. milk

Combine first 3 ingredients in large mixing bowl. Cut in shortening until crumbly. Store mix in airtight container. Combine 2 cups mix with milk; mix well. Knead on lightly floured surface. Roll to 3/4-inch thickness. Cut with biscuit cutter. Place on greased baking sheet. Bake at 450 degrees for 8 to 10 minutes. Yield: 1 quart mix.

Mrs. Stirling Welker
Scottsdale, Arizona

BACON BARS

> 1/2 c. shredded sharp process American
>   cheese
> 6 slices crisp-cooked bacon, crumbled
> 2 c. packaged biscuit mix
> 3 tbsp. bacon drippings

Combine cheese and bacon with biscuit mix in bowl. Prepare according to package directions for rich biscuits, substituting bacon drippings for oil. Knead as directed for rolled biscuits. Roll on floured surface to 10 x 6-inch rectangle. Cut into six 10 x 1-inch strips. Cut each into thirds crosswise to make 18 bars. Place 1 inch apart on baking sheet. Bake at 450 degrees for 10 minutes. Yield: 18 bars.

Sande J. Speck
Watertown, Washington

MASTER MIX

1/3 c. baking powder
1 tbsp. salt
2 tsp. cream of tartar
1/4 c. sugar
9 c. sifted all-purpose flour
2 c. shortening

Sift dry ingredients together 3 times into large bowl. Cut in shortening until crumbly. Store in airtight container at room temperature. Yield: 13 cups.

Biscuits

2 c. Master Mix
2/3 c. milk

Combine mix and milk in bowl; mix lightly. Knead 10 times on floured surface. Pat to 1/2-inch thickness. Cut with biscuit cutter. Place on baking sheet. Bake at 425 degrees for 10 to 12 minutes. Yield: 10 biscuits.

Waffles

2 tbsp. sugar
2 c. Master Mix
1 c. milk
1/4 c. oil
2 eggs, separated

Combine sugar and mix in bowl. Beat milk, oil and egg yolks together in small bowl; stir into mix. Fold in stiffly beaten egg whites. Bake in hot waffle iron until golden. Yield: 4 waffles.

Muffins

2 tbsp. sugar
3 c. Master Mix
1 c. milk
1 egg, beaten

Combine sugar and mix in bowl. Combine milk and egg in small bowl; beat well. Stir into mix until just moistened. Pour into greased muffin cups. Bake at 425 degrees for 20 minutes or until golden. Yield: 10 muffins.

Coffee Cake

3 c. Master Mix
1/2 c. sugar
2/3 c. milk
1 egg
1/4 c. (firmly packed) brown sugar
1 1/2 tsp. cinnamon

Combine mix and sugar in bowl. Beat milk and egg together; stir into mix. Pour into 2 greased 9-inch layer pans. Combine brown sugar and cinnamon in small bowl; mix well. Sprinkle over batter. Bake at 400 degrees for 25 minutes or until cake tests done.

Dumplings

2 c. Master Mix
1/2 c. milk

Combine mix and milk in bowl, stirring until just mixed. Drop from tablespoon into hot stew, tomato soup or hot fruit sauce. Cover. Steam without lifting cover for 12 minutes.

Renee Graff
Las Cruces, New Mexico

BUTTERED BREADSTICKS

6 tbsp. butter
2 c. biscuit mix
1 tbsp. sugar
1/2 c. milk

Melt butter in 13 x 9 x 2-inch baking pan in 400-degree oven. Combine remaining ingredients; stir until soft dough is formed. Beat until stiff but still sticky. Turn dough onto board lightly dusted with biscuit mix. Knead gently 10 times. Roll into 12 x 8-inch rectangle. Cut dough in half lengthwise. Cut each half into 16 strips. Coat each strip in melted butter; arrange in baking pan in 2 rows. Bake at 400 degrees for 12 minutes or until golden brown. Serve warm. Yield: 32 breadsticks.

Mrs. Floyd Craig
Nolan, Texas

CHEESE PINWHEELS

1 pkg. biscuit mix
3/4 c. grated cheese

Combine biscuit mix and 1 cup water in small bowl; mix well. Knead on floured board for 1 minute. Roll thin. Sprinkle with cheese. Roll as for jelly roll. Slice 1/4 inch thick. Place on baking sheet. Bake at 350 degrees for 10 minutes. Yield: 10-12 servings.

Mrs. Ruth Jordan
Alexander City, Alabama

CRESCENT ROLLS

1 pkg. dry yeast
2 1/2 c. biscuit mix
Melted butter

Dissolve yeast in 3/4 cup warm water in bowl. Add biscuit mix; beat vigorously. Turn onto floured surface. Knead until smooth. Roll into

12-inch circle. Cut into 16 wedges. Roll as for jelly roll from wide end. Place on greased cookie sheet, point side down. Cover with cloth. Let rise for 1 hour or until doubled in bulk. Bake at 400 degrees for 10 to 15 minutes or until golden brown. Brush with butter.

Esther Lake
Chandler, Arizona

ONION-CHEESE BREAD

1/2 c. chopped onion
Butter
1 egg, beaten
1/2 c. milk
1 1/2 c. biscuit mix
1 c. grated sharp cheese
2 tbsp. minced parsley

Saute onion in a small amount of butter in skillet until transparent. Combine egg and milk. Stir into biscuit mix in bowl until just mixed. Add onion, 1/2 cup cheese and parsley; mix well. Spread in greased 8 x 8 x 1 1/2-inch pan. Sprinkle with remaining cheese. Drizzle 2 tablespoons melted butter over top. Bake in 350-degree oven until bread tests done.

Kristie Boyer
Austell, Georgia

OVEN-BUTTERED CORN STICKS

4 tbsp. butter
2 c. biscuit mix
1 8 3/4-oz. can cream-style corn

Melt butter in 15 1/2 x 10 1/2-inch baking pan. Combine biscuit mix and corn in bowl; mix well. Knead 15 times on lightly floured board. Roll to 6 x 10-inch rectangle. Cut into 1 x 3-inch strips. Roll in butter in pan. Arrange in pan in single layer. Bake at 450 degrees for 10 to 12 minutes. Yield: 20 sticks.

Judy L. Revell
Marianna, Florida

QUICK CHEDDAR BREAD

3 1/3 c. biscuit mix
2 1/2 c. shredded sharp Cheddar cheese
2 eggs, slightly beaten
1 1/4 c. milk

Combine biscuit mix and cheese in bowl. Combine eggs and milk. Stir into cheese mixture until just mixed. Pour into greased and floured 9 x 5-inch loaf pan. Bake in 350-degree oven

for 55 minutes or until bread tests done. Remove from pan. Serve warm.

Mrs. Frances R. Tharpe
Hays, North Carolina

APPLE ROLLS

2 c. Bisquick
3/4 c. milk
1 c. chopped apples
1/2 tsp. cinnamon
1/2 c. sugar
2 tbsp. butter
Several drops of red food coloring

Blend Bisquick and milk in bowl until soft dough forms. Turn onto floured surface. Roll to 1/4-inch thickness. Spread with apples. Roll as for jelly roll. Cut into 1-inch thick slices. Place cut-side down in greased baking pan. Bring 1/2 cup water to a boil in saucepan. Add cinnamon, sugar, butter and food coloring, mixing well. Pour over rolls. Bake at 375 degrees for 35 to 40 minutes. Serve with light cream if desired. Yield: 4-5 servings.

Jeanne C. Jackson
Lehi, Utah

APPLE DOUGHNUTS

4 c. biscuit mix
1/2 c. sugar
2 c. canned apple slices, chopped
1/4 c. milk
2 tsp. vanilla extract
3 eggs
1/2 tsp. each cinnamon, nutmeg
1/4 tsp. ginger
Oil for deep frying
1/2 c. apple juice
1 1/2 tsp. lemon juice
4 c. confectioners' sugar
1/2 c. coconut, toasted

Combine biscuit mix and sugar in bowl. Add apples, milk, vanilla, eggs and spices. Stir until well blended. Turn onto well-floured surface. Knead until smooth. Roll dough to 1/2-inch thickness. Cut out with floured 3-inch doughnut cutter. Heat 2 inches oil in heavy saucepan. Fry doughnuts several at a time at 400 degrees for 1 minute per side or until evenly brown. Drain on paper towels. Combine apple juice and lemon juice in saucepan. Bring to a boil. Stir in confectioners' sugar. Beat until smooth. Spoon 2 tablespoons over each warm doughnut. Roll half the doughnuts in coconut. Yield: 2 dozen.

Joyce Antley
Melbourne, Florida

APPLE BISCUITS

1 c. crushed Wheat Chex
1/2 c. grated unpeeled apples
1/2 c. apple juice
2 c. biscuit mix
1/8 tsp. each nutmeg, cinnamon

Combine crushed cereal and apples in bowl. Pour juice over apple mixture. Combine dry ingredients. Add to apple mixture; mix well. Drop by spoonfuls onto buttered baking sheet. Bake at 450 degrees for 10 minutes. Yield: 16-18 servings.

Alice P. Lynum
N. Bellmore, New York

ZEBRA BREAD

2 c. biscuit mix
1/4 c. sesame seed
1/2 tsp. salt
2/3 c. milk

Combine biscuit mix, sesame seed and salt in bowl. Stir in milk vigorously. Beat for 20 strokes. Turn onto floured board. Knead 8 to 10 times. Divide dough into 3-inch balls. Flatten each ball into 1/8 to 1/4-inch thick circle. Grill circles 5 inches from medium-hot coals for 3 to 4 minutes on each side. Cut in half; butter with herb butter, if desired. Parmesan cheese, bacon bits, chives, chopped onions, peppers or mushrooms may be added for variation of flavor.

Cora Caldwell
Gooding, Idaho

BANANA AMBROSIA RING

1/2 c. flaked coconut
1/3 c. maple-flavored syrup
4 tbsp. melted butter
2 c. packaged biscuit mix
5 tbsp. sugar
1/2 c. mashed ripe banana
1 egg, slightly beaten
1 tsp. cinnamon

Combine coconut, syrup and 2 tablespoons butter in bowl. Spread coconut mixture in 5-cup ring mold. Combine biscuit mix and 3 tablespoons sugar in bowl. Stir in banana, egg and remaining melted butter. Beat vigorously for 1 minute. Spoon half the batter over coconut in mold. Mix 2 tablespoons sugar with cinnamon; sprinkle over batter. Dot with butter. Cover

with remaining batter. Bake in 375-degree oven for 20 minutes.

Jimmie Rae Hankins
Lexington, Alabama

CHERRY CREPES

1 c. sour cream
1/3 c. (firmly packed) brown sugar
1 c. biscuit mix
1 egg
1 c. milk
1 can cherry pie filling
1 tsp. orange extract

Blend sour cream and brown sugar in small bowl; set aside. Combine next 3 ingredients in bowl; beat until smooth. Pour 2 tablespoons batter into oiled 6-inch skillet; tilt from side to side until batter covers bottom evenly. Cook until lightly browned. Turn; brown other side. Fill each crepe with spoonful of sour cream mixture; roll. Place seam-side down in baking dish. Pour pie filling over crepes. Bake at 350 degrees for 5 minutes. Drizzle orange extract over crepes. Ignite before serving. Yield: 10-12 servings.

Barbara Brandon
Eudora, Arkansas

CINNAMON-BANANA MUFFINS

2 c. biscuit mix
2 1/4 tsp. cinnamon
Sugar
1 egg, beaten
1 c. milk
1/4 c. oil
3 bananas, mashed

Combine biscuit mix, 2 teaspoons cinnamon and 1/3 cup sugar in bowl. Add egg, milk and oil; mix well. Add bananas; stir until just mixed. Batter will be lumpy. Fill greased muffin cups 3/4 full. Combine remaining cinnamon and 1 tablespoon sugar. Sprinkle over muffins. Bake in 425-degree oven for 20 minutes. Yield: 18 muffins.

Mrs. Richard L. Moore
Lubbock, Texas

EASY SUGAR BUNS

2 c. Bisquick
Sugar

1 tsp. nutmeg
1/8 tsp. cinnamon
2/3 c. cream
1 egg, beaten
1/4 c. butter, melted

Combine Bisquick, 2 tablespoons sugar and spices in bowl. Add cream and egg; mix thoroughly. Fill greased muffin cups 1/2 full. Bake in 400-degree oven for 15 minutes. Dip into melted butter and sugar, coating all sides. Serve warm. Yield: 10-12 buns.

Mrs. Jo Anne Tuttle
Spencer, Iowa

FRENCH BREAKFAST PUFFS

2 c. biscuit mix
Sugar
1/4 tsp. nutmeg
2 tbsp. butter, softened
3/4 c. milk
1 egg
1/2 c. butter, melted
1 tsp. cinnamon

Combine biscuit mix, 1/4 cup sugar and next 4 ingredients in bowl. Beat vigorously with a spoon for 30 seconds. Fill greased muffin cups 2/3 full. Bake at 400 degrees for 15 minutes. Roll immediately in melted butter and mixture of 2/3 cup sugar and cinnamon. Serve hot. Yield: 12 medium muffins.

Dorothy Angelos
Deer River, Minnesota

QUICK HOT CROSS MUFFINS

2 c. packaged biscuit mix
1/4 c. sugar
1/4 tsp. salt
1 tsp. cinnamon
2 eggs, slightly beaten
3/4 c. milk
2 tbsp. oil
2 tsp. shredded orange rind
1/2 c. raisins, plumped
Confectioners' sugar frosting

Combine first 8 ingredients in bowl. Beat vigorously for 30 seconds. Add raisins. Fill greased muffin cups 2/3 full. Bake at 400 degrees for 15 to 18 minutes. Cool slightly. Pipe on crosses of frosting. Serve warm. Yield: 12 buns.

Linda Clark
Okanogan, Washington

VELVET CRUMB COFFEE CAKE

1 1/3 c. Bisquick
3/4 c. sugar
3 tbsp. shortening
1 tsp. vanilla extract
1 egg
3/4 c. milk
3 tbsp. butter, softened
1/3 c. (firmly packed) brown sugar
2 tbsp. cream
1/2 c. coconut
1/4 c. chopped nuts

Combine first 5 ingredients and 1/2 cup milk in mixer bowl. Beat at medium speed of electric mixer for 1 minute. Stir in remaining milk. Beat for 30 seconds. Pour into greased and floured 8 x 8-inch baking pan. Bake in 350-degree oven for 35 to 40 minutes. Combine remaining ingredients in bowl. Spread on hot coffee cake. Broil 3 to 4 inches from heat source for about 3 minutes or until brown. Yield: 6 servings.

Juanita Whiting
Monroeville, Alabama

BANANA-CORN BREAD MUFFINS

1 15-oz. package corn bread mix
1/2 c. sugar
1/4 tsp. baking powder
3 med. bananas, mashed
1 egg

Combine corn bread mix, sugar and baking powder in bowl. Add bananas, 1/4 cup water and egg. Beat for 1 minute. Line muffin tins with paper baking cups. Fill 2/3 full. Bake at 425 degrees for 15 to 20 minutes. Yield: 12 muffins.

Mrs. Charles R. Owen
Memphis, Tennessee

CHEESE-CORN MUFFINS

1 8-oz. package corn muffin mix
1 egg, beaten
1 8-oz. can cream-style corn
1/2 c. shredded sharp American process cheese
1/8 tsp. hot sauce

Combine all ingredients in bowl; mix well. Fill greased muffin cups 2/3 full. Bake at 425 degrees for 15 to 20 minutes or until muffins test done. Yield: 12 muffins.

Mrs. E. N. Franklin
Lynchubrg, Virginia

HOMEMADE CORNMEAL MIX

4 1/2 c. cornmeal
4 c. sifted all-purpose flour
1/2 c. sugar (opt.)
1/3 c. baking powder
4 tsp. salt
1 c. shortening

Combine first 5 ingredients in large bowl; blend well. Cut in shortening until crumbly. Store in covered container at room temperature. Yield: 3 quarts.

Corn Bread

2 1/2 c. Homemade Cornmeal Mix
1 c. milk
1 egg

Combine all ingredients in bowl. Beat for 1 minute or until smooth. Pour into greased 8-inch square baking pan. Bake in 425-degree oven for 20 to 25 minutes. Yield: 9 servings.

Corn Sticks

Prepare batter as for Corn Bread. Pour into hot greased corn stick pans. Bake in 425-degree oven for 20 to 25 minutes. Yield: 14 Corn Sticks.

Corn Muffins

3 c. Homemade Cornmeal Mix
1 1/4 c. milk
1 egg, beaten

Place mix in bowl. Make well in center. Pour milk and egg into well. Stir until just mixed. Fill greased muffin cups 2/3 full. Bake in 425-degree oven for 12 to 15 minutes. Yield: 12 muffins.

Cornmeal Griddle Cakes

3 c. Homemade Cornmeal Mix
1 3/4 c. milk
2 eggs

Combine all ingredients in bowl; mix until almost smooth. Bake on hot lightly greased griddle. Turn when tops are bubbly. Bake until brown. Yield: 1 1/2 dozen.

Photograph for this recipe above.

CORN BREAD DELUXE

1 8-oz. package corn bread mix
1 c. whole kernel corn, drained
3 tbsp. shortening

Prepare corn bread using package directions. Add corn; mix well. Melt shortening in baking pan. Pour in corn bread. Bake at 450 degrees for 40 minutes or until brown. Cut into squares. Serve hot. Yield: 4-6 servings.

Rosalind Clark
Pittsburgh, Pennsylvania

CORN BREAD JELLY ROLL

1 pkg. corn bread mix
2 tbsp. oil
1 c. berry jam
3/4 c. confectioners' sugar

Prepare corn bread mix according to package directions in bowl. Add 1/4 cup water and 2 tablespoons oil; stir until just mixed. Cook on hot greased griddle, as for pancakes. Place 1 tablespoon jam in center of each griddle cake. Roll as for jelly roll. Secure with toothpicks. Roll in confectioners' sugar. Serve hot. Yield: 12 servings.

Mrs. Charles S. Carlisle
Pearl Harbor, Hawaii

CRANBERRY-CORN MUFFINS

1 8-oz. package corn muffin mix
1 7-oz. can jellied cranberry sauce,
   diced

Prepare muffin mix using package directions. Fold in cranberry sauce. Fill paper-lined muffin cups 2/3 full. Bake using package directions. Yield: 12 muffins.

Dianne Fynboh
Onamia, Minnesota

SPANISH CORN BREAD

1 12-oz. package corn muffin mix
1 12-oz. can whole kernel corn with
   sweet peppers
1/2 tsp. dry mustard
1 sm. onion, chopped
1 egg, beaten
2/3 c. milk

Combine muffin mix, corn, mustard and onion in bowl; mix well. Add egg and milk; stir until just mixed. Pour into greased baking pan. Bake

at 400 degrees for 20 minutes or until corn bread tests done. Serve warm. Yield: 9 servings.

Mrs. Julia Acker
West Branch, Michigan

JALAPENO CORN BREAD

3 c. corn bread mix
2 1/2 c. milk
1/2 c. oil
3 eggs, beaten
1 lg. onion, grated
1 c. canned cream-style corn
1 1/2 c. grated yellow cheese
1/2 c. chopped jalapeno peppers

Combine all ingredients in bowl; mix well. Pour into greased 13 x 9-inch pan. Bake at 400 degrees for 45 minutes or until golden brown.

Edith Donaldson
Anthony, New Mexico

CRANBERRY-ORANGE NUT BREAD

1 box orange muffin mix
1 c. whole cranberry sauce
1 c. chopped pecans

Prepare muffin mix according to package directions. Stir cranberry sauce with fork; add to muffin mix. Add pecans; stir until just mixed. Pour into greased loaf pans. Bake at 350 degrees for 30 minutes or until golden brown. Cool. Remove from pans. Yield: 36 servings.

Mrs. Edith Pollock
Kerens, Texas

QUICK DOUGHNUT BALLS

3 c. pancake mix
1/3 c. sugar
1 1/2 tsp. cinnamon
1/2 tsp. nutmeg
2 eggs, beaten
3/4 c. milk
Oil
Confectioners' sugar

Combine first 4 ingredients in bowl; mix well. Mix eggs, milk and 2 tablespoons oil in separate bowl; mix well. Stir into pancake mixture; mix thoroughly. Drop by teaspoonfuls into 375-degree deep fat, turning to brown on both sides. Drain on paper towels. Roll in confectioners' sugar.

Jacqueline Witt
Viburnum, Missouri

LOOPY LOOPS

2 1/2 c. pancake mix
Sugar
3 tbsp. brown sugar
1 tsp. nutmeg
1 egg, well beaten
1/2 c. milk
3 tbsp. butter, melted
Oil for deep frying
1 tsp. cinnamon

Combine pancake mix, 3 tablespoons sugar, brown sugar and 3/4 teaspoon nutmeg in bowl. Add egg, milk and butter; mix well. Turn onto lightly floured surface. Knead gently until dough is just combined. Roll to 1/3-inch thickness. Cut into 6 x 1/2-inch strips. Shape into loops gently. Press ends together lightly. Fry in 375-degree hot deep fat for 1 minute on each side. Drain. Combine 1 cup sugar, cinnamon and 1/4 teaspoon nutmeg. Roll loops in cinnamon-sugar. Yield: 2 1/2 dozen.

Janice Svingen
Round Lake, Minnesota

QUICK FRUIT BUNS

1 pkg. hot roll mix
2 tbsp. butter, melted
2 tbsp. golden seedless raisins
2 tbsp. chopped candied fruits and rinds
1/3 c. sugar
1 tsp. cinnamon
1/2 tsp. nutmeg
1 egg, lightly beaten
Confectioners' sugar icing

Prepare hot roll mix according to package directions. Add next 6 ingredients to roll mix; mix well. Cover with damp cloth. Let rise in warm place for 1 hour or until doubled in bulk. Turn onto lightly floured surface. Knead until smooth and elastic. Shape into 12 buns. Place on lightly greased baking sheet. Cover. Let rise for 45 minutes or until doubled in bulk. Mix egg and 1 tablespoon water. Brush over buns. Bake at 375 degrees for 15 minutes or until rolls test done. Cool slightly. Spread with confectioners' icing.

Mrs. S. H. King
Hampton, Virginia

SHORTCUT BOSTON BROWN BREAD

1 pkg. gingerbread mix
3/4 c. yellow cornmeal

3/4 c. flour
1 c. seedless raisins

Combine all ingredients in large bowl; mix well. Add 1 1/4 cups water; stir until just mixed. Pour into greased 9 x 5-inch pan. Bake at 375 degrees for 35 to 40 minutes. Remove from pan immediately. Serve warm or cold. Yield: 1 loaf.

Mrs. Joan Thuma
Genoa, Illinois

STRAWBERRY HOT CAKES

2 c. cake mix
1 egg, beaten
1/3 c. flour
1/3 c. chopped nuts
Sweetened strawberries
Whipped cream

Combine cake mix, egg and 1/2 cup water in bowl; mix well. Stir in flour and nuts. Drop by tablespoonfuls onto lightly greased preheated grill. Cook as for hot cakes. Spoon strawberries over hot cakes. Top with whipped cream. Serve immediately. Yield: 6-8 servings.

Marlene Caszatt
Whitehall, Michigan

CRUNCHY BREAD TWISTS

1 egg, beaten
1/4 c. Green Goddess salad dressing
2 c. herb-seasoned stuffing mix,
   coarsely crushed
1/2 c. grated Parmesan cheese
1 pkg. refrigerator crescent rolls

Combine egg and salad dressing in small bowl. Combine stuffing mix and cheese in bowl. Separate rolls into 4 rectangles. Pinch perforations together; flatten slightly with rolling pin. Cut each rectangle lengthwise into 1-inch strips. Dip each strip into egg mixture; roll in cheese mixture. Twist each strip several times; place on ungreased cookie sheet 1 inch apart. Bake at 375 degrees for 15 minutes or until golden brown. Yield: 16 twists.

Joann Gardner
Hampton, Virginia

GOLDEN BISCUITS

2 pkg. refrigerator butter flake rolls
1/2 c. melted butter
1/4 tsp. garlic salt
1/4 tsp. parsley flakes
1/2 tsp. onion flakes

Place rolls in 2 rows in loaf pan. Separate tops of rolls slightly. Combine remaining ingredients in bowl. Pour over rolls. Bake in 375-degree oven for 15 to 20 minutes or until golden. Bacon bits, shredded cheese, sesame seed or poppy seed may be added to the butter. Yield: 6-8 servings.

Cathy DiOrio
Burbank, Illinois

HERB RING-A-ROUND BREAD

1/2 stick butter
2 tsp. mixed salad herbs
1/8 tsp. nutmeg
2 pkg. refrigerator butter flake rolls

Melt butter in small saucepan; stir in herbs and nutmeg. Separate rolls; dip into butter mixture, coating both sides. Stand on edge in buttered 9-inch pie plate, working from the sides toward the center. Bake at 375 degrees for 20 minutes or until golden brown. Serve hot. Yield: 12 servings.

Paralee Coleman
Wellington, Texas

ITALIAN CRESCENTS

1 pkg. refrigerator crescent rolls
1/4 c. bottled barbecue sauce
1/4 tsp. Italian seasoning
2 long slices mozzarella cheese

Unroll dough; separate into 8 triangles. Mix barbecue sauce and Italian seasoning in cup. Cut cheese crosswise into eight 2-inch wide strips. Brush triangle with sauce mixture. Place cheese strip on top. Roll from wide end as for jelly roll. Place on ungreased cookie sheet. Bake at 375 degrees for 20 minutes or until rolls are golden. Serve hot. Yield: 8 rolls.

Mrs. Thomas R. Woehler
Bad Kissingen, Germany

ONION ROLLS

2 med. onions, sliced
1/4 c. butter
1/4 c. sugar
2 tbsp. poppy seed
1 pkg. refrigerator crescent rolls,
separated

Saute onions in butter in frypan until transparent. Add sugar and poppy seed. Place 1 spoonful onions on each crescent roll wedge. Roll from tip as for jelly roll. Bake according to package directions.

Delores Kluckman
Monteriedo, Minnesota

CARAMEL ROLLS

1/3 c. margarine
1/4 c. (firmly packed) brown sugar
1/3 c. Karo syrup
1/4 c. nut halves
12 brown and serve rolls, separated

Combine margarine, sugar and syrup in saucepan. Boil for 1 minute, stirring constantly. Spoon mixture into 12 muffin cups; sprinkle with nuts. Press rolls gently into cups. Bake at 375 degrees for 15 minutes or until brown. Cool for 30 seconds; invert pan onto waxed paper. Shake pan gently to remove rolls. Yield: 12 servings.

Iva Lea Schupp
Arkansas City, Kansas

QUICK CARAMEL ROLLS

1 pkg. frozen rolls, thawed
1/2 c. (firmly packed) brown sugar
1/2 pkg. butterscotch pudding mix
1/2 c. butter

Place rolls in greased 9-inch baking pan. Sprinkle brown sugar and butterscotch pudding mix over tops of rolls; dot with butter. Cover. Let stand overnight. Bake according to package directions.

Carmen M. Tripp
Faribault, Minnesota

MONKEY BREAD

3/4 c. sugar
1 tsp. cinnamon
2 pkg. refrigerator rolls
1/2 c. melted margarine
Confectioners' sugar icing

Combine sugar and cinnamon. Separate rolls. Dip into margarine then sugar mixture. Stand rolls on edge in casserole. Bake at 425 degrees for 20 to 25 minutes. Invert on serving plate. Drizzle with confectioners' sugar icing. Yield: 6-12 servings.

Mrs. Ella Adair
Tropic, Utah

HONEY-DOME COFFEE CAKE

1 can refrigerator Parkerhouse dinner
  rolls
1/4 c. butter
1/4 c. honey
1/2 c. chopped nuts
1/2 c. flaked coconut
2 tbsp. grated orange rind
2 tbsp. maraschino cherry halves

Separate dinner rolls. Melt butter in saucepan. Add honey; mix well. Combine next 4 ingredients in bowl; mix well. Dip rolls into honey mixture then nut mixture. Place in foil-lined 1 1/2-quart baking dish. Bake at 350 degrees for 40 to 45 minutes or until deep golden brown. Invert onto serving plate immediately. Serve warm. Yield: 12 servings.

Mrs. Shirley Bonomo
Spring Valley, Wisconsin

SESAME STICKS

1 pkg. refrigerator rolls
Milk
1 1/2 c. rice cereal, crushed
  coarsely
2 tsp. salt
1 tbsp. sesame seed
1 tbsp. caraway seed

Cut each roll in half; roll each into stick about 4 inches long. Brush with milk. Combine cereal crumbs, salt and seeds; roll sticks in mixture. Place on greased baking sheet. Bake in 400-degree oven for about 10 minutes or until lightly browned. Yield: 20 servings.

Eloise Palmer
Wetumpka, Alabama

SESAME FLAT ROLLS

1 8-oz. package or 10 refrigerator
  rolls
1 tbsp. margarine or butter,
  melted
Sesame seed

Place rolls on greased cookie sheet. Pat out with fingers until 3 inches across. Leave 1-inch space between rolls. Brush with margarine; sprinkle with sesame seed. Bake at 350 degrees for 10 minutes or until brown. May be made ahead

and placed in refrigerator or frozen. Place in 200-degree oven to reheat. Yield: 5 servings.

Betty Bell
Montgomery, Alabama

QUICK FRENCH BREAD

2 cans refrigerator rolls
1 egg white, slightly beaten
Sesame seed
Melted butter or garlic butter

Stand rolls on edge on cookie sheet. Press together and shape to form long loaf. Brush with egg white; sprinkle with sesame seed. Bake at 350 degrees for 35 to 40 minutes or until brown. Remove from oven; slice almost to bottom. Spread with melted butter; return to oven. Bake for several minutes. Serve hot. Yield: 6-8 servings.

June Mauser
Johnson City, Tennessee

QUICK CINNAMON ROLLS

1/4 c. sugar
1 tsp. cinnamon
1 pkg. refrigerator rolls
2 tbsp. melted butter or margarine

Mix sugar and cinnamon. Dip each roll in melted butter, then in cinnamon-sugar mixture. Place in pans. Bake according to package directions. Remove from oven; loosen rolls immediately.

Nell Anderson
Birmingham, Alabama

ORANGE-HONEY ROLLS

1/4 c. frozen Florida orange juice
  concentrate, thawed
2 tbsp. honey
1 6-oz. package soft dinner rolls
Raisins (opt.)

Combine orange juice concentrate and honey in bowl; blend. Place rolls on foil-lined baking sheet. Brush orange mixture over rolls. Sprinkle with raisins. Bake at 375 degrees for 15 minutes, brushing frequently with orange mixture. Drizzle confectioners' sugar icing over warm rolls, if desired. Yield: 9 rolls.

Photograph for this recipe on page 71.

SPECIAL DIET

BAKED WALNUT BROWN BREAD

1 1/4 c. sifted all-purpose flour
2 tsp. baking powder
3/4 tsp. soda
1 1/4 tsp. salt
1 1/4 c. graham flour
1 c. chopped walnuts
1 egg, lightly beaten
1/3 c. (firmly packed) brown sugar
1/2 c. light molasses
3/4 c. buttermilk
3 tbsp. melted shortening

Sift first 4 ingredients together into large bowl. Stir in graham flour and walnuts. Combine remaining ingredients in small bowl; beat well. Stir into dry mixture until just mixed. Spoon into 3 greased 1-pound cans. Bake at 350 degrees for 45 minutes or until bread tests done. Let stand for 10 minutes. Turn onto wire rack to cool. Yield: 3 loaves.

Photograph for this recipe on page 85.

DELICIOUS HIGH-PROTEIN DARK BREAD

2 pkg. yeast
1 tbsp. sugar
1 c. cottage cheese
1/4 c. butter
1 tbsp. salt
1 tbsp. honey
2 c. milk, scalded
3 c. whole wheat flour
1/2 c. rye flour
1/4 c. wheat germ
3 c. all-purpose flour
Butter, melted

Dissolve yeast and sugar in 1/2 cup warm water in large mixing bowl. Add cottage cheese, butter, salt and honey to milk in saucepan. Stir until butter is dissolved. Cool to lukewarm. Stir whole wheat flour, rye flour, wheat germ and cottage cheese mixture into yeast. Beat until smooth. Stir in enough all-purpose flour to make soft dough. Turn onto lightly floured board. Knead for 10 minutes or until smooth and elastic. Place in greased bowl, turning to grease surface. Cover. Let rise in warm place until doubled in bulk. Punch down. Divide dough in half. Shape each half into loaf. Place in 2 greased 9 x 5 x 8-inch loaf pans. Cover. Let rise until doubled in bulk. Place on low rack of preheated 375-degree oven so tops are in center of oven. Bake for 1 hour. Cover with foil during last 20 minutes if tops get too brown. Remove bread from pans. Brush with melted butter.

Mrs. Lorain O'Connell
Helena, Montana

OVEN FRENCH TOAST

1 egg, well beaten
Dash of salt
Sweetener to equal 2 tsp. sugar
1/4 tsp. cinnamon
1/2 c. milk
Bread slices

Combine egg, salt, sweetener and cinnamon in small bowl; mix well. Add milk; mix until blended. Place bread in baking dish; pour egg mixture over bread. Let stand in refrigerator overnight. Bake in 350-degree oven for 1/2 hour or until golden.

Cynthia L. Kiser
Parsons, Kansas

PROTEIN-PLUS MUFFINS

1 1/4 c. soy flour
2/3 c. dry milk powder
2 tsp. baking powder
1/2 tsp. salt
2 eggs, beaten
1 tsp. grated orange rind
3/4 c. orange juice
2 tbsp. honey
2 tbsp. oil
1/2 c. chopped pitted dates
1/4 c. chopped nuts

Combine dry ingredients in large bowl; mix well. Combine eggs, orange rind, juice, honey and oil in bowl; mix well. Add to dry ingredients, stirring until just mixed. Fold in dates and nuts. Fill greased muffin cups 2/3 full. Bake at 350 degrees for 1/2 hour or until brown. Yield: 12 muffins.

Marie Heltzel
Lake Butler, Florida

HIGH-PROTEIN WAFFLES

2 1/2 c. biscuit mix
1/4 c. sugar
3 tbsp. bacon bits
1 c. crushed high-protein cereal
1/2 c. each chopped nuts, wheat germ
2 tbsp. oil
3 eggs

2 1/2 c. milk
1/2 c. grape preserves
3 c. orange yogurt
1/4 tsp. nutmeg

Combine first 6 ingredients in large bowl. Add oil, eggs and milk. Stir until just mixed. Spoon 1 cup batter onto heated waffle iron. Cook according to directions. Combine grape preserves, orange yogurt and nutmeg in bowl; mix well. Top each waffle with grape topping.

Gloria Lupkoski
Saskatchewan, Canada

DATE MUFFINS

1 cake yeast
1/2 tbsp. salt
1 3/4 c. chopped dates
1 c. oatmeal
1/4 c. oil

Dissolve yeast in 1/4 cup warm water. Combine yeast mixture and 1 cup hot water with remaining ingredients in large bowl; beat until smooth. Fill lightly oiled muffin cups 1/2 full. Let rise until doubled in bulk. Bake at 350 degrees for 20 minutes. Yield: 14 muffins. 140 calories each.

Anne Michotte
Orlando, Florida

FRENCH-ENGLISH MUFFINS

4 English muffins, split
1 c. Egg Beaters
1 1/2 c. crushed corn flakes
1/4 c. margarine

Dip muffin halves in Egg Beaters, coating thoroughly. Coat with corn flakes. Brown muffin halves lightly on one side in 1 tablespoon margarine in skillet. Turn. Add 1 tablespoon margarine to skillet. Brown remaining side lightly. Repeat process until all ingredients are used. Serve hot with syrup, if desired. Yield: 4 servings.

Jean Holcomb
Tempe, Arizona

LOW-CHOLESTEROL BAKING MIX

9 c. sifted flour
1/3 c. baking powder
1/4 c. sugar

1 tbsp. salt
2 tsp. cream of tartar
2 c. nonfat dry milk
1 lb. noncholesterol margarine

Combine dry ingredients in large bowl; mix well. Cut in margarine until crumbly. Store in airtight container in refrigerator. Use in same manner as packaged biscuit mix. Yield: 13 cups mix.

Fleda Lambert
Duncanville, Texas

LOW-CHOLESTEROL WHOLE WHEAT MUFFINS

3/4 c. all-purpose flour
4 tsp. baking powder
1 tsp. salt
1 c. whole wheat flour
1/4 c. sugar
3 tbsp. corn-oil margarine
1 c. reconstituted nonfat dry milk
1/4 c. Egg Beaters

Sift dry ingredients together into bowl. Cut in margarine until crumbly. Mix dry milk and Egg Beaters in separate bowl. Add to dry ingredients; stir until just mixed. Drop ty spoonfuls into muffin cups. Bake at 425 degrees for 12 to 15 minutes or until muffins test done. Yield: 12 muffins.

Frances W. Fredd
Coatesville, Pennsylvania

NO-CHOLESTEROL HOBO BREAD

2 c. raisins
4 tsp. soda
2 c. sugar
1/2 tsp. salt
1/4 c. 100% corn oil
4 c. flour

Bring raisins and 2 cups water to a boil in saucepan. Add soda; mix well. Cover; let stand overnight. Add sugar, salt and corn oil; mix well. Add flour, 1 cup at a time, beating well after each addition. Spoon into 3 coffee cans oiled with corn oil, filling each can 1/2 full. Bake at 350 degrees for 1 hour. Cool. Remove from cans. Loaves may be frozen.

Mrs. Kathy Jordan
Ottawa, Kansas

NO-FRY DOUGHNUTS

1 pkg. yeast
Sugar
1/4 c. Mazola oil
1 tsp. salt
1/4 c. Egg Beaters
3 to 3 1/2 c. flour
Butter, melted
Cinnamon

Dissolve yeast and 1/2 teaspoon sugar in 1/4 cup warm water in small bowl. Set aside. Combine 3/4 cup warm water, 1/4 cup sugar, oil, salt and Egg Beaters in large bowl. Stir until sugar is dissolved. Stir yeast mixture. Add to sugar mixture, blending well. Add flour, 1 cup at a time, stirring until dough leaves side of bowl. Turn onto lightly floured board. Knead until smooth and elastic. Place dough in greased bowl, turning to grease surface. Cover. Let rise in warm place for 1 1/2 hours or until doubled in bulk. Punch down. Pat dough out on floured surface. Cut into desired shapes. Place on ungreased baking sheet. Let rise until doubled in bulk. Bake at 325 degrees for 10 to 12 minutes or until golden. Do not overbake. Dip into melted butter. Combine cinnamon and sugar to taste. Coat doughnuts with cinnamon mixture.

Lynette Enewold
Council Bluffs, Iowa

ONE-BOWL LOW-CHOLESTEROL WHITE BREAD

7 to 8 c. flour
2 tbsp. sugar
2 tsp. salt
1 pkg. dry yeast
1 tbsp. margarine, softened

Combine 2 1/2 cups flour, sugar, salt and yeast in large bowl; mix well. Add margarine; mix well. Add 2 1/2 cups very hot water gradually to flour mixture. Beat for 2 minutes at medium speed of electric mixer, scraping bowl occasionally. Add enough flour to make thick batter; beat for 2 minutes at high speed, scraping bowl occasionally. Stir in enough additional flour to make soft dough. Turn onto lightly floured board. Knead for 8 to 10 minutes or until smooth and elastic. Place in greased bowl, turning to grease surface. Cover. Let rise in warm place for 1 hour or until doubled in bulk. Punch dough down; turn onto lightly floured board. Divide dough in half; shape each half into loaf. Place in 2 greased 9 x 5 x 3-inch loaf pans. Cover. Let rise in warm place for 1 hour or until doubled in bulk. Bake in 400-degree oven for 40 to 45 minutes or until bread tests done. Remove from pans. Cool on wire racks.

Cheryl Moffat
Piedmont, Oklahoma

RANCH LOAVES

1 pkg. yeast
2 tbsp. sugar
2 tsp. salt
2 1/2 c. all-purpose flour
1/2 c. instant nonfat dry milk powder
1/2 c. (firmly packed) dark brown sugar
3 tbsp. margarine
2 tbsp. dark molasses
5 3/4 c. (about) whole wheat flour

Dissolve yeast in 2 cups warm water in large bowl. Stir in sugar, salt and all-purpose flour. Beat until smooth. Cover. Let rise in warm place for 1/2 hour or until light and spongy. Combine dry milk powder and 1/2 cup water in saucepan. Bring to a boil. Stir in next 3 ingredients; mix well. Cool to lukewarm. Stir yeast mixture down. Add brown sugar mixture and half the whole wheat flour. Blend thoroughly. Stir in enough remaining flour to make soft dough. Turn onto lightly floured board. Cover. Let rest for 10 minutes. Knead for 10 minutes or until smooth and elastic. Place dough in greased bowl, turning to grease surface. Cover. Let rise in warm place for 1 hour or until doubled in bulk. Punch down. Turn onto lightly floured surface. Divide dough in half. Shape each half into loaf. Place each loaf in greased 9 x 5 x 3-inch loaf pan. Cover. Let rise in warm place for 1 hour or until doubled in bulk. Bake at 350 degrees for 50 minutes or until bread tests done.

Beverly Dixon
Baltimore, Maryland

MINIATURE SALT-FREE LOAVES

1/2 cake yeast
1 tsp. sugar
4 c. sifted all-purpose or whole wheat
    flour
1 tbsp. oil
2 tbsp. salt-free butter or shortening

Dissolve yeast in 1 1/2 cups warm water. Let stand in warm place for 10 minutes or until bubbly. Combine sugar and flour in large bowl. Add oil; mix well. Stir in yeast. Blend until dough is soft and easy to handle. Divide dough in half. Shape each half to fit well-greased 4 1/2 x 2 1/2 x 1 1/2-inch loaf pan. Cover. Let rise in warm place for 35 to 45 minutes or until dough reaches tops of pans. Bake in center of 450-degree oven for 1/2 hour or until bread tests done. Brush tops with butter. Turn onto rack to cool.

Gail Bonhus
Chatfield, Minnesota

SODIUM-FREE BAKING POWDER

79.6 grams potassium bicarbonate
56.0 grams cornstarch
15.0 grams tartaric acid
112.25 grams potassium bitartrate

Combine all ingredients in bowl; mix well. Store in airtight container. Use 1 1/2 teaspoons sodium-free baking powder for each teaspoon regular baking powder.

Mrs. Ruth E. Schriber
Natchee, Ohio

BREAKFAST BARS

1/2 c. butter
3 c. miniature marshmallows
1/2 c. peanut butter
1/2 c. instant nonfat dry milk
1/4 c. orange-flavored breakfast drink
1 c. raisins
4 c. Cherrios

Melt butter and marshmallows in large saucepan over low heat, stirring constantly. Stir in peanut butter until mixed. Stir in milk and breakfast drink. Fold in raisins and Cherrios, stirring until evenly coated. Place in buttered 9 x 9 x 2-inch pan. Pat evenly with buttered fingers. Cool thoroughly. Cut into 1 1/2 x 1-inch bars. Yield: 145 calories per bar.

Shirley Edmondson
Montgomery, Alabama

APRICOT-PINEAPPLE KUCHEN

1 10-count pkg. flaky-style refrigerator biscuits
1 16-oz. can water-packed apricot halves, drained, quartered
1 c. unsweetened pineapple tidbits
6 tbsp. sugar
1 tsp. grated lemon rind

1/4 tsp. cinnamon
3/4 c. low-calorie sour cream
1 egg, beaten

Flatten biscuits in 13 x 9 x 2-inch baking pan, sealing edges together; build up edges around pan slightly. Bake in 350-degree oven for 5 minutes. Combine fruits, 4 tablespoons sugar, lemon rind and cinnamon in bowl; toss lightly. Spoon over biscuits. Blend sour cream with egg and remaining 2 tablespoons sugar in bowl. Drizzle over apricot mixture. Bake for 20 minutes longer. Yield: 123 calories per serving.

Kathleen Burchett
Jonesville, Virginia

DIET BLUEBERRY COFFEE CAKE

2 c. blueberries
Artificial sweetener to equal 7 tsp. sugar
Cinnamon, nutmeg to taste
4 eggs, separated
2 tsp. vanilla extract
1/2 tsp. butter extract
1/2 c. evaporated skim milk
4 slices enriched white bread, toasted, crumbled

Place blueberries in baking dish. Sprinkle with sweetener, cinnamon and nutmeg; set aside. Combine egg yolks, vanilla, butter extract and skim milk in small mixing bowl; mix well. Beat egg whites in small bowl until stiff. Fold egg whites and bread crumbs into egg yolk mixture. Pour over blueberries. Bake at 350 degrees for 55 minutes. Yield: 4 servings.

Kathy Adams
Dover, Delaware

FRENCH TOAST

4 eggs
1/2 c. skim milk
Dash of salt
6 slices slightly dry bread
2 tbsp. butter
4 tbsp. honey

Beat eggs slightly with milk and salt in shallow bowl. Dip bread slices into egg mixture one at a time, turning to coat both sides well. Saute slowly in half the butter in skillet. Turn once to brown both sides, adding remaining butter as needed. Cut in half diagonally. Drizzle with honey. Yield: 4 servings/275 calories per serving.

Virginia R. Garber
Grundy, Virginia

CINNAMON COFFEE CAKE

6 tbsp. margarine, softened
Sugar
1 tbsp. Sucaryl
2 eggs
2 c. (scant) flour
1/8 tsp. salt
1 tsp. each soda, baking powder
1 c. (scant) buttermilk
2 tbsp. cinnamon

Cream margarine, 1/2 cup sugar and Sucaryl in large bowl until light. Add eggs, one at a time, beating constantly. Mix flour, salt, soda and baking powder; add to creamed mixture alternately with buttermilk, beating well after each addition. Pour half the batter into greased baking pan. Mix 2 tablespoons sugar and cinnamon; sprinkle half over batter in pan. Add remaining batter; sprinkle remaining sugar mixture over top. Bake at 350 degrees for 40 minutes. Yield: 16 servings/94 calories per serving.

Mrs. Jo Anne Tuttle
Spencer, Iowa

APPLESAUCE TEA BREAD

2 c. sifted flour
3/4 c. Sweetness and Light
3 tsp. baking powder
1/2 tsp. each soda, cinnamon and salt
1 c. unsweetened applesauce
1 egg, beaten
2 tbsp. butter, melted
1/2 tsp. almond extract

Combine first 6 ingredients in bowl; mix well. Combine remaining ingredients in large bowl; mix well. Add flour mixture to applesauce mixture all at once. Stir until just mixed. Spoon into lightly greased loaf pan. Bake at 350 degrees for 1 hour or until bread tests done. Yield: 12 servings. 109 calories per serving.

Mrs. Ruth Torpey
Floral Park, New York

BANANA-NUT BREAD

1 tbsp. sugar substitute
3 or 4 bananas, mashed
2 eggs, well beaten
1 3/4 c. cake flour
3 tsp. baking powder
1/4 tsp. salt
1/4 c. chopped walnuts

Sprinkle sugar substitute over bananas in large bowl; stir until dissolved. Blend in eggs. Sift flour, baking powder and salt together. Add walnuts. Stir into banana mixture until just mixed. Pour batter into greased loaf pan. Bake at 350 degrees for 25 minutes. Reduce heat to 300 degrees. Bake for 35 to 40 minutes longer or until bread tests done. Yield: 20 slices. 59 calories per slice.

Eva Jane Schwartz
Gettysburg, Pennsylvania

CHERRY PARTY BREAD

2 c. biscuit mix
10 maraschino cherries, drained, chopped
1/4 c. chopped walnuts
1 1/4 c. skim milk
2 tbsp. Sucaryl solution
1 egg, well beaten

Combine biscuit mix, cherries and walnuts in bowl. Stir until well blended. Combine remaining ingredients in separate bowl; mix well. Add to cherry mixture, beating well. Pour into greased loaf pan. Bake at 350 degrees for 1 1/4 hours or until bread tests done. Yield: 15 servings/94 calories per serving.

Mrs. Dixie Strode
Gamaliel, Kentucky

CRANBERRY BREAD

2 c. sifted flour
2 tsp. baking powder
1 tsp. salt
1/2 tsp. soda
2 eggs, slightly beaten
3/4 c. unsweetened orange juice
1/4 c. oil
4 tsp. liquid Sweet-10
1 c. cranberries

Sift flour, baking powder, salt and soda into large bowl. Mix eggs, orange juice, oil and Sweet-10 in bowl; add to dry ingredients. Stir until just mixed. Stir in cranberries. Pour into greased 8 x 4-inch pan. Bake at 375 degrees for 55 to 60 minutes or until golden brown. Remove from pan; cool. Yield: 18 servings.

Sister Mary Carmelita
Cedar Rapids, Iowa

FRUIT-NUT BREAD

2 c. sifted flour
1 1/2 tsp. baking powder

1/2 tsp. soda
1/4 tsp. salt
1/3 c. skim milk
1 egg
2 tbsp. butter, melted
Artificial sweetener equivalent to
    1/2 c. sugar
1/2 c. dietetic jam
1/4 c. chopped nuts

Combine first 4 ingredients in mixing bowl. Combine milk, egg, butter and sweetener in small bowl. Add to flour mixture; stir until just mixed. Fold in jam and nuts gently. Spoon batter into lightly greased loaf pan. Bake at 350 degrees for 1 hour. Cool before slicing. Yield: 12 servings/Each = 1 bread plus 1 fat exchange.

Ellen Seelye
Lexington, Kentucky

LOW-CALORIE BROWN BREAD

2 c. sour milk
1 egg, beaten
1/2 c. molasses
1 tbsp. soda
1 tsp. salt
3 c. graham flour
2 c. white flour

Combine first 3 ingredients in bowl; blend thoroughly. Combine dry ingredients. Add to milk mixture gradually, beating well. Turn into loaf pan. Bake at 350 degrees for 1/2 hour or until bread tests done. Yield: 1 loaf.

Judith A. Svoboda
Springfield, Nebraska

LOW-CALORIE TEA BREAD

1 3/4 c. sifted flour
2 tsp. baking powder
1/4 tsp. soda
1/2 tsp. salt
1/4 c. melted shortening
2 eggs, well beaten
4 tsp. Sucaryl solution
1 tsp. vanilla extract
2 med. bananas, mashed

Sift dry ingredients into bowl. Combine shortening, eggs, Sucaryl and vanilla in separate bowl; mix well. Add to flour mixture, stirring until just mixed. Fold in bananas. Turn into greased 8 x 4 x 3-inch loaf pan. Bake at 350

degrees for 1 hour and 10 minutes. Yield: 15 servings/98 calories per serving.

Lula Smith
Sand Springs, Oklahoma

NUT BREAD

2 c. sifted flour
3 tsp. baking powder
1/4 tsp. salt
2 tbsp. sugar
1/2 tsp. soda
1/2 c. coarsely chopped nuts
2 eggs
3/4 tsp. liquid Sucaryl
1 c. buttermilk

Sift first 5 ingredients into bowl. Stir in nuts. Beat eggs in separate bowl until thick. Add Sucaryl; stir in buttermilk. Add egg mixture to flour mixture; stir until just mixed. Turn into greased loaf pan. Bake at 350 degrees for 40 minutes or until golden brown. Cool on rack for 10 minutes. Remove from pan. Cool thoroughly. Slice 1/4 inch thick. Yield: 36 slices/40 calories per slice.

Virginia O. Savedge
Eastville, Virginia

STEAMED PINEAPPLE-DATE BREAD

1 1/2 c. sifted flour
1 tsp. each soda, salt
1/4 tsp. each cinnamon, nutmeg
1/2 c. chopped dates
2 tbsp. margarine
1 egg, beaten
1/2 c. crushed pineapple, drained
2 tbsp. sugar
1 1/2 tsp. Sweet 'N Low
1/2 c. chopped pecans

Sift dry ingredients together. Combine dates and margarine in 1 cup boiling water in bowl; set aside. Combine egg, pineapple, sugar and Sweet 'N Low in bowl. Add date mixture; mix well. Add flour mixture; stir until just mixed. Stir in pecans. Pour into well-greased and floured 2-pound coffee can. Place can in Crock-Pot; place 8 folds of paper toweling over top. Cover. Cook on high setting for 3 hours. Do not lift cover.

Emma Catherine Lawson
Carrizozo, New Mexico

ORANGE MARMALADE-NUT BREAD

2 c. sifted flour
1 1/2 tsp. baking powder
1/2 tsp. soda
1/4 to 1/2 tsp. salt
1/3 c. skim milk
1 egg
2 tbsp. butter, melted
1 tbsp. Sucaryl solution
1/2 c. dietetic orange marmalade
1/4 c. chopped walnuts

Combine dry ingredients in large bowl. Combine next 4 ingredients in small bowl; mix well. Add to flour mixture; stir until just mixed. Fold in marmalade and walnuts gently. Spoon into lightly greased loaf pan. Bake at 350 degrees for 1 hour and 40 minutes. Cool before slicing. Yield: 12 servings/110 calories per serving.

Mrs. Elsie M. Fahlgren
Winnipeg, Manitoba, Canada

ALL-BRAN MUFFINS

2 1/2 tsp. soda
2 c. buttermilk
1 c. All-Bran
1/2 c. margarine, softened
1 c. Sugartwin
2 eggs
2 c. Bran Buds
2 1/2 c. flour
1/2 tsp. salt
1 tsp. cinnamon
1/2 c. raisins

Dissolve soda in buttermilk in bowl; set aside. Pour 1 cup boiling water over All-Bran in bowl. Let stand. Cream margarine and Sugartwin in separate bowl. Add eggs; beat well. Add buttermilk mixture and Bran Buds; mix well. Sift dry ingredients into creamed mixture; mix well. Fold in All-Bran and raisins. Spoon into muffin tins. Bake at 400 degrees until lightly browned. Yield: 18 muffins/Each = 4 bread plus 2 fat exchanges.

Janice McDonald
Moraga, California

APPLE MUFFINS

1 2/3 c. all-purpose flour
2 tsp. sugar substitute
2 1/2 tsp. baking powder
1/2 tsp. salt
1 tsp. cinnamon
1/4 tsp. nutmeg
1 egg, lightly beaten
2/3 c. skim milk
1/4 c. melted shortening
1 c. minced apples

Sift first 6 ingredients together into mixing bowl. Combine egg, milk and shortening in bowl; mix well. Add to dry ingredients. Blend until just mixed. Batter should be lumpy. Fold in apples. Fill lined muffin cups 2/3 full. Bake in 400-degree oven for 20 to 25 minutes. Yield: 12-14 muffins.

Sister M. Tabitha
Omaha, Nebraska

BANANA MUFFINS

2 c. sifted flour
2 tsp. baking powder
1 tsp. salt
1/2 tsp. each soda, nutmeg
1 egg, slightly beaten
1 c. ripe bananas, mashed
1/3 c. skim milk
1/3 c. oil
2 tsp. Sweet-10

Sift dry ingredients together into mixing bowl. Combine remaining ingredients in small bowl; mix well. Add to dry ingredients; stir until just mixed. Fill greased and floured muffin cups 2/3 full. Bake at 375 degrees for 20 to 25 minutes or until golden brown. Yield: 12 muffins/Each = 1 1/2 bread plus 1 fat exchange.

Joan Casavant
Torrington, Connecticut

CHEWY GRANOLA MUFFINS

1 c. granola
1 c. rolled oats
1/2 c. Bisquick
1/4 c. Sugartwin
1/2 c. raisins
1/4 c. chopped pecans
1/4 c. oil
2 eggs, beaten
2/3 c. milk

Mix first 6 ingredients in large bowl. Add oil, eggs and milk. Stir until just moistened. Fill greased muffin cups 2/3 full. Bake in preheated 425-degree oven for 15 to 20 minutes or until muffins test done. Serve warm or cold.

Carline Cuttrell
Petty, Texas

LOW-CALORIE MUFFINS

1 c. flour
3 tsp. baking powder
1/2 tsp. salt
1 tsp. cinnamon
5 egg whites
3 tbsp. sugar
1 tsp. cream of tartar
1 tsp. grated orange rind
1/4 tsp. almond flavoring

Sift first 4 ingredients together; set aside. Add 5 tablespoons water to egg whites in bowl. Beat until soft peaks form. Add sugar gradually, beating until stiff. Fold dry ingredients lightly into egg whites. Add cream of tartar; beat well. Add orange rind and flavoring; mix well. Fill greased muffin cups. Bake at 375 degrees until golden brown. Yield: 16 servings/36 calories per serving.

Grace M. Shepard
Williamston, South Carolina

PINEAPPLE MUFFINS

1 slice white bread
1 egg, beaten
1/2 c. pineapple in own juice
1/4 c. nonfat dry milk
1 tsp. vanilla extract
1 tsp. artificial sweetener

Break bread into small pieces in bowl. Add remaining ingredients. Beat until well mixed. Pour into nonstick muffin cups. Bake at 375 degrees for 20 to 25 minutes. Yield: 4 servings.

Mary Vipond
Aledo, Illinois

PANCAKE SUBSTITUTE

1 slice whole wheat bread, crumbled
1 sm. apple, peeled, thinly sliced
1 egg, beaten
Dash of salt
1/2 tsp. cinnamon

Combine all ingredients in small bowl. Stir until bread crumbs are thoroughly moistened. Place mixture on grill; brown evenly on both sides. Serve with diet margarine.

Bertie M. Powell
Hixson, Tennessee

DIET APPLE PANCAKE

1 slice bread, crumbled
1 egg, beaten
1/3 c. instant nonfat dry milk
Artificial sweetener to equal 2 tsp.
*   sugar*
Cinnamon to taste
1 apple, grated

Combine crumbled bread and egg in bowl; mix well. Add dry milk, sweetener, cinnamon and 1 tablespoon water; mix well. Stir in 1/4 grated apple. Pour into nonstick skillet. Sprinkle remaining apple over batter. Brown on both sides over medium-low heat. Serve with diet margarine and diet syrup.

Elaine Pugh
Hugoton, Kansas

DESSERT PANCAKES

3 eggs, separated
1/4 tsp. salt
3/4 c. cottage cheese, drained
1/4 c. sifted flour
1 tbsp. butter

Beat egg yolks with salt in bowl until thick. Add cottage cheese and flour; mix lightly. Beat egg whites in bowl until stiff but not dry. Fold into egg yolk mixture. Drop batter by spoonfuls into 1/2 tablespoon butter in hot skillet. Brown lightly on both sides. Add remaining butter as needed. Serve with maple syrup or fruit sauce. Yield: 6 servings/115 calories per serving.

Mrs. Judith Sudheimer Payne
Halsey, Oregon

ALL-RYE QUICK BREAD

2 c. rye flour
1/2 tsp. salt
2 tsp. baking powder
2/3 c. instant nonfat dry milk
1 tbsp. honey
2 tbsp. oil

Combine flour, salt, baking powder and dry milk in large bowl. Stir honey, 1 cup water and oil together in separate bowl; mix well. Add to flour mixture; stir until smooth. Place in greased and floured cast-iron frypan. Pat dough with floured hands to 1/2-inch thickness. Prick dough generously with fork. Bake at 350 degrees for 10 minutes or until well browned.

Mrs. Ethel M. Poley
Narrowsburg, New York

SESAME CRACKERS

1 1/3 c. whole wheat flour
1 c. all-purpose flour
1/4 c. soy flour
1/4 c. sesame seed
1/3 c. wheat germ
1/4 c. (firmly packed) brown sugar
1 tsp. salt
1/2 c. oil

Combine dry ingredients in large bowl. Sprinkle with oil and 1 cup water; mix well. Turn onto floured surface. Knead until smooth and elastic. Divide dough; roll into thin circles. Cut into desired shapes. Prick with fork. Place on baking sheet. Bake at 325 degrees until crisp and lightly browned.

Gwladys Jeanneret
Kettle Falls, Washington

SOY FLOUR WAFFLES

1 3/4 c. all-purpose flour
1/4 c. low-fat soy flour
1/4 tsp. soda
1 1/2 tsp. baking powder
2 eggs, separated
1 3/4 c. buttermilk
5 tbsp. butter, melted

Sift dry ingredients together into bowl. Beat egg yolks in separate bowl until light. Add buttermilk and butter; beat well. Add to dry ingredients, stirring until just mixed. Beat egg whites until stiff; fold into batter. Cook in nonstick waffle iron according to directions. Yield: 6 waffles/290 calories each.

Patricia Ann Spaeth
Tulsa, Oklahoma

SPROUT FLAT BREAD

2 c. rye flour
3/4 c. nonfat dry milk
1/2 c. each sesame seed, sunflower seed
Dash of salt (opt.)
1/2 c. rye or wheat sprouts
3 tbsp. oil
1 egg, well beaten

Combine first 5 ingredients in large bowl; mix well. Stir in sprouts, oil and 1 cup water; mix well. Fold in egg. Spread 1/4 to 1/2 inch thick on greased and floured baking sheet. Bake at 450 degrees for 10 to 12 minutes. Brown under broiler. Cut into squares. Serve hot.

Kathy Bradford
Provo, Utah

THIRTY-MINUTE WHOLE WHEAT ROLLS

1 c. oil
3/4 c. sugar
6 pkg. yeast
1 tbsp. salt
3 eggs, beaten
10 1/2 c. whole wheat flour

Combine 3 1/2 cups warm water, oil, sugar and yeast in large bowl. Let stand for 15 minutes. Add salt and eggs; mix well. Add flour gradually, stirring until well blended. Turn onto floured surface. Knead until smooth and elastic. Shape as desired. Place on baking sheet. Let rise in warm place for 10 minutes. Bake at 425 degrees for 10 to 15 minutes or until brown. May substitute 1/2 cup honey for sugar.

Patricia Nelson
Elko, Nevada

NATURAL SUGARLESS BANANA BREAD

2 c. oat flour
1 c. instant nonfat milk powder
3/4 tsp. soda
1 1/4 tsp. cream of tartar
1/4 tsp. salt
1/2 c. chopped peanuts
2/3 c. sunflower seed
2 eggs
1 c. mashed bananas
1 tbsp. vanilla extract
1/3 c. butter, melted

Combine first 7 ingredients; set aside. Combine next 3 ingredients in large bowl; beat well. Add butter; mix well. Add dry ingredients; blend thoroughly. Pour into buttered loaf pan. Bake at 350 degrees for 45 minutes or until bread tests done.

Nancy Roark
San Mateo, California

CRACKED WHEAT BREAD

4 3/4 to 5 3/4 c. flour
3 tbsp. sugar
4 tsp. salt
3 pkg. dry yeast
1/2 c. milk
3 tbsp. Fleischmann's margarine
1 c. cracked wheat

Combine 2 cups flour, sugar, salt and yeast in large mixer bowl; mix thoroughly. Combine

1 1/2 cups water, milk and margarine in saucepan. Heat over low heat to 120 degrees. Add to dry ingredients gradually. Beat with electric mixer for 2 minutes at medium speed, scraping bowl occasionally. Add cracked wheat. Beat at high speed for 2 minutes, scraping bowl occasionally. Stir in enough additional flour to make stiff dough. Turn onto lightly floured board. Knead for 8 to 10 minutes or until smooth and elastic. Divide dough in half. Roll each piece into 12 x 8-inch rectangle. Roll as for jelly roll from short end. Seal edges. Fold ends under; place seam-side down in 8 1/2 x 4 1/2 x 2 1/2-inch loaf pan. Cover. Let rise in warm place for 1 1/2 hours or until doubled in bulk. Bake at 400 degrees for 1/2 hour or until bread tests done.

Photograph for this recipe below.

WHOLE WHEAT-BRAN BREAD

3/4 c. milk
1 c. whole bran cereal
3 tbsp. sugar
4 tsp. salt
6 tbsp. Fleischmann's margarine
1/3 c. dark molasses
3 pkg. dry yeast
3 c. whole wheat flour
3 1/2 to 4 1/2 c. all-purpose flour

Combine 1 cup water and milk in saucepan. Bring to a boil. Stir in next 5 ingredients. Cool to lukewarm. Combine 3/4 cup warm water and yeast in large bowl; stir until dissolved. Add cereal mixture and whole wheat flour; beat until smooth. Add enough all-purpose flour to make stiff dough. Turn onto lightly floured board. Knead for 8 to 10 minutes or until smooth and elastic. Cover with towel. Let rest for 15 minutes. Divide dough in half. Shape each half into smooth round ball. Flatten each ball to 6 inches in diameter. Place on greased baking sheets. Let rise in warm place, until doubled in bulk. Bake at 400 degrees for 1/2 hour or until bread tests done. Cool on wire racks. Yield: 2 loaves.

Photograph for this recipe below.

SUGAR-FREE BANANA-WHEAT QUICK BREAD

1/4 c. diet margarine
2 tbsp. orange juice
1 egg
3 c. thinly sliced ripe bananas
1 3/4 c. whole wheat flour
1 tsp. Sucaryl
1 tsp. each salt, soda
1/2 c. chopped nuts (opt.)

Combine margarine, orange juice and egg in large bowl; beat well. Add bananas; mix well. Combine dry ingredients. Stir into creamed mixture; add nuts. Blend at low speed of electric mixer; beat for 3 minutes at medium speed. Pour into greased and floured loaf pan. Bake at 325 degrees for 1 hour or until bread tests done. Store in refrigerator. Freezes well.

Myra Houck
Ashe, North Carolina

NO-KNEAD WHOLE WHEAT BREAD

4 tsp. dry yeast
2 tsp. honey
5 c. whole wheat flour
3 tbsp. molasses
1/2 tbsp. salt
1/3 c. wheat germ
1/2 tbsp. butter
1 tbsp. sesame seed

Dissolve yeast in 2/3 cup warm water in small bowl. Add honey; mix well. Let stand until bubbly. Warm flour in large bowl in 250-degree oven for 20 minutes. Add molasses and 2/3 cup warm water to yeast mixture; mix well. Add yeast mixture, salt, wheat germ and 1 1/3 cups warm water to flour; mix well. Dough may be sticky. Turn dough into well-buttered loaf pan. Sprinkle with sesame seed. Let rise in warm place until doubled in bulk. Bake at 400 degrees for 30 to 40 minutes or until brown and crusty. Cool before cutting.

Melody Busch
Goodland, Kansas

BUTTERMILK-BRAN MUFFINS

3 c. whole bran
2 c. buttermilk
2 eggs, slightly beaten
1/2 c. oil
1 c. raisins
1 c. sugar

2 1/2 c. unbleached flour
2 1/2 tsp. soda

Combine bran and 1 cup boiling water in bowl. Let stand until cool. Add buttermilk, eggs and oil; mix well. Stir in raisins. Mix remaining ingredients together. Add to bran mixture; mix well. Spoon into greased muffin cups. Bake at 425 degrees for 20 minutes. Batter can be stored in refrigerator for up to 2 weeks. Yield: 16-18 muffins.

Glenda Kimsey
Bothell, Washington

REFRIGERATOR HIGH FIBER MUFFINS

2 c. 100% bran cereal
1 c. shortening
2 c. sugar
4 eggs, well beaten
1 qt. buttermilk
5 c. unbleached flour
1 tsp. salt
5 tsp. soda
4 c. All-Bran cereal

Pour 2 cups boiling water over 100% bran cereal in bowl. Cream shortening, sugar and eggs together in separate bowl. Add 100% bran cereal mixture and buttermilk; mix well. Sift flour, salt and soda together. Add all at once with All-Bran to creamed mixture. Stir until well moistened. Fill greased muffin cups 1/2 full. Bake at 400 degrees for 15 minutes. Store in tightly covered container in refrigerator. Keeps for at least 6 weeks.

Mrs. Virginia Claypool
Marshall, Illinois

SPECIAL BRAN MUFFINS

1 c. stone-ground whole wheat flour
1 tsp. soda
1 1/2 c. bran
1/2 c. raisins
1 egg, well beaten
1/2 c. honey
3/4 c. milk
2 tbsp. butter, softened

Combine dry ingredients and raisins in large bowl; set aside. Beat egg in separate bowl until foamy. Add honey in fine stream, beating constantly. Stir in milk and butter. Stir into dry ingredients until just mixed. Spoon into well-greased muffin cups. Bake at 400 degrees for 20 to 30 minutes.

Mrs.Nancy M. Ross
Plant City, Florida

FOREIGN

AUSTRIAN HONEY-NUT BREAD

2 1/2 tbsp. butter
1 c. honey
1 egg
2 1/2 c. sifted flour
1 tsp. each salt, soda
3/4 c. buttermilk
3/4 c. white raisins (opt.)
3/4 c. chopped nuts

Cream butter and honey in bowl. Add egg; mix well. Sift flour, salt and soda together. Add to creamed mixture alternately with buttermilk, mixing well after each addition. Fold in raisins and nuts. Pour into greased loaf pan. Bake at 300 degrees for 1 hour and 40 minutes.

Mrs. John Riner
Contra Costa County, California

AUSTRIAN SWEET BREAD

1/2 c. milk, scalded
1/2 c. sugar
1/2 tsp. salt
1/4 c. margarine
1 pkg. yeast
2 eggs, beaten
2 c. flour
2 tbsp. fine bread crumbs
14 whole blanched almonds
1/2 c. seedless raisins
1/2 tsp. grated lemon rind

Combine milk, sugar, salt and margarine in bowl; mix well. Cool to lukewarm. Dissolve yeast in 1/4 cup warm water. Stir into milk mixture. Add eggs and flour; beat vigorously for 5 minutes. Cover. Let rise in warm place for 1 1/2 hours or until doubled in bulk. Sprinkle bread crumbs over sides and bottom of well-greased 1 1/2-quart casserole. Arrange almonds on bottom. Stir dough down; beat well. Stir in raisins and lemon rind. Place in casserole. Let rise in warm place for 1 hour or until doubled in bulk. Bake at 350 degrees for 50 minutes or until bread tests done.

Lula Smith
Sand Springs, Oklahoma

BRAZILIAN COFFEE CAKE

1 c. seedless raisins
Strong coffee
1/2 tsp. cinnamon
2/3 c. shortening
1 c. sugar
2 eggs

1 1/2 c. sifted flour
1/2 tsp. each baking powder, soda
1/4 tsp. salt
1/2 c. chopped nuts
1 1/2 c. confectioners' sugar

Combine raisins, 2/3 cup coffee and cinnamon in bowl; mix well. Set aside. Cream shortening and sugar in bowl. Add eggs one at a time, beating well after each addition. Sift dry ingredients together. Add to egg mixture alternately with coffee mixture, mixing well after each addition. Stir in nuts. Spread in greased 10 x 15 x 1-inch jelly roll pan. Bake at 350 degrees for 20 to 25 minutes or until cake tests done. Add enough additional coffee to confectioners' sugar to make thin frosting. Spread over warm cake. Cool. Cut into 36 bars.

Mary Janice Johnson
Richardson, Texas

CANADIAN POPOVERS

3 eggs
1 c. milk
1 c. sifted flour
1/8 tsp. salt

Beat eggs in bowl until thick and lemon-colored. Add milk; beat well. Sift flour with salt. Add to egg mixture; beat until smooth. Fill large, well-greased muffin cups 2/3 full. Bake at 425 degrees for 15 minutes. Reduce temperature to 350 degrees. Bake for 1/2 hour longer.

Mrs. Sandy North
Hickory, North Carolina

CZECHOSLOVAKIAN BREAD

1 pkg. dry yeast
3/4 c. milk, lukewarm
1/4 c. sugar
1 tsp. salt
1/4 c. shortening
2 eggs
3 1/2 to 3 3/4 c. flour
1/4 c. butter, softened
1/2 c. (firmly packed) brown sugar
1/4 c. milk
1/2 tsp. each vanilla, lemon extracts
2 c. pecans, finely ground

Dissolve yeast in 1/4 cup warm water in bowl. Stir in next 4 ingredients and 1 egg; mix well. Add enough flour to make soft dough. Turn onto lightly floured board; let rest for 10 minutes. Knead until smooth and elastic. Place in greased bowl, turning to grease surface. Cover with damp cloth. Let rise in warm place until doubled in bulk. Punch down. Turn onto board; cover. Let rise for 15 minutes. Combine butter, brown sugar and milk in saucepan; heat until butter melts. Remove from heat. Beat 1 egg; add slowly to warm mixture. Mix well. Stir in flavorings and pecans. Divide dough in half. Turn half onto floured board; roll paper thin into 16 x 20-inch rectangle. Spread 1/2 of the filling over dough. Roll as for jelly roll from long side. Repeat for remaining half. Place in 9 x 13-inch baking pan; form into U-shape. Let rise for 1 hour. Bake at 325 degrees for 40 to 45 minutes. Yield: 12 servings.

Mrs. Harold E. Leifeste
Brindisi, Italy

CZECHOSLOVAKIAN KOLACHE

1 c. milk, scalded
1/2 c. shortening
3/4 c. sugar
1 tsp. salt
1 pkg. dry yeast
3 eggs, beaten
4 1/2 c. flour
2/3 c. each cooked prunes, cooked
    apricots
1 sm. can crushed pineapple
1 1/2 tbsp. quick-cooking tapioca

Combine milk, shortening, 1/2 cup sugar and salt in bowl. Cool to lukewarm. Add yeast; stir well. Add eggs and flour. Mix until soft dough forms. Turn onto floured board. Knead until smooth and elastic. Place in greased bowl, turning to grease surface. Cover. Let rise in warm place until doubled in bulk. Shape into 1 1/2-inch balls. Press flat. Place on baking sheet. Let rise until doubled in bulk. Make indentation in center of each, using two fingers. Combine remaining ingredients in saucepan. Cook over low heat until tapioca is tender and mixture is thick. Spoon into roll indentations. Let rise for several minutes longer. Bake at 325 degrees for 12 to 15 minutes or until light brown. Yield: 2 1/2 dozen.

Mrs. Mary Witt
Buffalo, Wyoming

DANISH ALMOND PASTRY

14 tbsp. margarine
2 c. all-purpose flour
Sugar
1 pkg. yeast
1 egg, beaten

4 oz. almond paste
7 tbsp. butter
2 tsp. almond extract
1 sm. package raisins
1 egg yolk, well beaten
1/2 c. slivered almonds or pecans

Cut margarine into flour in bowl until crumbly. Add 1 tablespoon sugar; mix well. Dissolve yeast in 3 tablespoons warm water. Add egg and yeast mixture to flour mixture; mix well. Shape into ball. Cover. Refrigerate for 6 hours or overnight. Roll dough on waxed paper to 11 x 18-inch rectangle. Combine 1/3 cup plus 1 tablespoon sugar and next 3 ingredients in bowl. Blend thoroughly. Stir in raisins. Spread filling down center of pastry. Fold short ends in. Bring long ends together over filling. Pinch edges together to seal. Place on baking sheet. Brush with egg yolk. Sprinkle almonds over top. Bake at 375 degrees for 25 to 30 minutes.

Alice Holmes
Athens, Georgia

DUTCH APPLE FLIPS

2 pkg. yeast
3 eggs, beaten
2 tsp. salt
4 1/2 c. flour
2 c. milk
5 lg. tart apples, peeled
1 1/2 c. raisins
1/2 c. chopped, mixed candied peel
1 tart apple, diced
Oil for deep frying
Confectioners' sugar

Dissolve yeast in a small amount of warm water in bowl. Set aside. Combine eggs, salt and flour in bowl; mix well. Make hole in center of mixture. Pour yeast mixture into center. Add milk; blend well. Divide dough into 2 portions. Slice apples into 1-inch rings. Combine apples with 1 portion dough. Let dough rise in warm place until doubled in bulk. Combine raisins, candied peel and diced apple with remaining dough. Let rise in warm place until doubled in bulk. Heat oil in Dutch oven to 375 degrees. Dip 2 tablespoons into hot oil. Pick up spoonful of dough with 1 spoon; form ball with other spoon. Drop in hot oil, turning to brown all sides. Drain on absorbent paper. Serve warm or cold, sprinkled with confectioners' sugar.

Mrs. Barend Eversen
Rantoul, Illinois

DUTCH FUNNEL CAKES

2 c. milk
2 eggs, beaten
2 c. flour
1/2 tsp. salt
1 tsp. baking powder
Oil for deep frying
Confectioners' sugar

Combine milk and eggs in bowl; mix well. Set aside. Sift 1 1/2 cups flour, salt and baking powder together into bowl. Pour egg mixture into flour mixture; blend well. Add additional flour to make thick batter. Fill 9-inch skillet 2/3 full with oil. Heat to 375 degrees. Pour batter into 1/2-inch funnel. Drizzle batter from funnel into hot oil. Spirals and other shapes may be made by a turn of the finger. Turn to brown on both sides. Sprinkle with confectioners' sugar. Serve hot. Yield: 8-10 servings.

Mrs. Margaret Ford
Converse, Indiana

EAST INDIAN BREAD

2 tbsp. shortening
2 c. sifted all-purpose flour
1/2 tsp. salt
1/2 c. shredded sharp process American
cheese
Oil for deep frying

Cut shortening into flour and salt in bowl until crumbly. Add cheese; mix well. Add 1/2 to 2/3 cup water, stirring to make soft dough. Knead and pound dough for 10 to 15 minutes. Cover. Let stand for 1/2 hour. Roll very thin on lightly floured surface. Cut into 4-inch circles. Fry in deep fat at 375 degrees until puffed, turning to brown both sides. Drain on paper towels. Keep warm in 200-degree oven. Yield: 16 servings.

Mrs. Larry King Simmering
Adak, Alaska

ENGLISH CRUMPETS

2 cakes yeast
4 c. sifted flour
1 tbsp. salt
Butter

Dissolve yeast in 4 cups lukewarm water. Add flour and salt; beat well. Cover. Let rise in warm place for 1 hour or until doubled in bulk. Beat down. Place greased muffin rings on greased hot griddle. Fill muffin rings 1/2 full with dough. Cook over low heat until well risen and brown on underside. Turn to brown on other side. Serve with butter.

Mrs. Daisymae Eckman
Pawnee City, Nebraska

ENGLISH ORANGE TEATIME BREAD

1 c. ground orange rind
1 c. sugar
3 c. flour
3 tsp. baking powder
1 tsp. salt
1 c. milk
1 tbsp. oil
1 egg, beaten

Combine 1 cup water, orange rind and sugar in saucepan. Cook for 15 minutes, stirring constantly. Cool. Sift dry ingredients together into bowl. Add milk, oil, orange rind mixture and egg. Stir until just mixed. Pour into 2 greased and floured bread pans. Bake at 350 degrees for 45 minutes. Slice thin. Bread freezes well.

Betty M. Sykes
Pottsville, Pennsylvania

ENGLISH SCONES

2 c. flour
3 tsp. baking powder
1 tsp. salt
Sugar
6 tbsp. butter
1/2 c. currants (opt.)
1 egg
1 egg, separated
1/2 c. milk

Sift flour, baking powder, salt and 2 tablespoons sugar into mixing bowl. Cut in butter until crumbly. Add currants. Beat 1 egg and egg yolk together in bowl. Add enough milk to beaten eggs to measure 3/4 cup. Stir enough egg mixture into flour mixture to moisten. Turn dough onto floured board. Knead lightly. Roll into circle, 1/2 inch thick. Cut into wedges. Beat reserved egg white slightly. Brush tops of wedges. Sprinkle with additional sugar. Place on lightly oiled cookie sheet. Bake at 425 degrees for 12 to 15 minutes. Yield: 1 dozen scones.

Katharine Rigby
Lancaster, Ohio

ENGLISH YORKSHIRE PUDDING

1 c. all-purpose flour
1 tsp. salt
Shortening
1 c. milk
2 eggs, well beaten

Sift flour and salt together into mixer bowl. Cut in 1 tablespoon shortening until crumbly. Add milk and eggs. Beat at high speed of electric mixer for 10 minutes. Chill thoroughly. Heat empty muffin tin in oven. Melt 1/4 cup shortening. Pour 1 teaspoon shortening into each muffin cup. Fill 1/2 full with batter. Bake at 425 degrees for 1/2 hour. Yield: 12 servings.

Mrs. R. E. Bowman
Colorado Springs, Colorado

FINNISH CARDAMOM BREAD

3 pkg. dry yeast
1/2 c. milk, scalded
5 tbsp. butter
1 1/2 tsp. salt
Sugar
2 tsp. finely ground cardamom
3 eggs, beaten
4 1/2 to 5 c. sifted flour
1 egg white

Dissolve yeast in 1/2 cup warm water. Mix milk, butter, salt and 1/2 cup sugar in bowl. Cool to lukewarm. Add yeast, cardamom and eggs; mix lightly. Add enough flour to make stiff dough. Knead on floured surface for 5 to 8 minutes or until smooth and elastic. Place in greased bowl, turning to grease surface. Cover. Let rise in warm place for 45 minutes. Punch down. Divide into 3 portions. Shape each portion into long roll. Place rolls close together on greased cookie sheet. Braid rolls. Beat egg white with 2 tablespoons sugar until stiff peaks form. Spread on braid. Cover. Let rise for 45 to 50 minutes. Bake in 375-degree oven for 40 minutes or until bread tests done.

Mrs. Anne George
Ridgefield, Connecticut

FRENCH BABAS WITH APRICOT-RUM SYRUP

1/3 c. milk, scalded
1 pkg. yeast

1 c. flour
1 3/4 c. sugar
1/8 tsp. salt
2 eggs
1/4 c. seedless raisins
4 1/2 oz. rum
4 tbsp. butter, softened
1 1/2 c. apricot nectar
2 tsp. lemon juice
Sweetened whipped cream

Cool milk to lukewarm in large bowl. Dissolve yeast in milk. Let stand for 10 minutes. Add flour, 1/4 cup sugar, salt and eggs; mix thoroughly. Cover with towel. Let rise in warm place for 1 hour or until doubled in bulk. Soak raisins in 1/2 ounce rum. Add butter to flour mixture. Beat until shiny and no longer sticky. Add raisins; blend well. Fill greased muffin cups 1/2 full. Cover with waxed paper. Let rise for 2 hours or until doubled in bulk. Bake at 400 degrees for 12 minutes or until muffins test done. Remove with fork. Place in dessert bowls. Combine remaining ingredients except whipped cream in bowl. Stir until sugar is dissolved. Pour over Babas, turning until syrup is absorbed. Top with whipped cream.

Mrs. L. Hyland
Orlando, Florida

FRENCH BREAD

1 pkg. dry yeast
1 tbsp. salt
6 to 6 1/2 c. all-purpose flour
Cornmeal

Sprinkle yeast over 2 cups warm water in large mixing bowl. Add salt and 4 cups all-purpose flour; beat until well mixed. Add enough remaining flour to make stiff dough. Turn onto floured board. Knead until smooth and elastic. Place dough in bowl. Cover with damp cloth. Let rise in warm place for 2 1/2 hours or until tripled in bulk. Punch down. Let rise for 35 to 40 minutes or until doubled in bulk. Divide dough into 4 equal portions. Roll each portion into 15-inch loaf. Sprinkle cookie sheet with cornmeal. Place rolls over cornmeal. Make 1/2-inch deep cut down center of each roll. Let rise for 2 hours. Bake in preheated 400-degree oven for 40 to 45 minutes or until bread tests done.

Frances Summers
Florence, Oklahoma

FRENCH BREAD MADE EASY

1 pkg. dry yeast
1 tbsp. sugar
1 1/2 tsp. salt
1 tbsp. shortening
4 c. sifted all-purpose flour

Sprinkle yeast into 1/2 cup warm water; stir until dissolved. Place sugar, salt and shortening in large bowl. Add 1 cup warm water. Stir until dissolved. Add yeast mixture; mix well. Add flour. Stir dough with spoon 5 times at 10 minute intervals. Turn onto lightly floured board. Shape into 2 balls. Let rest for 10 minutes. Roll each ball into 10 x 8-inch rectangle. Roll from long side as for jelly roll. Seal edges. Place rolls on greased cookie sheet side by side. Slash top of rolls diagonally 6 times. Cover with towel. Let rise for 1 1/2 hours. Bake at 400 degrees for 1/2 hour.

Mrs. Betty James
Chatsworth, California

FRENCH CREOLE CAKE

1/2 c. rice
1/2 cake yeast
3 eggs, well beaten
1/2 c. sugar
3 tbsp. flour
1/2 tsp. nutmeg
Oil for deep frying
Confectioners' sugar

Add rice to 3 cups rapidly boiling water in saucepan. Cook until very soft. Chill. Dissolve yeast in 1/2 cup warm water in bowl. Mash rice; add to yeast mixture. Let rise overnight. Add eggs, sugar and flour to rice mixture; beat thoroughly. Let rise for 15 minutes. Add nutmeg; blend well. Drop by spoonfuls into deep fat at 375 degrees, turning to brown both sides. Drain on absorbent paper. Sprinkle with confectioners' sugar.

Mrs. Allen S. Lawrence
Sinton, Texas

FRENCH CROISSANTS

1 pkg. yeast
1 tsp. sugar
3 c. flour
1/2 tsp. salt
1 c. butter
1 egg, beaten

Dissolve yeast in 1 cup warm water. Stir in sugar. Combine flour, salt, 1/4 cup butter and

yeast mixture in bowl; mix well. Knead until smooth. Cover; let rest for 20 minutes. Roll into large rectangle on floured surface. Place remaining butter in center of dough. Fold dough in thirds from narrow ends. Chill for 1/2 hour. Roll; fold again. Chill for 1 hour. Roll, fold and chill again. Roll to 1/4-inch thickness. Cut into squares. Cut each square diagonally. Brush with beaten egg. Roll from wide side. Place on baking sheet. Let rise in warm place for 1/2 hour. Bake at 425 degrees for 15 minutes or until brown.

Mrs. Frances Chwalinska
Philadelphia, Pennsylvania

FRENCH MUFFINS

1/3 c. shortening
1 c. sugar
1 egg
1 1/2 c. sifted flour
1 1/2 tsp. baking powder
1/2 tsp. salt
1/4 tsp. nutmeg
1/2 c. milk
6 tbsp. butter, melted
1 tsp. cinnamon

Combine shortening, 1/2 cup sugar and egg in bowl; mix thoroughly. Sift together flour, baking powder, salt and nutmeg. Stir into egg mixture alternately with milk, beating well after each addition. Fill greased muffin cups 2/3 full. Bake at 350 degrees for 20 to 25 minutes or until golden brown. Roll immediately in melted butter, then in mixture of remaining sugar and cinnamon. Serve hot.

Myra Sorensen
Richfield, Utah

FRENCH PANCAKES

3 eggs
1 1/2 c. milk
1/2 c. cream
1/2 c. butter, melted
1 c. sifted flour
1 tbsp. sugar
1 tsp. salt

Beat eggs until creamy in bowl; add milk and cream. Beat for 1 minute. Add melted butter. Beat until well blended. Sift flour, sugar and salt together. Add to egg mixture. Beat well. Fry in lightly greased hot skillet. Keep batter thin. Turn and roll pan to spread batter. Turn to brown both sides. Serve hot with butter and jelly. Fold or roll.

Beverly L. Haas
Taylor, North Dakota

FRENCH SAVARIN CAKE

2 pkg. yeast
1/2 c. milk, scalded
1/3 c. sugar
1 tsp. salt
2/3 c. butter, melted
4 c. sifted flour
1 1/2 tsp. vanilla extract
4 eggs, beaten
Confectioners' sugar icing
Almonds
Candied fruits

Dissolve yeast in 1/4 cup lukewarm water in bowl. Set aside. Combine milk, sugar, salt and butter in bowl; cool to lukewarm. Add enough flour to make soft dough; mix well. Add yeast mixture, vanilla and eggs; beat well. Add enough flour to make stiff dough; beat until smooth. Cover. Let rise in warm place until doubled in bulk. Punch down. Turn into well-greased 10-inch tube pan. Let rise in warm place until doubled in bulk. Bake at 350 degrees for 35 minutes. Remove from pan. Cool. Drizzle with confectioners' sugar icing. Decorate with almonds and candied fruits. Yield: 12-15 servings.

Mrs. D. T. Hamilton
Michie, Tennessee

GERMAN APPLE BREAD

1/2 stick butter
1 1/2 c. sifted all-purpose flour
Sugar
1 tsp. baking powder
1 egg
1 egg yolk
3 tbsp. milk
6 or 7 apples, thinly sliced
Cinnamon
Currants
Whipped cream (opt.)

Cut butter into flour in bowl until crumbly. Add 1/4 cup sugar; mix well. Stir in next 4 ingredients; mix well. Turn onto floured surface. Knead until smooth. Press over bottom and side of greased pizza pan. Arrange apples in overlapping single layer. Sprinkle with sugar and cinnamon to taste. Sprinkle currants over top. Bake at 350 degrees for 45 minutes. Cut

into wedges. Serve warm with whipped cream. Yield: 8 servings.

Mrs. Raymond Beery
Sedalia, Missouri

GERMAN BREAD

5 eggs, beaten
2 3/4 c. (firmly packed) brown sugar
1 c. grated chocolate, melted
1 tsp. each cinnamon, allspice and
*   baking powder*
2 c. sifted flour
1/4 c. milk
1 c. chopped almonds
2 egg whites
2 tbsp. confectioners' sugar

Combine eggs and brown sugar in bowl; beat thoroughly. Add chocolate; mix well. Sift together next 4 ingredients. Add to creamed mixture alternately with milk, mixing well after each addition. Add almonds; blend well. Spread 1/2 inch thick in greased shallow baking pans. Bake at 350 degrees for 20 minutes. Beat egg whites until stiff peaks form; add confectioners' sugar gradually, beating until stiff. Frost cake. Bake until slightly browned. Cut into strips. Yield: 100 strips.

Mrs. Douglas Kendrick
Washington, D.C.

GERMAN BREAD BALLS

1 1/2 pkg. yeast
1 qt. warm potato water
2 tsp. salt
All-purpose flour
3/4 c. hot mashed potatoes
1 c. cream
Sugar
3 eggs, beaten
2 tsp. cardamom
2 1/2 oz. rose water
1 1/2 c. raisins
Oil for deep frying

Combine yeast and potato water in large bowl; stir until dissolved. Add salt and enough flour to make soft dough; mix well. Let rise in warm place until doubled in bulk. Combine hot potatoes and cream; add to flour mixture. Add 1/2 cup sugar and next 4 ingredients; mix well. Let rise in warm place until doubled in bulk. Drop by spoonfuls into deep fat at 375 degrees, turning to brown both sides. Drain on paper towels. Dip into sugar. Serve warm. Yield: 50-75 balls.

Mrs. Marlow Anderson
Dix, Nebraska

GERMAN OVEN PANCAKE

1/2 c. flour
3 eggs, slightly beaten
1/2 c. milk
2 tbsp. butter, melted
1/4 tsp. salt

Beat flour and eggs together in bowl. Add remaining ingredients; mix well. Pour into cold greased 10-inch baking dish. Bake in preheated 450-degree oven for 20 minutes. Pancake will puff into big bubbles while baking. Cut into wedges. Serve with melted butter, powdered sugar and lemon. Yield: 2 servings.

Mrs. Fran Heckman
Waupaca, Wisconsin

GERMAN ZWIEBACK

2 pkg. dry yeast
1 c. milk
1 egg, beaten
1 tsp. salt
3 c. flour

Dissolve yeast in warm milk in bowl. Add egg. Sift salt and flour together. Add to yeast mixture gradually. Let rise until doubled in bulk. Punch down. Let rise until doubled in bulk. Shape into 1 1/2-inch balls. Place 2 together, 1 on top of other. Place on baking sheet. Let rise for 30 minutes. Bake at 350 degrees for 10 to 15 minutes.

Mrs. John H. Adams, Jr.
Gila Bend, Arizona

PITA BREAD HEROES

1 pkg. dry yeast
2 c. flour
1 tbsp. oil
1/2 tsp. salt
1/8 tsp. sugar
2 c. drained sauerkraut
1/2 c. sliced pimento-stuffed olives
1/3 c. chopped onion
1/2 c. diced seeded tomato
2 tbsp. olive oil
1/2 lb. corned beef, sliced
1/2 lb. salami, sliced

Combine yeast and 3/4 cup flour in mixer bowl. Mix 2/3 cup warm water, oil, salt and sugar together. Add to flour mixture. Beat at low speed of electric mixer for 1/2 minute, scraping side of bowl. Beat at high speed for 3 minutes. Stir in remaining flour. Turn onto lightly floured surface. Knead for 5 minutes or until smooth and elastic. Cover. Let rise for 1/2 hour. Punch down. Divide into 6 equal portions. Shape into balls. Let rise for 10 minutes. Roll into 5-inch circles. Place on baking sheet; cover. Let rise for 20 minutes. Bake at 400 degrees for 10 minutes or until light brown. Cool. Cut in half. Split each half to make pocket. Combine sauerkraut, olives, onion and tomato in bowl. Sprinkle with olive oil. Toss lightly. Fill pita with corned beef, salami and sauerkraut mixture.

Photograph for this recipe on page 97.

GREEK HONEY-NUT BREAD

1 pkg. dry yeast
2 1/2 to 3 c. sifted all-purpose flour
3/4 c. milk
4 tbsp. margarine
1/4 c. sugar
1/2 tsp. salt
1 egg
1/2 tsp. grated lemon rind
1/2 c. each light raisins, chopped figs
*   and chopped walnuts*
1/4 c. honey

Combine yeast with 1 cup flour in mixer bowl. Heat milk, margarine, sugar and salt in saucepan until just warm, stirring constantly to melt margarine. Add to yeast mixture. Add egg and lemon rind. Beat at low speed of electric mixer for 1/2 minute, scraping bowl constantly. Beat for 3 minutes at high speed. Stir in enough remaining flour to make moderately stiff dough. Turn onto lightly floured surface. Knead for 5 to 10 minutes or until smooth and elastic. Shape into ball. Place in lightly greased bowl, turning to grease surface. Cover. Let rise in warm place for 1 to 1 1/2 hours or until doubled in bulk. Knead in fruits and walnuts. Let rest for 10 minutes. Shape into round loaf. Place in greased 9 x 1 1/2-inch round baking pan. Let rise for 45 minutes or until doubled in bulk. Bake in 375-degree oven for 1/2 hour. Brush with honey while hot.

Nolaine H. Ferrell
Williamson, West Virginia

GREEK SWEET BREAD

1/4 c. milk, scalded
1 pkg. yeast
1/4 lb. butter, softened
3/4 c. sugar

3 eggs, beaten
1/2 c. mashed potatoes
2 cinnamon sticks
1/4 tsp. baking powder
5 to 6 c. flour
1 egg yolk, beaten

Cool milk to lukewarm. Add yeast; stir until dissolved. Cream butter and sugar in bowl. Add eggs; blend thoroughly. Stir in yeast mixture. Add potatoes; mix well. Add cinnamon sticks to 1 cup boiling water in saucepan; boil for 5 minutes. Cool to lukewarm. Remove cinnamon sticks. Stir liquid into yeast mixture. Add baking powder and enough flour to make stiff dough; mix well. Turn onto floured surface; knead until smooth and elastic. Place in greased bowl, turning to grease surface. Cover. Let rise in warm place until doubled in bulk. Divide into 3 portions. Shape each portion into long rope. Place close together on greased baking sheet. Braid. Brush top with beaten egg yolk. Garnish with walnuts or sesame seed. Bake at 350 degrees for 1 hour.

Mrs. N. S. Harrison
Wheeling, West Virginia

HUNGARIAN RUM-BUTTER BISCUITS

1/2 c. butter
1 c. sifted flour
1/2 tsp. salt
2 tbsp. rum
3 egg yolks

Cut butter into flour in bowl until crumbly. Combine salt, rum and 2 egg yolks in bowl; mix well. Stir into flour mixture. Knead lightly. Refrigerate until chilled. Roll out 1/4 inch thick on lightly floured surface. Cut into 2-inch rounds. Brush with remaining slightly beaten egg yolk. Bake at 350 degrees for 10 minutes or until golden. Yield: 10 servings.

Mrs. Bea Myers
Tulare, California

CREPES FRANGIPANE

1 c. all-purpose flour
1/4 tsp. salt
5 eggs
2 c. milk
1/2 c. butter, melted
3/4 c. sugar
2 egg yolks

1/2 c. ground almonds
1 tsp. vanilla extract
1/2 tsp. almond extract
Confectioners' sugar
Whipped cream
Chocolate curls

Combine 3/4 cup flour and salt in bowl. Add 3 eggs, 1 cup milk and 3 tablespoons butter; beat until smooth. Pour 2 to 3 tablespoons batter into lightly buttered 8-inch skillet. Rotate skillet until batter covers bottom. Cook over medium heat until light brown. Turn. Cook for 30 seconds. Repeat to make 12 crepes. Stack crepes between sheets of waxed paper. Set aside. Combine sugar and 1/4 cup flour in saucepan. Add 1 cup milk gradually. Bring to a boil, stirring constantly. Boil for 1 minute, stirring constantly. Beat 2 eggs and egg yolks together in bowl. Stir a small amount of hot mixture into eggs; stir eggs into hot mixture. Cook for 1 minute longer. Remove from heat. Stir in 3 tablespoons butter, almonds, vanilla and almond flavoring. Cool. Spread 3 tablespoons filling on each crepe. Fold in half. Fold into quarters. Arrange in shallow baking dish. Brush with 2 tablespoons butter. Bake in 350-degree oven for 10 to 15 minutes or until heated through. Sprinkle with confectioners' sugar. Serve warm with whipped cream and chocolate curls.

Photograph for this recipe below.

HUNGARIAN BUTTERHORNS

1 1/2 c. sugar
4 c. sifted flour
1/2 tsp. salt
1 c. butter
1 pkg. yeast
2 tsp. vanilla extract
3 egg yolks, beaten
1 c. sour cream
Confectioners' sugar
3 egg whites
3/4 c. finely chopped nuts
Confectioners' sugar icing

Sift 1/2 cup sugar, flour and salt together in bowl. Cut in butter until crumbly. Add yeast, 1 teaspoon vanilla, egg yolks and sour cream. Mix until smooth. Divide into 10 portions. Roll each portion into circle on board covered with confectioners' sugar. Cut each into 8 wedges. Beat egg whites in bowl until stiff peaks form. Add remaining sugar gradually, beating until sugar is dissolved. Fold in nuts and remaining vanilla. Place 1 teaspoon meringue on wide end of each wedge. Roll from wide end as for jelly roll. Place on greased baking sheet, point-side down. Let rise for 1/2 hour. Bake at 400 degrees until brown. Frost with confectioners' sugar icing while warm.

Mrs. John Batiste
Fort Knox, Kentucky

HUNGARIAN COFFEE CAKE

1 pkg. dry yeast
3/4 c. lukewarm milk
1 c. sugar
1 tsp. salt
1 egg, beaten
1/4 c. shortening
3 1/2 to 3 3/4 c. sifted flour
1 tsp. cinnamon
1/2 c. each finely chopped nuts,
*   seedless raisins*
1/2 c. butter, melted

Dissolve yeast in 1/4 cup warm water in mixing bowl. Stir in milk. Add 1/4 cup sugar and salt; mix well. Add egg, shortening and half the flour; mix well. Add enough remaining flour to make stiff dough; beat well. Turn onto lightly floured board. Knead for 5 minutes or until smooth and elastic. Place in greased bowl, turning to grease surface. Cover with damp cloth. Let rise in warm place until doubled in bulk. Punch down. Let rise for 30 to 40 minutes or

until doubled in bulk. Shape into balls, using 2 tablespoons dough for each. Combine remaining sugar, cinnamon and nuts. Roll each ball in melted butter, then in nut mixture. Place half the balls in well-greased tube pan. Sprinkle with half the raisins. Press raisins in lightly. Repeat layers. Let rise for 45 minutes. Bake at 375 degrees for 35 to 40 minutes. Yield: 6-8 servings.

Helen Janice Hale
Somerset Kentucky

HUNGARIAN SOUR CREAM TWISTS

3 1/2 c. sifted flour
1 tsp. salt
1/2 c. each butter, shortening
1 pkg. dry yeast
3/4 c. sour cream
2 eggs
1 tsp. vanilla extract
1 c. sugar

Sift flour and salt into mixing bowl; cut in butter and shortening until crumbly. Dissolve yeast in 1/4 cup warm water. Stir into flour mixture. Add sour cream, eggs and vanilla; mix well. Cover with damp cloth. Refrigerate for 2 hours. Roll half the dough on sugared board into 8 x 16-inch oblong. Fold ends into center, overlapping. Sprinkle with sugar. Roll again to same size. Repeat again. Roll to 1/4 inch thick. Cut into 1 x 4-inch strips. Twist ends in opposite directions, stretching dough slightly. Shape into horseshoes on ungreased baking sheet. Press ends to pan to hold shape. Repeat with remaining dough. Bake in 375-degree oven for 15 minutes or until light brown. Remove from baking sheet immediately. Yield: 4 dozen.

Elizabeth M. Stevenson
Windsor, New York

ICELANDIC PANCAKES

3 eggs
2 c. milk
1 c. flour
1/2 tsp. salt
1/2 tsp. vanilla extract
1 tbsp. sugar
Butter, melted

Combine all ingredients except butter in blender container. Process for several seconds. Heat 8-inch skillet. Brush lightly with butter. Pour batter, 2 tablespoons at a time, into skillet, tilting to cover bottom. Fry until lightly browned. Turn; brown on other side. Keep warm. Serve with syrup or whipped cream and fresh fruit. Yield: 6-7 servings.

Mrs. C. N. Sheridan
Tupelo, Mississippi

IRISH SODA SCONES

1 lb. flour
1 tsp. each soda, cream of tartar
1/2 tsp. salt
1 tbsp. margarine
Buttermilk

Sift dry ingredients into large bowl. Cut in margarine until crumbly. Add enough buttermilk to make stiff dough. Turn onto floured surface. Knead lightly. Roll to 1/2-inch thickness. Cut into desired shapes. Place on baking sheet. Bake at 350 degrees for 15 minutes, turning to brown both sides. May be baked on griddle.

Virginia S. McEwen
Rockford, Alabama

IRISH SODA BREAD

3 c. sifted self-rising flour
2 tbsp. sugar
1/2 tsp. soda
1 tsp. caraway seed
1 1/2 c. milk
1/2 c. margarine, melted
3/4 to 1 c. raisins

Sift flour, sugar and soda together into mixing bowl. Stir in caraway seed. Combine milk, margarine and raisins in bowl. Add all at once to flour mixture; stir until just mixed. Turn into greased 4 1/2 x 8 1/2-inch pan. Bake in preheated 400-degree oven for 40 to 45 minutes or until bread tests done. Remove from pan immediately. Cool on rack. Serve warm or cool. Yield: 1 loaf.

Mrs. Hazel Johnson
Lake City, Tennessee

ISRAELI HONEY CAKE

3 eggs
1 c. sugar
2 tbsp. oil
3 1/2 c. sifted flour
2 tsp. baking powder
1 tsp. soda
1/2 tsp. each salt, ginger
1/4 tsp. nutmeg
1 tsp. cinnamon
Dash of ground cloves
1 c. each honey, coffee

1/2 c. chopped walnuts
Confectioners' sugar

Beat eggs and sugar in bowl. Stir in oil until smooth. Sift next 8 ingredients together in bowl. Combine honey and warm coffee; mix well. Add egg mixture to dry ingredients alternately with coffee mixture, beating well after each addition. Fold in walnuts. Pour into greased and floured round cake pan. Bake at 325 degrees for 50 minutes. Remove from pan. Sprinkle with confectioners' sugar. Serve within several hours. Yield: 12 servings.

Mrs. Gloria E. Suthowski
Bremerhaven, Germany

CLASSIC ITALIAN BREAD

6 1/4 c. flour
1 tbsp. salt
1 cake yeast
1/4 c. olive oil

Pour flour into bowl. Make well in center. Add 2 cups warm water and salt. Crumble in yeast; mix thoroughly. Add olive oil. Knead until smooth and elastic. Cover. Let rise in warm place until doubled in bulk. Punch down. Knead well. Let rise until doubled in bulk. Shape into 2 loaves. Place in oiled bread pans. Let rise until doubled in bulk. Bake at 350 degrees for 1 hour or until bread tests done. May be formed into round mounds and placed on oiled cookie sheet to bake. Yield: 2 loaves.

Mrs. John Beale
Columbus, Ohio

ITALIAN RYE BREAD

1 cake yeast
6 c. flour
4 c. rye flour
2 1/2 tbsp. caraway seed
1 tsp. salt
Cornmeal

Dissolve yeast in 3 cups warm water in large bowl. Add flours, caraway seed and salt; mix well. Turn onto floured surface. Knead until smooth and elastic. Place in greased bowl, turning to grease surface. Cover. Let rise in warm place until doubled in bulk. Turn onto floured surface. Knead. Shape into 8 small round loaves. Place on cookie sheet sprinkled with cornmeal. Bake at 400 degrees for 30 to 40 minutes. Yield: 8 small loaves.

Mrs. James Bower
Lakeside, Montana

ITALIAN BISCOTTI

1 c. butter
1 c. sugar
3 eggs
3 c. flour
3 tsp. baking powder
1/2 tsp. salt
1 tsp. lemon extract
1 c. chopped pecans

Cream butter and sugar in bowl. Add eggs one at a time, beating well after each addition. Sift flour, baking powder and salt together. Add to creamed mixture. Add lemon extract and pecans; mix well. Turn onto floured board. Knead until smooth. Shape into 2 oval loaves. Place on greased baking sheet. Bake at 350 degrees for 1/2 hour. Cut into 1/2-inch slices while warm. Arrange on baking sheet. Toast on both sides. Yield: 25 Biscotti.

Mrs. Raymond Gatti
Ft. Carson, Colorado

ITALIAN CROSTATA

3 c. flour
1/2 c. sugar
Pinch of salt
3 tbsp. (heaping) baking powder
2 sticks margarine
2 eggs
1/4 c. milk
1 tsp. vanilla extract
1 jar prune butter
1 jar strawberry jam
1 c. chopped pecans

Combine first 4 ingredients in bowl. Cut in margarine until crumbly. Beat eggs, milk and vanilla in bowl. Add to flour mixture; mix well. Refrigerate until chilled. Turn onto floured board. Do not handle dough too much. Reserve portion of dough for top. Roll dough between 2 sheets of waxed paper to fit cookie sheet. Place on greased and floured cookie sheet. Combine remaining ingredients in bowl; mix well. Spread over dough. Roll reserved dough. Cut into strips. Arrange in criss-cross pattern over prune-butter mixture. Bake at 350 degrees for 35 to 40 minutes. Yield: 36 bars.

Mrs. Jerry D. Smith
Patrick, Ohio

ITALIAN SWEET BISCUITS

2 c. plus 2 tbsp. sifted all-purpose
flour

4 tsp. baking powder
1/4 tsp. salt
3 eggs, lightly beaten
4 tbsp. sugar
1/4 c. oil
1 tsp. almond extract
2 tsp. light cream
4 tsp. confectioners' sugar
Food coloring

Sift first 3 ingredients together. Combine eggs, sugar, oil and almond extract in bowl; mix well. Stir in dry ingredients; mix well. Shape into 1-inch balls with floured hands. Place on greased cookie sheet 1 1/2 inches apart. Bake in 400-degree oven for 10 minutes or until golden. Cool. Mix cream and confectioners' sugar in bowl. Add food coloring. Spread on biscuits. Yield: 24 biscuits.

Ina Maranzini
Merion, Pennsylvania

MEXICAN FLOUR TORTILLAS

2 c. flour
2 tsp. salt
5 tbsp. shortening

Mix flour and salt in bowl. Cut in shortening until crumbly. Add 3/4 cup hot water. Knead to mix well. Pinch off 2-inch pieces. Roll on floured surface to 1/8-inch thickness. Cook on greased hot griddle. Yield: 1 1/2 to 2 dozen.

Mrs. George Lee Newcomb
Antigo, Wisconsin

MEXICAN SOPAPILLAS

2 c. flour
3 tsp. baking powder
1/2 tsp. salt
1 tbsp. shortening
Oil for deep frying

Sift dry ingredients together in bowl. Cut in shortening until crumbly. Add 1/2 cup warm water gradually, stirring with fork. Dough will be crumbly. Turn onto lightly floured surface. Knead until smooth. Divide in half. Let stand for 10 minutes. Roll each half into 10 x 12 1/2 x 1/8-inch rectangle. Cut into 3-inch squares. Fry, several at a time, in deep fat at 400 degrees for 30 seconds on each side. Yield: 40 sopapillas.

Mrs. Robert Thompson
Superior, Arizona

NORWEGIAN FLAT BREAD

1 c. shortening
2 c. graham flour
2 c. buttermilk
1 tsp. each soda, salt
7 to 8 c. flour
Cornmeal

Cut shortening into graham flour in bowl until crumbly. Add buttermilk, soda, salt and enough flour to make stiff dough. Shape into small balls. Roll each ball into thin circle on surface sprinkled with flour and cornmeal. Bake on hot greased pancake griddle until light brown, turning often.

Hazel Tonseth
Lyons, South Dakota

POLYNESIAN BANANA BREAD

1 c. shortening
2 c. sugar
1 tsp. vanilla extract
4 eggs
1 c. mashed bananas
2 1/2 c. all-purpose flour
2 tsp. soda
1/4 c. chopped black walnuts

Cream shortening, sugar and vanilla together in bowl. Add eggs one at a time, beating well after each addition. Add bananas; mix well. Sift flour and soda together. Fold into creamed mixture. Mix in walnuts. Pour into 3 greased and floured 4 x 8-inch loaf pans. Bake at 350 degrees for 40 minutes. Yield: 3 loaves.

Mrs. George Barnes
Corpus Christi, Texas

PORTUGUESE SWEET BREAD

1 cake yeast
2 potatoes
2 1/2 c. sugar
Salt
10 eggs, beaten
1/2 lb. butter, melted
10 c. flour

Dissolve yeast in 1/4 cup warm water. Boil potatoes in water to cover in saucepan until tender. Drain, reserving liquid. Mash potatoes in bowl until smooth; add reserved liquid. Add yeast, 1/2 cup sugar and 1/2 teaspoon salt. Mix thoroughly. Cover. Let stand overnight. Add eggs, butter, 2 cups sugar and 1 tablespoon salt to yeast mixture; beat well. Place flour in large mixing bowl. Pour sugar mixture into center of flour; mix well. Knead thoroughly for 15 minutes or until smooth and elastic. Let rise in warm place until doubled in bulk. Divide dough into 4 portions. Knead each portion. Place in 4 greased baking pans. Let rise until doubled in bulk. Bake at 350 degrees for 1 hour. Yield: 4 loaves.

Mrs. Guy Youngberg
Londonderry, Ireland

SPANISH BUNUELOS

4 eggs, beaten until lemon colored
1/2 c. milk
1/4 c. butter, melted
3 c. flour
1 tbsp. sugar
Oil for deep frying
Sugar
Cinnamon

Combine eggs, milk and butter in bowl. Add dry ingredients; mix well. Shape into 1-inch balls. Roll balls on slightly floured board into pancakes. Fry in hot deep oil until golden. Drain. Mix sugar and cinnamon. Sprinkle on bunuelos.

Mrs. Bruce Barker
Granite City, Illinois

SPANISH DOUGHNUTS

4 tbsp. butter, cut in pieces
1/8 tsp. salt
1 1/4 c. flour
3 eggs
1/4 tsp. vanilla extract
Oil for deep frying
1/2 tsp. cinnamon
1/2 c. sugar

Combine butter, 1/2 cup water and salt in saucepan. Bring to a boil. Remove from heat. Add flour; beat with wooden spoon until smooth. Return to heat. Beat for 2 minutes longer. Remove from heat. Cool. Add eggs one at a time, beating well after each addition. Add vanilla; beat until mixture is satiny. Force mixture through 1/2-inch wide fluted tip cookie press. Cut into 2-inch strips with wet scissors. Drop several at a time into deep fat at 350 degrees. Fry for 2 minutes on each side. Drain. Combine cinnamon and sugar. Roll doughnuts in cinnamon-sugar mixture.

Pat Jenkins
San Jose, California

SPANISH STUFFED ROLLS

4 to 5 hard dinner rolls, split
1/4 c. chopped seeded green chilies
1/2 lb. butter, softened
1 clove of garlic, crushed
1 c. mayonnaise
1/2 lb. Cheddar cheese, shredded

Toast rolls on one side. Mix chilies, butter and garlic in bowl. Spread mixture on untoasted side of roll. Mix mayonnaise and cheese in bowl. Spread over chili mixture to edges. Broil until brown and puffy. Serve at once. Yield: 4-5 servings.

Ms. Emily Mullins
Rome, Georgia

SWEDISH LIMPA

1/4 c. (firmly packed) brown sugar
2 tsp. caraway seed
2 tbsp. shortening
2 tsp. salt
1 pkg. dry yeast
4 c. sifted flour
2 c. sifted rye flour
Milk

Combine 1 1/2 cups water, brown sugar, caraway seed, shortening and salt in saucepan. Bring to a boil. Simmer for 5 minutes. Pour into large bowl. Add 1 cup water. Dissolve yeast in 1/2 cup lukewarm water. Add 2 cups flour to brown sugar mixture; mix well. Add yeast; mix well. Stir in remaining flour and 1 1/2 cups rye flour. Sprinkle 1/4 cup rye flour on bread board. Turn dough onto board. Knead until smooth and elastic, working in remaining rye flour if necessary. Place dough in greased bowl, turning to grease surface. Cover. Let rise in warm place until doubled in bulk. Punch down. Divide in half. Shape each half into ball. Place on lightly greased baking sheet. Make 4 slashes 1/2 inch deep across tops of loaves. Cover. Let rise until doubled in bulk. Bake at 400 degrees for 40 to 45 minutes. Cool on rack. Brush with milk. Bake for 2 minutes longer if shiny crust is desired. Yield: 2 loaves.

Lula Patrick
Monticello, Kentucky

SWEDISH RYE BREAD

1 pkg. yeast
Sugar
1 c. milk, scalded

1/4 c. molasses
1 1/2 tbsp. shortening
1 c. rye flour
2 1/2 tsp. salt
5 1/2 to 6 1/2 c. flour
Butter, melted

Dissolve yeast and 1 tablespoon sugar in 1/2 cup warm water. Combine milk and molasses in large bowl; stir in shortening. Cool to luke-warm. Add rye flour. Beat until smooth. Add salt, 1/3 cup sugar, yeast mixture, 1 1/2 cups water and 2 cups flour. Beat until blended. Work in enough remaining flour to make soft dough. Turn dough onto floured surface. Knead until smooth and elastic. Place dough in greased bowl, turning to grease surface. Cover. Let rise in warm place until doubled in bulk. Shape dough into 3 loaves. Place on greased baking sheets. Let rise until doubled in bulk. Bake at 375 degrees 1/2 hour. Brush tops of loaves with butter. Bake for 5 minutes longer.

Mrs. Nancy Kores
Scottsdale, Arizona

RUSSIAN CHEESE BLINTZES

1/2 c. flour
5 eggs
Butter, melted
Salt to taste
1 lb. hoop cheese, grated
1 tbsp. sugar
Sm. amount of sour cream
Cherry pie filling
Crushed pineapple, drained
1/4 c. rum

Sift flour into 1 cup water in bowl; beat well. Add 3 eggs, 2 2/3 tablespoons butter and salt; beat until blended. Melt a small amount of butter in small skillet. Pour enough batter into skillet to make paper-thin pancake. Cook until brown on bottom. Turn onto cloth-covered board. Repeat process, using remaining batter. Combine cheese, 2 eggs, sugar, sour cream and salt in bowl; mix well. Place a small amount of cheese mixture on each pancake. Fold sides in; roll to enclose filling. Place in buttered baking dish. Bake at 375 degrees for 1 hour, turning pancakes once. Combine pie filling and pineapple in saucepan. Heat. Heat rum; pour over pie filling. Set aflame. Spoon over blintzes. Yield: 18 blintzes.

Mrs. Gerald Fink
Yuma, Arizona

HOLIDAY

HOLIDAY SURPRISE

1 13 3/4-oz. package hot roll mix
1 egg
1/2 c. finely chopped walnuts
1 tsp. cornstarch
1/4 c. orange juice
1 tbsp. brown sugar
1 c. prepared mincemeat
1/3 c. chopped walnuts
1/4 c. chopped candied cherries

Prepare hot roll mix according to package directions, using egg. Fold in finely chopped walnuts. Cover. Let rise for 30 to 40 minutes until doubled in bulk. Combine cornstarch and orange juice in small saucepan. Cook until thick, stirring constantly. Stir in brown sugar, mincemeat, chopped walnuts and chopped cherries. Roll dough on lightly floured surface to 14 x 10-inch rectangle. Lift carefully onto greased baking sheet. Spread filling down center third of dough. Cut slits from sides to filling at 1-inch intervals. Fold strips at an angle across filling, alternating from side to side. Fold ends under. Cover. Let rise for 30 minutes. Bake at 350 degrees for 30 minutes. Cool. Frost with confectioners' sugar glaze. Decorate with walnut halves and candied cherries.

Photograph for this recipe on page 111.

RESOLUTION CAKE

1/2 c. milk, scalded
3/4 c. sugar
1 tsp. salt
1/2 c. margarine
1 tbsp. grated lemon rind
2 pkg. yeast
Eggs
5 1/2 c. flour
Sesame seed
Blanched almonds

Blend first 5 ingredients in small bowl. Cool. Dissolve yeast in 1/2 cup warm water in large bowl. Add milk mixture, 3 eggs and half the flour; beat well. Add enough remaining flour to make soft dough. Turn onto floured board. Knead until smooth and elastic. Place in greased bowl, turning to grease surface. Cover. Let rise in warm place for 1 hour or until doubled in bulk. Punch down. Divide into 2 equal portions. Pat dough into 2 greased 9-inch round baking pans. Cover. Let rise until doubled in bulk. Brush tops lightly with beaten eggs. Sprinkle with sesame seed. Decorate with almonds.

Bake at 350 degrees for 25 minutes or until cake tests done. Turn onto wire rack to cool.

Hortense Holcomb
Butte, Montana

SUGAR BOWL BREAD

2 pkg. yeast
1/2 c. sugar
2 tsp. salt
2/3 c. instant dry milk
2 eggs
1/2 c. shortening
1/2 tsp. yellow food coloring
1 c. raisins
1/2 c. finely chopped toasted almonds
7 2/3 c. sifted all-purpose flour
3 c. sifted confectioners' sugar
1 tsp. lemon juice
1 tsp. grated lemon rind

Dissolve yeast in 1/2 cup warm water in large bowl. Add next 8 ingredients and 1 1/2 cups water; mix well. Stir in 1/2 of the flour; beat well. Add enough remaining flour to make soft dough. Turn onto lightly floured board. Knead until smooth and elastic. Place in greased bowl, turning to grease surface; cover. Let rise in warm place for 45 minutes or until doubled in bulk. Punch down. Divide dough into 4 equal portions. Fill 4 well-greased 1-pound coffee cans 1/2 full. Let rise until doubled in bulk. Place cans on baking sheet. Bake at 375 degrees for 40 minutes. Remove from cans. Place on rack. Combine remaining ingredients and 3 tablespoons water in small bowl; blend well. Drizzle over top of bread. Decorate as desired.

Janice Lyons
Phoenix, Arizona

BRAIDED EASTER BREAD

4 tbsp. sugar
4 tbsp. butter
1 1/2 tsp. salt
1 c. milk, scalded
1 pkg. yeast
1 egg, beaten
4 c. flour

Cream sugar, butter and salt in small bowl. Add to cooled milk in large bowl. Mix yeast, 1/4 cup warm water and egg in small bowl. Stir to dissolve yeast. Add to milk mixture; blend well. Add 2 cups flour; beat until smooth. Add remaining flour; mix well. Turn onto floured surface. Knead until smooth and elastic. Cover. Let rise for 2 hours or until doubled in bulk. Punch down. Let rise for 1 hour or until doubled in bulk. Separate into 3 equal portions. Roll each into long rope. Braid; let rise for 45 minutes or until doubled in bulk. Bake at 325 degrees for 1/2 hour or until bread tests done.

Mrs. H. J. Stevens
Raleigh, North Carolina

EASTER BASKET BREAD

1 pkg. dry yeast
1 pkg. lemon pudding mix
1/4 c. margarine
1/2 tsp. salt
3/4 c. milk, scalded
4 to 4 1/2 c. sifted flour
4 eggs
6 eggs in shell
Candy decorettes

Dissolve yeast in 1/4 cup warm water. Combine next 4 ingredients in large bowl. Mix until butter is melted. Cool to lukewarm. Add 1 1/2 cups flour; mix well. Beat 3 eggs in small bowl. Add eggs and yeast to flour mixture; beat well. Add enough remaining flour to make soft dough. Turn onto lightly floured surface. Knead for 10 minutes or until smooth and elastic. Place in greased bowl, turning to grease surface. Cover. Let rise in warm place for 1 hour and 15 minutes or until doubled in bulk. Punch down. Let rise for 1 hour or until doubled in bulk. Turn onto lightly floured surface. Divide into 3 equal portions. Shape into balls. Cover. Let rest for 10 minutes. Roll each ball into rope 20 inches long. Braid ropes. Fit into greased 10-inch round cake pan. Tuck uncooked whole eggs into braid until almost covered. Cover. Let rise for 45 minutes or until doubled in bulk. Beat remaining egg with 1 tablespoon water in small bowl. Brush on loaf. Sprinkle with candy decorettes. Bake in 375-degree oven for 25 minutes or until bread tests done. Eggs may be dyed before placing in braid.

Mrs. Lindy Mann
Aiken, South Carolina

EASTER MORN COFFEE CAKE

3 c. sifted all-purpose flour
4 tsp. baking powder
1/2 tsp. salt

2 tsp. grated lemon rind
3/4 c. butter
1 c. sugar
1 tsp. vanilla extract
3 eggs
1/2 c. milk
1/2 c. apricot preserves
1 c. flaked coconut
3/4 c. chopped nuts
1 1/2 c. sifted confectioners' sugar

Sift together flour, baking powder and salt into bowl. Stir in lemon rind; set aside. Cream butter in large bowl. Add sugar gradually; beat well. Add vanilla. Add eggs one at a time, beating well after each addition. Combine milk and 1/4 cup apricot preserves. Add to creamed mixture alternately with dry ingredients, blending after each addition. Spread 1/3 of the batter over bottom of greased and floured 10-inch tube pan. Reserve 1/3 cup coconut for topping. Spoon half the remaining coconut and half the nuts over batter, 1 inch from edge on pan. Top with half the remaining batter. Spoon remaining coconut and nuts over batter. Cover with remaining batter. Bake at 350 degrees for 40 to 45 minutes. Cool in pan for 10 minutes. Remove from pan. Heat remaining preserves and 1 tablespoon water in small saucepan. Remove from heat. Stir in confectioners' sugar. Spread over top of warm cake allowing glaze to drip down sides. Sprinkle reserved coconut over top.

Photograph for this recipe below.

EASTER BUNNY BREAD

1 1/2 c. flour
1 tsp. each baking powder, soda and
  cinnamon
1/4 tsp. salt
1/2 c. seedless raisins
1/4 c. chopped pecans
1 c. sugar
2/3 c. oil
2 eggs
1/2 tsp. vanilla extract
1 1/2 c. grated carrots

Sift dry ingredients together. Mix raisins and pecans with 2 tablespoons flour mixture in small bowl. Blend sugar and oil in large bowl. Add eggs and vanilla; beat well. Add flour mixture and carrots; mix well. Stir in raisin mixture. Turn into greased loaf pan. Bake at 350 degrees for 1 hour or until bread tests done. Cool in pan on rack. Yield: 6-8 servings.

Mrs. Thomas Johnston
Atlanta, Georgia

EASTER CHEESE BREAD

1 cake yeast
Flour
1/2 tsp. each salt, pepper
3/4 c. grated Parmesan cheese
3 eggs, beaten
1 c. milk, scalded
Olive oil

Dissolve yeast in 6 tablespoons warm water. Sift 4 cups flour, salt and pepper into large bowl. Stir in cheese. Make well in center of flour mixture. Pour in yeast, eggs, warm milk and 2 tablespoons olive oil; blend well. Turn onto lightly floured board. Knead until smooth and elastic, adding enough flour to make stiff dough. Place in greased bowl, turning to grease surface. Cover. Let rise in warm place for 1 1/2 to 2 hours or until doubled in bulk. Punch down. Let rise for 30 to 45 minutes or until doubled in bulk. Turn onto floured board. Knead. Shape into round loaf. Place in 10-inch pie pan. Cover. Let rise until doubled in bulk. Brush top with olive oil. Bake at 350 degrees for 1 hour or until loaf tests done.

Mrs. Walter H. Huber
Langley, Virginia

GRECIAN HALVAH

3/4 c. butter, softened
3 c. sugar

4 eggs
2 c. farina
1 c. chopped almonds
1 tsp. cinnamon

Cream butter and 1 cup sugar in bowl. Add eggs one at a time, beating well after each addition. Add farina, almonds and cinnamon; mix well. Fill greased 7 x 11-inch baking pan 1/2 full. Bake at 350 degrees for 35 to 40 minutes. Combine remaining sugar with 4 cups water in saucepan. Baste hot Halvah with syrup until all is absorbed. Cool. Cut into squares.

Hazel Tassis
Imperial, California

RISEN POTATO BREAD

3/4 c. milk
3/4 c. potato water
1 c. butter
2/3 c. sugar
2 tsp. salt
2 pkg. dry yeast
7 to 8 c. flour
1 c. mashed potatoes
3 eggs, beaten
Raisins to taste (opt.)

Scald milk with potato water in saucepan. Add butter, sugar and salt; stir until melted. Dissolve yeast in 1/2 cup warm water. Let stand for 10 minutes. Sift 4 cups flour into bowl. Add milk mixture, potatoes, eggs and yeast; beat until smooth. Stir in enough remaining flour to make soft dough. Stir in raisins. Turn onto floured surface. Knead until smooth and elastic. Place in greased bowl, turning to grease surface. Cover. Let rise in warm place for 1 hour or until doubled in bulk. Shape into loaves. Place in greased loaf pans. Let rise for 1 hour or until doubled in bulk. Bake in 400-degree oven for 10 minutes. Reduce temperatue to 350 degrees. Bake for 1/2 hour longer or until brown. Dough may be refrigerated for 3 to 4 days before shaping into loaves.

Mrs. Carley Smith
Prattville, Alabama

RUSSIAN EASTER BREAD

1 1/4 c. milk, scalded
1/2 c. each sugar, butter
2 cakes yeast
5 c. flour
4 eggs, beaten
1 tsp. salt

1 tbsp. each grated orange rind, lemon
   rind
1 c. raisins

Combine milk, sugar and butter in large bowl. Cool. Dissolve yeast in small amount of milk mixture. Add to remaining milk mixture. Add half the flour; beat well. Combine eggs and salt; beat until thick. Add to milk mixture; mix well. Add remaining ingredients. Beat until bubbles appear. Divide dough in half. Turn into 2 greased loaf pans. Cover. Let rise in warm place until doubled in bulk. Punch down. Let rise until doubled in bulk. Bake at 350 degrees for 45 minutes. Yield: 2 loaves.

Carrie Fisher
Merced, California

HOT CROSS BUNS

2 pkg. dry yeast
1/4 to 1/3 c. milk, scalded
1/2 c. oil
1/3 c. sugar
3/4 tsp. salt
3 1/2 to 4 c. sifted all-purpose flour
1 tsp. cinnamon
3 eggs, beaten
2/3 c. currants
1 egg white, slightly beaten
3/4 c. sifted confectioners' sugar

Dissolve yeast in 1/2 cup warm water. Combine next 4 ingredients in large bowl; cool to lukewarm. Combine 1 cup flour and cinnamon; stir into milk mixture. Add eggs; beat well. Stir in yeast and currants; mix well. Stir in enough remaining flour to make soft dough. Cover. Let rise in warm place until doubled in bulk. Punch down. Turn onto lightly floured surface. Cover. Let rest for 10 minutes. Roll to 1/2-inch thickness; cut into rounds. Shape into buns. Place 1 1/2 inches apart on greased baking sheet. Cover. Let rise until doubled in bulk. Cut crosses on tops of buns with sharp knife. Brush tops with egg white. Bake at 375 degrees for 15 minutes; cool slightly. Mix confectioners' sugar with remaining egg white; place in pastry tube. Outline crosses on buns with icing. Yield: 2 dozen.

Betty Goorhouse
Hudsonville, Michigan

EASTER ORANGE ROLLS

1 1/4 c. milk, scalded
1/2 c. shortening
1 tsp. salt
1/3 c. sugar
1 pkg. yeast
2 eggs, well beaten
Grated orange rind
Orange juice
5 c. flour
1 c. confectioners' sugar, sifted

Combine first 4 ingredients in large bowl; mix well. Cool to lukewarm. Stir in yeast until dissolved. Add eggs, 2 tablespoons orange rind and 1/4 cup orange juice; mix thoroughly. Add enough flour to make soft dough; mix well. Cover. Let stand for 10 minutes. Turn onto lightly floured surface. Knead until smooth and elastic. Place in greased bowl, turning to grease surface. Let rise in warm place for 2 hours or until doubled in bulk. Punch down. Turn onto floured surface. Roll to 1/2-inch thickness. Cut into 6 x 1/2-inch strips. Knot each strip. Place on greased baking sheet. Cover. Let rise until doubled in bulk. Bake at 400 degrees for 15 minutes. Combine 2 tablespoons orange juice, 1 teaspoon orange rind and confectioners' sugar in bowl. Spread on rolls.

Mrs. Wanda Gray
Coosada, Alabama

GOBLIN DOUGHNUTS

3 1/3 c. pancake mix
1/3 c. sugar
1 tsp. cinnamon
1/2 tsp. mace
1/4 tsp. cardamom
1/3 c. shortening
2 eggs, beaten
Milk
Oil for deep frying
1 c. sifted confectioners' sugar
1/2 tsp. vanilla extract

Combine first 5 ingredients in large bowl. Cut in shortening until crumbly. Add eggs and 2/3 cup milk; mix thoroughly. Turn onto lightly floured board. Knead gently for several seconds. Roll out to 1/2-inch thickness. Cut with floured doughnut cutter. Fry in hot deep fat for 2 minutes or until brown. Drain on absorbent paper. Cool. Blend confectioners' sugar, 4 tablespoons milk and vanilla in small bowl until smooth. Drizzle glaze on doughnuts. Decorate with chocolate shot or nonpareils. Yield: 12 doughnuts.

Jane Carson
Reno, Nevada

CELEBRATION BUTTERHORNS

2 c. sifted flour
1 c. butter, softened
1 egg yolk
3/4 c. sour cream
3/4 c. sugar
1 tbsp. cinnamon
1/2 c. chopped walnuts

Combine flour, butter, egg yolk and sour cream in bowl; mix well. Shape into ball; wrap well. Refrigerate for 2 to 3 hours. Cut into 4 portions. Roll into circles. Cut each into 8 wedges. Combine remaining ingredients. Sprinkle each wedge with filling. Roll up from wide end. Place on ungreased cookie sheet. Bake at 375 degrees for 10 minutes. Yield: 24 butterhorns.

Alma Leiser
Freeport, Long Island, New York

FIRECRACKER POPOVERS

2 eggs, beaten
1 c. milk
1 tbsp. melted shortening
1 c. sifted all-purpose flour
1/2 tsp. salt
1/4 c. grated sharp Cheddar cheese
Pinch of cayenne pepper (opt.)

Combine eggs, milk and shortening in bowl. Add flour and salt. Beat until smooth. Fold in cheese and pepper. Fill hot, oiled muffin cups 1/2 full. Bake in preheated 450-degree oven for 15 minutes. Reduce temperature to 350 degrees. Bake for 15 to 20 minutes longer or until popovers test done. Do not open oven door for first 25 minutes of baking time. Yield: 8-12 servings.

Mrs. Marjorie Westmore
Daleville, Missouri

HALLOWEEN SPUDNUTS

1 3/4 c. milk, scalded
1/2 c. shortening
Sugar
1/2 c. mashed potatoes
1 pkg. dry yeast
2 eggs, beaten
1/2 tsp. vanilla extract
6 1/2 to 7 c. sifted flour
1 tsp. baking powder
2 tsp. salt
Oil for deep frying
Cinnamon
1/4 c. (firmly packed) brown sugar

1/4 c. light corn syrup
36 pecan halves
36 to 48 raisins

Combine milk, shortening, 1/2 cup sugar and potatoes in bowl; mix well. Cool to lukewarm. Sprinkle yeast over 1/2 cup warm water, stirring until dissolved. Add yeast to milk mixture. Stir in eggs and vanilla. Sift 6 1/2 cups flour with baking powder and salt. Add to potato mixture gradually; mix well. Add enough remaining flour to make soft dough. Place in greased bowl, turning to grease surface; cover. Let rise for 1 1/2 hours or until doubled in bulk. Turn onto floured surface. Roll to 1/2-inch thickness. Cut with floured doughnut cutter. Cover with cloth. Let rise for 30 minutes or until doubled in bulk. Drop several at a time into deep fat at 375 degrees, turning to brown both sides. Drain on paper towels. Shake doughnuts in bag containing sugar and cinnamon or spread with confectioners' sugar icing. Place 1 teaspoon brown sugar, 1 teaspoon syrup, 1/2 teaspoon water, 3 pecan halves and 3 or 4 raisins in each of 12 greased 2 1/2-inch muffin cups. Arrange 4 doughnut centers in each cup. Cover with cloth. Let rise for 30 minutes or until doubled in bulk. Bake at 350 degrees for 25 to 30 minutes. Yield: 4 dozen doughnuts, 1 dozen rolls.

Mrs. Linda Russell
Mountainair, New Mexico

CORNUCOPIA CRANBERRY BREAD

2 c. flour
1/2 tsp. soda
2 tbsp. butter, softened
1 c. sugar
1 egg
1/2 tsp. salt
3/4 c. orange juice
1 c. chopped cranberries
1/2 c. chopped walnuts

Sift flour and soda together. Cream butter and sugar in large bowl. Add egg and salt; beat well. Add flour mixture alternately with orange juice, blending well after each addition. Fold in cranberries and walnuts. Turn into greased loaf pan. Bake at 350 degrees for 1 hour.

Mrs. R. L. Jones
Atlanta, Georgia

FESTIVE PUMPKIN BREAD

1 3/4 c. flour
3/4 tsp. salt

1/4 tsp. baking powder
1 tsp. soda
1/2 tsp. each cloves, cinnamon, allspice,
ginger and nutmeg
1 1/2 c. sugar
1/2 c. oil
2 eggs
1 c. pumpkin
1/2 c. each raisins, chopped nuts

Sift first 9 ingredients together. Cream sugar and oil in large bowl. Add eggs one at a time, beating well after each addition. Blend 1/3 cup water and pumpkin in bowl. Add pumpkin mixture alternately with dry ingredients to sugar mixture, blending well after each addition. Stir in raisins and nuts. Pour into 2 small greased and floured loaf pans. Bake at 350 degrees for 45 minutes or until bread tests done.

Sarah Marshall
Charleston, West Virginia

HARVEST SWEET POTATO BISCUITS

2 c. sifted flour
4 tsp. baking powder
1 tsp. salt
2/3 c. sugar
1/2 c. shortening
2 c. mashed sweet potatoes
1/4 c. milk

Sift first 4 ingredients together into bowl. Cut in shortening until crumbly. Stir in sweet potatoes. Add milk; mix well. Turn onto floured board. Knead lightly. Roll to 1/2-inch thickness. Cut with 2-inch biscuit cutter. Place on greased baking sheet. Bake in 475-degree oven for 12 to 15 minutes.

Mrs. Sam Hill
Morrilton, Arkansas

PILGRIM'S MINCEMEAT COFFEE RINGS

3/4 c. milk, scalded
1/2 c. sugar
2 tsp. salt
1/2 c. margarine
2 pkg. yeast
1 egg, beaten
4 c. flour
1 lg. jar mincemeat

Combine first 4 ingredients in large bowl; mix well. Cool to lukewarm. Dissolve yeast in 1/2 cup warm water. Stir into milk mixture. Add egg and 2 cups flour; beat until smooth. Add remaining flour; blend well. Cover. Refrigerate for 2 hours or overnight. Divide dough in half. Turn onto floured surface. Roll each half into rectangle. Spread with mincemeat. Roll as for jelly roll from long end. Place rolls in circle in greased, round 9-inch baking pan, pressing ends together. Cut 4 slashes on top of each circle. Cover. Let rise in warm place until doubled in bulk. Bake at 350 degrees for 1/2 hour. Cool. Frost with confectioners' sugar frosting.

Kar Lynn Roberts
Pine Bluff, Arkansas

PLYMOUTH ROCK APPLE BREAD

1/2 c. butter
1 c. sugar
2 eggs
1 tsp. vanilla extract
2 c. flour, sifted
1 tsp. soda
1/2 tsp. salt
1/3 c. sour milk
1 c. chopped apples
1/3 c. chopped walnuts

Cream butter and sugar in bowl. Add eggs and vanilla; beat well. Combine flour, soda and salt. Add to creamed mixture alternately with sour milk, beating well after each addition. Fold in apples and walnuts. Place in greased loaf pan. Bake at 350 degrees for 55 minutes or until bread tests done. May substitute orange juice for milk.

Mrs. Dean Holmes
Warner Robins, Georgia

THANKSGIVING PUMPKIN MUFFINS

Sugar
1 c. sifted flour
2 tsp. baking powder
1/2 tsp. each cinnamon, nutmeg
1/4 tsp. salt
1/4 c. butter
1 egg, beaten
1/2 c. canned pumpkin
1/2 c. evaporated milk
1/2 c. raisins

Sift 1/2 cup sugar and next 5 ingredients in large bowl. Cut in butter until crumbly. Combine next 4 ingredients in bowl; blend well. Add to flour mixture; stir until just mixed. Fill greased muffin cups 2/3 full; sprinkle each with 1/4 teaspoon sugar. Bake at 400 degrees for 20 minutes or until brown. Yield: 16 muffins.

Mrs. Ralph Houston
Frankfort, Kentucky

TURKEY DAY TOMATO BREAD

2/3 c. malted cereal granules
1 1/3 c. milk, scalded
1/4 c. shortening, melted
2 eggs, well beaten
1 c. chopped tomatoes
2 1/4 c. sifted flour
3/4 c. sugar
3 tsp. baking powder
1 1/2 tsp. salt

Combine cereal granules and milk in large bowl. Cool. Stir in next 3 ingredients; mix well. Sift remaining ingredients together. Add flour mixture to cereal mixture. Stir until just mixed. Turn into greased loaf pan. Bake at 375 degrees for 50 minutes or until bread tests done. Cool in pan for 10 minutes. Turn onto rack. Wrap in foil; cool overnight before slicing.

Mrs. Leon P. Smith
Port Arthur, Texas

ADVENT ORANGE LOAF

2 med. oranges, quartered
1/4 c. shortening, melted
1 1/4 c. (firmly packed) brown sugar
2 eggs, beaten
2 1/2 c. sifted flour
3 tsp. baking powder
1/2 tsp. each soda, salt
1/2 c. chopped pecans
1/2 c. chopped red and green gumdrops

Force oranges through food grinder; reserve 1/4 cup juice. Combine oranges with next 3 ingredients in large bowl; beat well. Sift dry ingredients together. Add to orange mixture alternately with reserved juice, beating well after each addition. Fold in pecans and gumdrops. Pour into greased loaf pan. Bake at 325 degrees for 1 hour or until bread tests done. Yield: 1 loaf.

Carrie Mason
Dodge City, Kansas

CAROLLERS' STOLLEN

3 1/2 c. milk, scalded
2 pkg. yeast
10 c. flour
1 tsp. salt
2 1/2 c. butter, melted
1 1/2 c. sugar
2 tsp. grated lemon rind
5 egg yolks

2 oz. Brandy
1 lg. each raisins, mixed candied fruit
1 pkg. glazed cherries
1 lb. pecans, chopped
1/2 c. confectioners' sugar

Cool milk. Dissolve yeast in 1/2 cup lukewarm water. Set aside for 10 minutes. Add to milk in large bowl. Sift 6 cups flour with salt. Add to yeast mixture; mix well. Let rise in warm place until doubled in bulk. Add 1 1/2 cups butter, sugar, lemon rind, egg yolks and Brandy to dough; mix well. Add remaining flour slowly, working in until dough leaves side of bowl. Add fruits and pecans; knead well. Divide dough into 5 equal portions. Shape into ovals. Place in greased loaf pan. Cut 2 rows of slashes down length of oval. Let rise until doubled in bulk. Bake at 350 degrees for 1 hour. Cool slightly. Spoon remaining melted butter over loaves. Sprinkle with confectioners' sugar. Garnish with red and green cherries. Store in cool place. Yield: 5 loaves.

Mrs. Jackie Carlisle
Houston, Texas

CHRISTMAS MORAVIAN SUGAR CAKE

1 pkg. yeast
1 c. milk, scalded
2 eggs, slightly beaten
1/2 c. sugar
2 tsp. salt
1 c. mashed potatoes
Butter, softened
5 c. flour
2 c. (firmly packed) light brown sugar
2 tsp. cinnamon

Dissolve yeast in 2/3 cup warm water in large bowl. Cool milk. Add milk, next 4 ingredients and 1/2 cup butter; beat until smooth. Add enough flour to make stiff dough. Place in greased bowl; cover. Let rise in warm place for 1 hour. Punch down. Divide in half. Shape each half into cake. Place in 11 x 15-inch baking pan. Brush tops with melted butter. Let rise until doubled in bulk. Make holes evenly in cake with thumb. Combine brown sugar, cinnamon and 1/2 cup butter in bowl; mix well. Fill holes in cake with mixture. Bake at 325 degrees for 20 minutes. Yield: 18 servings.

Naomi Honaker
Bethel, Alaska

CHRISTMAS MORNING COFFEE CAKE

1/2 c. shortening
3/4 c. sugar
1 tsp. vanilla extract
3 eggs
2 c. flour
1 tsp. each baking powder, soda
1 c. sour cream
1/2 c. butter, softened
1 c. (firmly packed) brown sugar
2 tsp. cinnamon
1 c. chopped walnuts

Cream first 3 ingredients together in large bowl. Add eggs one at a time, beating well after each addition. Sift dry ingredients together. Add to creamed mixture alternately with sour cream, blending well after each addition. Blend remaining ingredients in small bowl. Alternate layers of batter and brown sugar mixture in greased tube pan. Bake at 350 degrees for 50 minutes. Cool. Drizzle confectioners' sugar icing over top and sides. Yield: 8 servings.

Louise Spencer
Columbia, Tennessee

FESTIVE APRICOT-BRAN MUFFINS

3/4 c. diced dried apricots
6 tbsp. sugar
1/4 c. finely chopped red glace cherries
1 c. sifted all-purpose flour
2 1/2 tsp. baking powder
1/2 tsp. salt
1/4 tsp. nutmeg
1 c. All-Bran cereal
3/4 c. milk
1 egg
1/4 c. shortening
12 red glace cherry halves

Cover apricots with very hot water in bowl. Let stand for 10 minutes. Drain well. Toss lightly with 2 tablespoons sugar and cherries. Set aside. Sift next 4 ingredients and 4 tablespoons sugar together. Set aside. Combine cereal and milk in large bowl. Let stand for 1 to 2 minutes or until most of liquid is absorbed. Add egg and shortening; beat well. Add dry ingredients and apricot-cherry mixture to cereal mixture, stirring until just mixed. Fill greased muffin cups 2/3 full. Garnish each with cherry half. Bake at 400 degrees for 25 minutes or until golden brown. Yield: 1 dozen.

Photograph for this recipe on this page.

CHRISTMAS COFFEE CROWN

1 1/2 c. diced dried apricots
2 1/4 c. All-Bran cereal
1 c. sugar
1/3 c. oil
Almond extract
2 eggs, slightly beaten
1 1/2 tsp. baking powder
1 1/2 tsp. soda
1 1/2 tsp. salt
2 1/4 c. all-purpose flour
1 c. chopped almonds
2/3 c. confectioners' sugar
1 tbsp. milk
Dried apricot halves

Combine first 4 ingredients and 2 1/4 cups hot water in large bowl; stir until mixed. Cool. Stir in 3/4 teaspoon almond extract and eggs; mix well. Combine dry ingredients. Add flour mixture and almonds to apricot mixture. Stir until just mixed. Turn into greased 10-inch bundt pan. Bake at 350 degrees for 50 minutes or until cake tests done. Cool in pan for 10 minutes. Invert onto rack. Cool for 20 minutes. Blend confectioners' sugar, milk and 2 drops of almond extract in small bowl. Spoon over cake. Garnish with apricot halves. Cut into 1/2-inch slices.

Photograph for this recipe below.

SANTA'S CINNAMON ROLLS

2 c. sour cream
2 pkg. dry yeast
1/4 c. margarine, softened
Sugar
2 tsp. salt
2 eggs
6 c. flour
Butter, softened
Cinnamon

Heat sour cream to lukewarm in saucepan over low heat. Dissolve yeast in 1/2 cup warm water in large bowl. Add sour cream, margarine, 1/3 cup sugar, salt, eggs and 2 cups flour. Beat until smooth. Stir in remaining flour until dough leaves side of bowl. Turn dough onto floured surface. Knead for 10 minutes or until smooth and elastic. Place in greased bowl, turning to grease surface. Cover. Let rise in warm place for 1 hour or until doubled in bulk. Punch down. Turn onto floured surface. Roll half the dough to 1/4-inch thick rectangle. Spread with butter. Sprinkle with sugar and cinnamon to taste. Roll as for jelly roll. Cut into 1 1/2 to 2-inch slices. Place in greased baking pan. Repeat process with remaining dough. Bake at 375 degrees for 20 to 25 minutes. Frost as desired. Yield: 3 dozen rolls.

Mrs. Raymond Leahey
Asaka, Japan

SEASON'S GREETINGS SAGE BREAD

1 c. milk, scalded
3 tbsp. sugar
1 tbsp. each salt, instant minced onion
Butter
2 pkg. dry yeast
4 1/2 c. sifted flour
2 tsp. leaf sage, crumbled

Combine milk, sugar, salt, instant onion and 2 tablespoons butter in small bowl. Cool to lukewarm. Dissolve yeast in 1 cup warm water in large bowl. Add milk mixture. Stir in flour and sage. Beat vigorously, about 100 strokes, scraping bowl often. Cover. Let rise in warm place for 1 hour or until doubled in bulk. Punch down. Spoon into greased 10-cup tube pan. Bake at 375 degrees for 1 hour or until bread tests done.

Mary Carter
Yuma, Arizona

WISE MEN'S FRUIT BREAD

2 c. milk, scalded
1/2 c. shortening
2/3 c. sugar
2 tsp. salt
1/4 tsp. crushed cardamom
1 tsp. cinnamon
2 pkg. yeast
2 eggs, beaten
8 c. flour
1 c. each white raisins, maraschino
    cherries and shredded citron
Butter, melted

Combine first 6 ingredients in bowl; mix well. Cool to lukewarm. Soften yeast in 1/4 cup warm water. Add to milk mixture. Add eggs; mix well. Add 4 cups flour; beat well. Add fruits and remaining flour; mix well. Let rise in warm place until doubled in bulk. Punch down. Turn onto floured surface. Knead lightly. Divide dough into 2 to 4 portions, depending on size braid desired. Shape each portion into 3 long ropes. Place 3 ropes together on greased cookie sheet. Braid. Repeat with remaining dough. Let rise until doubled in bulk. Bake at 350 degrees for 45 minutes. Brush warm bread with butter. Yield: 24 servings.

Mrs. Gary Wiltse
Broadus, Montana

TWELVE DAYS OF CHRISTMAS STOLLEN

1/2 c. butter
1/2 c. milk, scalded
1 pkg. dry yeast
Eggs
1/4 c. sugar
1 tsp. salt
1 c. raisins
1/2 c. chopped candied red and green
    cherries
1/2 c. chopped almonds
3 1/2 to 4 c. flour

Melt butter in milk in small bowl. Cool. Dissolve yeast in 1/2 cup warm water. Beat 1 egg in large bowl. Add yeast, milk mixture and next 5 ingredients; mix well. Add flour gradually, beating well after each addition. Cover. Let rise in warm place until doubled in bulk. Turn onto floured surface. Knead lightly. Divide dough into 2 equal portions. Shape into loaves. Place on greased baking sheet. Cover. Let rise until doubled in bulk. Brush tops with 1 tablespoon beaten egg. Bake at 350 degrees for 1/2 hour or until bread tests done. Yield: 2 loaves.

Janice Turner
Sioux City, Iowa

ABBREVIATIONS USED IN THIS BOOK

Cup . . . . c.   Large . . . . .lg.

Tablespoon . . . . .tbsp.   Package . . . . pkg.

Teaspoon . . . . .tsp.   Small . . . . .sm.

Pound .lb.   Dozen . . . . doz.

Ounce . . . . oz.   Pint . . . . pt.

MEASUREMENTS

3 tsp. = 1 tbsp.   2 c. sugar = 1 lb.

2 tbsp. = 1/8 c.   5/8 c. = 1/2 c. + 2 tbsp.

4 tbsp. = 1/4 c.   7/8 c. = 3/4 c. + 2 tbsp.

8 tbsp. = 1/2 c.   2 2/3 c. powdered sugar = 1 lb.

16 tbsp. = 1 c.   2 2/3 c. brown sugar = 1 lb.

5 tbsp. + 1 tsp. = 1/3 c.   4 c. sifted flour = 1 lb.

12 tbsp. = 3/4 c.   1 lb. butter = 2 c. or 4 sticks

4 oz. = 1/2 c.   2 pts. = 1 qt.

8 oz. = 1 c.   1 qt. = 4 c.

16 oz. = 1 lb.   A few grains = less than 1/8 tsp.

1 oz. = 2 tbsp. fat or liquid   Pinch = as much as can be taken

2 c. fat = 1 lb.   between tip of finger and thumb

2 c. = 1 pt.

SUBSTITUTIONS

1 tablespoon cornstarch (for thickening) = 2 tablespoons flour (approximately)

1 cup sifted all-purpose flour = 1 cup plus 2 tablespoons sifted cake flour

1 cup sifted cake flour = 1 cup minus 2 tablespoons sifted all-purpose flour

1 teaspoon baking powder = 1/4 teaspoon baking soda plus 1/2 teaspoon cream of
        tartar

1 cup bottled milk = 1/2 cup evaporated milk plus 1/2 c. water

1 cup sour milk = 1 cup sweet milk into which 1 tablespoon vinegar or lemon juice
        has been stirred; or 1 cup buttermilk

1 cup sweet milk = 1 cup sour milk or buttermilk plus 1/2 teaspoon baking soda

1 cup cream, sour, heavy = 1/3 cup butter and 2/3 cup milk in any sour-milk recipe

1 cup cream, sour, thin = 3 tablespoons butter and 3/4 cup milk in sour-milk recipe

1 cup molasses = 1 cup honey

INDEX

PHOTOGRAPHY CREDITS

Favorite Recipes®
of Home Economics Teachers
COOKBOOKS

Add to
Your Cookbook Collection
Select from These ALL-TIME
Favorites

BOOK TITLE	ITEM NUMBER
Holiday Season Cookbook (1981) 160 Pages	14621
Breads (1981) 128 Pages	14656
Meats (1981) 128 Pages	14648
*Salads * Vegetables* (1979) 200 Pages	05576
Desserts—Revised Edition (1962) 304 Pages	01422
Quick and Easy Dishes—Revised Edition (1968) 256 Pages	00043
Dieting To Stay Fit (1978) 200 Pages	01449
Foods From Foreign Nations (1977) 200 Pages	01279
Life-Saver Cookbook (1976) 200 Pages	70335
Canning, Preserving and Freezing (1975) 200 Pages	70084
New Holiday (1974) 200 Pages	70343
Americana Cooking (1972) 192 Pages	70351

FOR ORDERING INFORMATION

Write to:
Favorite Recipes Press
P. O. Box 77
Nashville, Tennessee 37202

BOOKS OFFERED SUBJECT TO AVAILABILITY.